Card Sharps, Dream Books,
& Bucket Shops

Card Sharps, Dream Books, & Bucket Shops

GAMBLING IN 19TH-CENTURY AMERICA

ANN FABIAN

Cornell University Press

ITHACA AND LONDON

First published 1990 by Cornell University Press

Library of Congress Cataloging-in-Publication Data

Fabian, Ann Vincent.
  Card sharps, dream books, and bucket shops : gambling in 19th
-century America / Ann Vincent Fabian.
    p. cm.
  Includes bibliographical references (p.).
  Includes index.
  ISBN 0-8014-2501-8 (alk. paper)
  1. Gambling—Social aspects—United States—History—19th century. I. Title.
HV6715.F33 1990
394'.3—dc20   90-55121

Printed in the United States of America

⊗ The paper in this book meets the minimum requirements of the American National Standard for Information Sciences—Permanence of Paper for Printed Library Materials, ANSI Z39.48-1984.

For Isabelle, Andrew, & Chris

Contents

Acknowledgments

In a perverse reaction to the orderly categories of social history, I set out several years ago to study some nineteenth-century wanderers who would have escaped even the census takers' careful scrutiny and to pursue some unbelievers who never joined churches. I turned up a few stories of professional gamblers who seemed to be consummate wanderers and unbelievers, shunning stable communities and organized religion and dissenting as well from the patterns of rational accumulation that bent nineteenth-century Americans toward individual gain and national economic growth. I was led from gamblers back to texts on gambling and from the texts on gambling back to larger economic and cultural structures in which American gamblers operated.

The search for texts on gambling was full of small and happy accidents, and I am indebted to the archivists who saw fit to preserve some of the less serious products of the nineteenth-century American imagination. I found the sources for this book scattered throughout the library system of Yale University, in the Beinecke Library, in Sterling Memorial Library, in the stacks of Seely-Mudd Library, and in the collections on the history of medicine at the Medical School. I also found material in the Astor and Lenox Collection and in the Rare Book Room of the New York Public Library, in the Saram Ellison Collection of the Society of American Magicians at the Lincoln Center Branch of the New York Public Library, and in the Bella C. Landauer Collection and the general collections at the New-York Historical Society. I thank the staffs of those institutions where I so frequently worked and the librarians who so often assisted my research. At a

Acknowledgments

much earlier stage the research was assisted materially by a fellowship from the Mrs. Giles Whiting Foundation.

I could never have written this book without the enormous generosity of my colleagues and friends. The project has been sustained in numerous ways by those who have made up the American Studies Program at Yale University. They taught me that the risks of interdisciplinary research were risks worth taking, and they created an atmosphere in which interdisciplinary scholarship simply appeared normal and natural. I thank Robert Byer, Amy Kaplan, Katherine Morrissey, Theresa Murphy, Leslie Rado, Marni Sandweiss, Lynn Wardley, Robert Westbrook, and Bryan Wolf for listening to ideas half-formed and for suggesting ways to fill voids in my knowledge out of their own enormous reserves. Joel Bernard, Jon Butler, William Cronon, Michael Denning, George Miles, William Parker, and Harry Stout all took time from their own work to read early drafts of various chapters and returned them to me with stringent criticisms and kind suggestions. William Reese always offered me his hospitality and his boundless knowledge of Americana. He also gave me, one by one, the dream books that inspired the third chapter. Elizabeth Kaspar volunteered her skills as a reader and editor, and where the prose is felicitous, it is often to her credit.

Peter Agree at Cornell University Press treated this book with care and patience. He found a wonderful reader in William Leach, whose critical but enthusiastic reading of the manuscript made me want to write the book I did. James Livingston also gave the manuscript a careful reading and forced me to clarify just where I stood on market speculation and on the construction of value in the late nineteenth-century economy. Marilyn M. Sale edited the manuscript with a sure and careful hand.

Through the stages of this project, I have constantly relied on Howard Lamar's knowledge of history and on his wisdom about writing history. I am very fortunate to have been his student. This book could never have been written without the immense help and remarkable intellectual example of Jean-Christophe Agnew. He was always present as a critic and friend, and he read many versions of the manuscript.

In our many moves in and around Connecticut and New York and in two trips across the Atlantic, Christopher Smeall took it for granted that I would pack notes and books and go on writing. He never

Acknowledgments

seemed to find it strange that I sat in our Paris apartment and wrote about wheat farmers who, a century before, had had trouble with the Chicago Board of Trade. When he had time, he was a strict and helpful editor. I also thank my parents, Robert and Virginia Fabian, who sustained this work in many ways, and a very generous group of au pairs, Sylvia McAslin, Christine Fouquet, Fabienne Gadouais, Corine Robin, and Sophie Terrisse, who have enriched all our lives and taken wonderful care of Andrew and Isabelle. Andrew and Isabelle have always found this book a curious project. Now that it is finally finished, it is for them and for their father.

ANN FABIAN

Larchmont, New York

Card Sharps, Dream Books,
& Bucket Shops

Introduction

In the 1820s Robert Bailey, a Virginian who had given up gambling to write about it, described an elaborate trick he had used to entice a man to bet on the contents of a needle case. Seven decades later, John Philip Quinn, a Chicago gambler and itinerant reformer, wrote of gamblers still profiting by versions of Bailey's ruse. Such tricks, frequently sketched in books designed to expose gamblers' wiles, are described as though they exist outside of time, outside of history, in the curious and constant realm of human greed.

In the seventy years that separated Quinn from Bailey, however, the economic consequences, the cultural significance, and even the definition of gambling changed enormously.[1] Lotteries and gaming grew morally troublesome in capitalist America as citizens openly embraced the virtues of prudence, thrift, rationality, and productive labor. I explore how the culture of the emerging capitalist economy dealt with the irrational and selfish aspects of gain so well preserved in gambling.

Public lotteries were common in the American colonies, and in the early nineteenth century, cities, states, and Protestant churches still looked to revenue raised in lotteries to finance expensive construction projects; many schools, bridges, roads, and jails could not have been built without the support of a public willing to wager on the outcome of a drawing. The lottery was a form of indirect taxation, a means of spreading the risks of finance and development but, in the perceptions of some, at a moral cost. By the late 1830s many northern states began to turn against lotteries as anachronistic and dangerous.

Introduction

In this early period gambling also flourished in many less official forms. In the South, rich planters, dazzled by examples of eighteenth-century English aristocrats, bet openly among themselves with money made for them by the labor of slaves. They staged horse races and cockfights and entertained themselves playing cards. In taverns in northern cities, poorer men bet on dogs and cocks and on the turn of a card and the throw of the dice. Private games were sometimes disrupted by the appearance of professional gamblers, and early in the century a few professionals won their living from crowds gathered at markets, fairs, and militia musters.

These few wandering professionals changed the nature of the games they played, but they were also symptoms of the social and economic forces that altered gambling itself in the nineteenth century. By 1810 prosperous philanthropic reformers began to argue that gambling undermined the economic stability they thought necessary to ensure public welfare and personal well-being: gamblers, whether rich or poor, were little better than thieves and parasites and hardly worthy of the trust needed to assure the smooth workings of economic transactions in a world of strangers. The gamblers they described sought profits when they had produced nothing, offering nothing in exchange for the money they made. Reformers used gambling to build a model of economic rationality and to talk about political as well as economic behavior. Gambling transactions, they argued, were dangerous to a republic of rational profit seekers because they encouraged false hopes for quick profits. False hopes fostered destabilizing passions, and wild passions distorted the careful political and economic deliberations necessary for an honest electorate. Deluded by false hopes for ready gain, those who would gamble menaced the very structures of trust and credit on which an expanding economy, and ultimately the republic, depended.

Opposition to gambling never coalesced into a single-minded crusade, but opposition bore fruit over the century, and by the late 1890s most forms of gambling (especially the lottery) were illegal. All men and women did not suddenly stop gambling, for private gaming and gambling in numbers and policy continued, but in the ideal communities described by state laws and local ordinances people had foresworn the foolish and irrational expectations that lay behind gambling and embraced the search for slow and honest gain. The rational search for gain was constructed, in part, in opposition to the gambling at the margins of society. Reformers frequently criticized gaming among the very rich, attacking it as aristocratic pretense, but they reserved most of their reforming zeal for the gambling of the very poor—African Americans and poor immigrants, especially the Chinese.

But gambling was marginalized only to be domesticated at the end of the century, when risk and rapid gain reappeared as essential ingredients in rational capitalist speculation. The "new" gamblers, who profited from the operations of stock and commodities exchanges, presented themselves as virtuous, rational citizens by delineating their differences from the "old," evil gamblers. Over the course of the nineteenth century, the definition of gambling as a transgression changed and it changed in response to particular ideological developments in nineteenth-century American capitalism. At times one finds a version of Puritan fears of corrupted leisure repeated in the debates on gambling, and at times one encounters repetitions of the warnings about excessive gaming that had characterized even the most tolerant eighteenth-century communities. But the debate over gambling was not always everywhere the same, and one can read objections to gambling as speculations on particular developments in the capitalist economy and on the nature of individuals who were to make economic decisions.[2] Those who gambled and those who wrote about gambling as well as those who wrote about the economy with the aid of gambling metaphors frequently raised the very questions that troubled serious political economists. They used gambling, both overtly and implicitly, to construct the ordered economic rationality so necessary to a liberal political economy. What was to assure stability in individuals bent on gain? When would the search for wealth turn dangerous and destructive? Who had a right to profits generated by the ever more rapid transfer of property and by the seemingly magical fertility of speculative markets?

At times during the last century the search for answers to such questions became particularly pressing. And just as gambling enabled some of small means to speculate in financial matters, debates about gambling enabled some, who might otherwise have hesitated to address economic issues, to speculate on financial matters. For those whose interests lay in building an economy based on ordered gain, gambling became increasingly dangerous. Its dangers increased as individuals moved from intimate and reciprocal economies to economies governed by relations between strangers and designed to end in asymmetrical accumulations. In reciprocal economies (best exemplified in the nineteenth-century United States by small communities of neighbors and friends), gambling entailed the continual flow of money within the group, the constant transfer of property, and necessarily in amounts within the reach of all players. The same structural considerations could be applied to rich communities as to poor. What was wagered and lost one day was bound to return, as games were replayed, contests restaged, and races rerun. Bets may well have carried great symbolic weight, but continuing fair contests assured the possibility of return.[3]

Such simple structural assurances of return disappeared when individuals began to gamble in a commercial economy. People not only bet with strangers, but they bet with strangers who were resolute in their own search for gain. Gambling was no longer an action that kept money moving but an action that threatened to drain precious resources as gambling strangers crept away with ill-gotten gains.

The American gamblers of advice books and popular fiction were the direct descendants of the venerable seducers who had long inhabited a literature designed to facilitate moves from innocence to experience, moves of country boys into cities and into manhood. But in the 1840s American writers added to their warnings about gambling the very important contention that in the real world no one gambled anymore. In an economy inhabited only by rational profit seekers, speculation and gambling at the highest levels militated against gambling as a form of play. Professional gamblers hid behind a pretense of luck, and they used the illusion of luck to lure the foolish into wagering their money, particularly money they had borrowed, money they had inherited, or money that had been entrusted to them in the course of the innumerable financial errands that ensured the continuity of commercial life. With all this money swirling around, a belief in the possibility of a lucky return was dangerous indeed. Those who appeared to gamble lived in fact by plots and schemes as the dark criminal doubles of rational businessmen. Descriptions of gambling were continually turned to prescriptive ends, and writers warned young readers that no individual ambitious for prosperity would risk the sure losses of gambling transactions.

Gambling thus became a "negative analogue," the one form of gain that made all other efforts to get rich appear normal, natural, and socially salubrious. To condemn gambling was to condone the speculative profits generated by the transfer of land and stock and by the sale of contracts for agricultural commodities. While such speculative profits had once appeared dangerous and destructive, they were surely less so than the illusory profits of gambling. As Karen Halttunen has argued, the bourgeoisie who relished opportunities for speculative gain and often aspired to live off the labor of others quieted their own lingering doubts by condemning gambling and constructed an image of themselves as virtuous and productive citizens by banishing their gambling doubles.[4]

But the split between virtuous speculation and vicious gambling could never be maintained with absolute precision: gambling contained too much of capitalist virtue to stand exalted as unalloyed vice. Southern planters who bet with money made for them by their slaves could hardly condemn a gambler's search for easy gain, and northern capitalists who celebrated the great profits that came of great risks could hardly condemn a gambler's small risks and tireless search for money.[5]

The many ambiguities that have barred gambling from the pantheon of great social vices have made it both difficult to suppress and difficult to study. Gamblers avoided local regulations with technological innovations and often with the protection of local citizens. Historians of gambling have written the history of gambling with a sensational antiquarianism that has kept it forever on the margins of nineteenth-century cultural and economic history.[6]

I have tried to examine gambling and writings about gambling to explore just how the construction of the nineteenth-century economy came to exclude those who continued to gamble. Exclusion gave gamblers and gambling an important place in the rhetoric of popular economics. With a delicate mix of repulsion and attraction, reformers, reporters, and popular authors described gamblers who had rejected the careful calculations that held individuals locked in the embrace of a market society. Freed from this type of careful calculation, gamblers wandered through the economic universe of popular fiction with an easy daring that was becoming increasingly rare both for wage laborers and for an acquisitive and ambitious middle class.

Popular histories have followed gamesters through the nineteenth century. Although I have chosen to analyze gambling's relation to the evolution of the economic rationality which shaped a capitalist economy rather than return to sensational materials, sensational accounts do suggest that gambling had a distinct tie to certain economic formations. Popular accounts place gamblers in wild and unsettled moments in certain economies—particularly frontier economies in extractive industries—where labor was not yet fully governed by the industry, sobriety, and frugality that molded daily life to the rhythms of industrial production. In Gold Rush California, for instance, profits appeared to come from risk and daring and not from sound practice. Money was not earned in slow and steady toil; it fell suddenly, like manna. And the miners who won their money in lucky windfalls turned and gambled their profits on unlikely wagers.[7]

Cowboys and sailors also gambled when they were not working. They operated on similar frontiers of commerce, moving from a world of work governed by the completion of certain necessary tasks into the commercialized leisure of cattle towns and port cities. Their work served commercial ends, but daily life on long drives or on board ship was free from the constant clamor of commercial transactions that ordered life on the job, whether in offices or in factories.[8]

In the 1830s and 1840s, reformers and popular novelists described gambling along the Mississippi River. The frenzied real-estate transactions that made the flush times in the Mississippi Valley generated wealth that was easily wagered. For the next fifty years popular writers repeated tales of quick gain and easy loss and used them to reinforce the lesson that money confided in trust or money won too easily was money readily lost in idle play and on foolish wagers. Dime novelists writing in the 1880s used the Mississippi Valley's surviving myths of easy wealth to create the fictional river gamblers who lived by graceful airs and careful ruses, and they sold their tales to the northern readers who were increasingly confined to the small and uncertain gains of wage labor.[9]

For slightly different reasons, young clerks on Wall Street were also singled out as likely gamblers. Theirs was a different sort of economic frontier, but equally distant from the concrete pattern of productive labor which remained the center of a moral economy throughout most of the nineteenth century. Reformers worried that clerks and brokers supported gambling houses on the edges of the financial district and that they continued speculating there (probably with other people's money) long after legitimate markets had closed. Although they attacked gambling, reformers recognized that profits on the stock markets were often the results of lucky gambles and that it was difficult to assert a vast moral difference between stock markets and gambling casinos.

Such moral confusion has plagued the whole long history of gambling in the United States. I have tried to capture that confusion and to follow a history of gambling through the language of those who opposed it, through the actions of those who continued to gamble, and through the metaphors of those who used gambling to comment on the origin of profits in stock and commodities markets and to legitimate gain in the new commercial economy. To do this I have had to turn to a variety of texts and figures and to argue by comparison, by juxtaposition, and by contrast. I have tried to consider the motives of African Americans who bet on the numbers as well as the complaints of disgruntled farmers who attacked gambling speculators. Gambling and ideas about gambling, I argue, helped people place themselves in the economy.

I begin with the story of Robert Bailey, a Virginian who in the early years of the nineteenth century fashioned both a gambler's career and a reformer's career based on a loose mix of aristocratic pretense and commercial aspiration. Bailey's mix struck several of his contemporaries as particularly unsavory, and he encountered direct and personal opposition to his gaming, to his gaming establishments, and to his reformed persona. He was attacked in public as a blackguard and scoundrel, and he was denounced and thrown into jail. Bailey's repeated efforts to commercialize his gaming, however, suggest he straddled a sort of cultural divide and gambled at the opening of a market economy. Bailey's curious position is illuminated in the contrast of the opposition he encountered with earlier objections to gambling. In the middle of the eighteenth century, a few Virginia clergymen had sensed the dangers of excess gambling in a slaveholding society, and they had warned gamblers of the harm they risked bringing on themselves and their communities.

In the 1830s Dr. Charles Caldwell told his students at Transylvania University in Lexington, Kentucky, that their gambling threatened the good order of their minds, as well as the good order of their small community. Like the eighteenth-century Virginia ministers, he described gambling as a sign of deeper social disorders. But Caldwell also saw psychic disorders. He considered gamblers victims of dangerous passions and he mapped a human mind in which greed and gain were balanced by emotions of a higher order. He ignored the dispassionate commercial aspirations of a figure like Bailey and went on to praise the upstanding citizens of Vicksburg who had risen up against gambling and hanged five faro dealers. The violence seemed to him a timely measure and the proper reaction of a community deeply threatened.

The response to a perceived threat of gambling also took more sober forms, although the reasoned responses to gambling shared with the Vicksburg lynching the effort to make gambling appear a marginal activity, a pastime of the very poor, the corrupt, the evil, and the irrational. In northern cities in the 1820s, wealthy philanthropic reformers sensed dangers in the gambling among the working poor. Gambling seemed a sign of surplus, a sign of an excess of cash which was better invested in savings banks than in lottery tickets. Members of the New York Society for the Prevention of Pauperism, for instance, joined the promoters of savings banks in announcing that savings accounts, and not lottery winnings, would best see the poor through hard times. The working poor who put money into savings accounts and gave up betting on the lottery or betting in a friendly game of chance may well have seen saving as a route to independence, but organized philanthropists put their own construction on saving: the very act of putting money aside in a slow and orderly fashion taught important lessons in frugality. Savings banks had other virtues as well, and even small savings accounts helped turn the economies of the laboring poor into a pool of capital available for wealthy entrepreneurs.

Sober reformers often attracted strange allies, and in the second chapter I explore the career of Jonathan Harrington Green, one antebellum reformer who tried to build a business out of gambling reform. He singled out gambling as the peculiar sin of young clerks tempted to wager others' money in great commercial cities. He wrote a number of sensational books, all of them based on complex revelations of greed and chicanery and all of them designed to illustrate the simple fact that, in a financial world governed by self-interest and by a rational search for gain, no one really gambled anymore. Green's efforts to suppress gambling were largely futile.

In the 1840s and 1850s reporters in the northern papers described gambling by African-American men and women. They were particularly struck by their passion for policy. Policy play allowed side bets on official lotteries, but it continued as "numbers" long after most nineteenth-century lotteries had closed. White writers looked with wonder and disquiet at the superstitions and dreams that informed policy play and worried that simple play revealed dangerous ways of thinking. Policy players, trapped in irrational superstitions, could never be turned into the good citizens needed to run an economy of rational profit seekers. Reformers argued that policy play offered no real hope of a return, and they tried to explain that the folly of players meant great profits for the criminal businessmen who had organized the numbers rackets in northern cities. Reformers exposed the ways policy financed organized crime out of the minute speculations of the very poor, but they phrased their appeals to policy players through a rational common sense the poor who continued to play policy did not, by definition, possess. The dreams and superstitions of policy players, however, continued to offer a distinct commentary on capitalist economics.

Late in the century, angry farmers took up the moral discourse that had grown up around gambling and used accusations of greed and undue gain to challenge those who profited from speculations in agricultural commodities. I turn to them, and to Populist complaints about gambling and speculation, in the fourth chapter. Farmers remarked that by the late 1870s far more produce changed hands on the commodities exchanges than was grown in their fields and that traders who made money on the constant transfer of property were the direct descendants of the evil gamblers who lived as parasites on the productive economy. Traders brought nothing to market and they offered no real exchange for the profits they made.

Speculators, especially the members of the Chicago Board of Trade, responded to the farmers' challenge. They fended off accusations of gambling by turning against the small and often criminal bucket shops, where they admitted that speculators gambled on price fluctuations. They painted themselves as guardians of legitimate commodities markets, as solid citizens who constructed the markets that made the transfer of produce possible. They justified their profits by asserting the natural evolution of speculative markets but also by engineering the important shifts in meaning that turned their own gambling into virtuous speculation. They made themselves into virtuous producers by transforming prices into products produced and speculative markets into a social service. Their redefinitions of prices and productive labor did not go uncontested, and antagonisms were criss-crossed with shifting meanings. The speculators' claims to the virtues of production, along with their ability to generate immense profits from the sale of wheat that did not exist, represented a significant alteration in calculations of moral and economic value in market society. The long labor to distinguish the evils of gambling bore curious fruit. By the beginning of the twentieth century, the great market gamblers had moved from the periphery of the financial universe to its moral center. They had domesticated the vice of gambling.

By the 1890s recreational gambling, with the important exception of the sport of horse racing, was largely prohibited by local ordinance and state law. Men and women were asked to give up the games of chance which fostered an unnatural or irrational thirst for gain and encouraged expenditure without an immediate return, while enhanced opportunities for speculative gain were made available in commercial markets. Prohibition proved a brief interlude, and over the last century we have slowly returned to recreational gambling. In the 1980s increasing numbers of cities and states have legalized gambling games. Legalization is presented, in part, as a defense against powers of organized crime so deeply entrenched that lawmakers have no recourse but imitation. Lotteries have spread through contiguous states as lawmakers try to prevent citizens crossing borders to bet their money, adding to a neighbor's revenue base rather than to their own.

The return to gambling also reflects the long-term economic changes that have undercut the moral foundations of the ways we once told ourselves we earned and spent our money. In studying gambling in the nineteenth century, I have tried to trace the cultural history of certain aspects of the economic imagination, to understand how the moral values of a world based on production and productive labor gave way before the miraculous fertility of speculative capitalism.[10] Some have told the story by tracing the transformation of an economy based on production to an economy based on consumption.[11] Gambling was neither production nor consumption, and its study provides a different view of the debates abut the morality of great profits and about the origins of value.

Gambling has reappeared in the twentieth century as a product to be consumed, initially in Las Vegas on the coattails of the entertainment industry. It now stands as an industry in its own right. The gambling industry produces games and it markets the rights to take risks and to harbor wild hopes as products to be consumed. This is indeed consumption at a very high level of abstraction. Such formulations would have been impossible for those in the nineteenth century who understood that gambling was the antithesis of both production and consumption.

If the evolution of a rational economy in the nineteenth century precluded the possibility of gambling, the twentieth-century celebration of consumption has increased the occasions to gamble. State lotteries hire advertisers to overcome the middle-class resistance to games of chance. We have largely abandoned the nineteenth-century belief in the deep morality of production, but we have not constructed a vital substitute. When popular writers now investigate the problems created by the gambling industry, they rephrase century-old fears about the dangers of gambling. We hear that state-run lotteries, like lotteries in the 1830s, are a regressive tax, falling most heavily on those who can least afford to pay; that casino gambling encourages waste and fraud; that employees addicted to sports betting are too distracted to work; that athletes, seduced by the culture of gambling, are induced to bet on or even against their own teams; that stock and commodity traders live by gambling and, worse, that they manipulate the prices that generate their profits; that communities depending on casino income are plagued by economic instability and political corruption; and that individuals addicted to betting fall victim to passions they cannot control and end by squandering personal sanity and family fortunes.[12]

Even if our consumers' tolerance for gambling would have seemed strange to nineteenth-century commentators, they would have recognized the patterns of passion, addiction, and corruption which linger in discussions of gambling. Recognition of dangers seems the vestige of an older productive economy, but an economy whose moral structures disintegrated as it moved to embrace speculative gain by shunning the irrational passions fostered by recreational gambling. The lingering sense of danger also suggests that our moral structures have not quite kept pace with economic innovation. For ethical direction we turn to the remnants of virtues designed for an economy based on production, yet we live in a speculative economy freed from the constraints of both producers and consumers. At times figuring out just what it means to gamble has provided the intellectual guidelines for the ethical structures of casino capitalism.

Rich Men, Poor Men

The term GAMBLING implies an incorporation of all that is corrupt and nefarious in principle, seductive in example, and ruinous in effect. It makes irrevocable havoc of family, fame, fortune, morality, social endearment, private worth, and public usefulness, and of every thing else that renders youth lovely, age venerable, or life desirable—of every thing that does honor to the living, or embalms and hallows the memory of the dead.
—Charles C. Caldwell, 1835

I have often anathematized the spirit of Trade which reigns triumphant, not only on the 'Change, but in our halls of legislation, and even in our churches. Thought is sold under the hammer, and sentiment in its holiest forms stands labelled for the market. Love is offered to the highest bidder, and sixpences are given to purchase religion for starving souls.
—Lydia Maria Child, 1841

When Robert Bailey published his autobiography, *The Life and Adventures of Robert Bailey from his Infancy up to December, 1821,* he announced that he had abandoned his career as a gambler and gambling-house proprietor and that he intended to support himself, his sixteen-year-old wife, and their twin sons, Esau and Jacob, with the proceeds from the sale of his book and from his patented faro box. Bailey promised to instruct the young in the evils of gaming, especially dishonest gaming, and to use his own life to illustrate the futility of a gambler's search for wealth. Because he had designed a dealing device meant to guarantee the appearance of an honest game, Bailey stood to profit both from gambling and from efforts to suppress it. His story was shaped by his conflicting interests, and he could never decide exactly where he stood on the ethical and financial issues he raised.

Bailey was not alone in his financial indecision. In both the slave-

holding South and the early industrial North, virtues and their opposing vices were reconstructed to fit the needs of the emerging market
economy of the early republic. Despite differences in economic systems, gambling entered moral and financial dialogues in both the
South and the North, and it provides a useful lens on constructions
of economic virtue in a market economy. In neither instance was
gambling an unalloyed vice (a perfect substance, that is, for the construction of pure virtue), for in the South it was kin to the celebration
of leisured wealth that characterized rich slaveholders and in the North
to the celebration of venturesome risk that engaged budding capitalists. Nevertheless, attempts to prohibit, to eliminate, or to control
gambling helped construct definitions of moral gain and moral expenditure in a commercial economy. Bailey's case provides a good example of the role of gambling in a changing economy. There were other
exemplary figures and exemplary incidents. The reasoned speeches of
Charles Caldwell, the impassioned violence at Vicksburg, as well as
the sober financial reforms of northern philanthropists all illuminate
the ways gambling and debates about it helped create the moral and
psychological structures for an economy based on gain.

Bailey's social desires and financial ambitions run opposite to those
of northern mechanics and artisans who abandoned "traditional" patterns of recreation (drinking and sporting) in response either to their
own images of communities of republican labor or to the demands of
ambitious employers and reformers who sought to build a work force
instilled with the joys of industry and frugality.[1] Bailey sought success
in lavish expenditure rather than in careful accumulation, in the socia-
bility of the inn and tavern rather than in the sober privacy of the
home, and in the decadent play of aristocrats rather than in steady toil.

In the early nineteenth century, state legislatures in the North and
South passed laws prohibiting gambling in public. In both regions
laws were designed to regulate the behavior of the poor and working
class in inns and taverns and to protect unwary travelers from the
cheats of professional gamblers. In general, southern legislation was
concerned more with the vice, disorder, and loss that might come out
of excessive gaming than with gaming itself, and laws ignored private
bets among the wealthy. In the North gambling in private was discouraged by injunctions to save and to spend in only the most rational
fashion, and gambling in public was specifically prohibited by local
ordinances.[2] People continued to gamble in private, so that laws

against gambling were little more than optimistic fictions of an ideal bourgeois financial republic, but by the mid 1830s northern states banned most games and most no longer permitted lotteries as official ways to raise revenue.

Although particular games sometimes crossed frontiers of geography, economy, and class, what it meant to gamble or to oppose gambling varied enormously. Southern slaveholders might celebrate their world view as they gambled with wealth produced by women and men whose labor they controlled. As the historian Timothy Breen argued, they used high-stakes wagers to display their competitiveness, individualism, and materialism, but they also acted out a cavalier indifference to the origins of the money they used for play.[3] Northern mechanics and merchants intent on building a republican society that displayed the logic of free labor and acquisitive individualism could tolerate no such aristocratic pretense and no such indifference to the origins and future of wealth. Those who continued to gamble in the North did not endorse careful, rational accumulation and they seemed to refuse to hold property as a sacred trust. According to clergymen and reformers, poor workers who gambled in the lottery, purchased policy slips, or wasted money in games with friends risked in wagers the small surpluses meant to ensure their independence from charity in hard times. Those who played with their money were not saving surpluses to see their families through periods when labor was bound to be scarce.

The gambling vice thus had different regional constructions. Northerners used legal, moral, and institutional means to counter the remnants of a gambling vice. In certain instances southerners voiced legal and moral opposition as well, and in a notable case in the summer of 1835 the people of Vicksburg became polarized over the dangers posed by outsiders they labeled gamblers, and "respectable citizens" rose up and hanged five men.

The Adventures of Mr. Bailey

Robert Bailey was born in Maryland in 1773. His father was killed in the Revolution and his widowed mother survived as a tavern keeper and schoolteacher. According to his own account, Bailey apprenticed himself to a farmer to escape an abusive stepfather. But he had better things in mind, and Bailey later remembered that as a youth he was more interested in learning to dance than in farming or learning to read or write. He delighted in his graceful moves from the field to the dance floor, but he discovered that his social skills could take him only so far. He pursued wealthy young women who had been charmed by his graceful steps, but his suits invariably ended in his exposure as a poor farm boy and in his rejection by prospective fathers-in-law.

He always maintained he was a better dancer than scholar, and although he boasted of his illiteracy, he managed to take in enough of school to write a lengthy autobiography, which he marketed by selling subscriptions throughout Virginia. In four months of schooling he said he learned to "write a tolerable hand, and I cyphered as far as the double rule of three, but I could not spell." His skill at calculation was sufficient to win at cards, but his formal education did little for his social ambition. Bailey saw that both dancing and writing would serve him as forms of communication and that so long as he was interested in luring women to bed and men to the gaming table, dancing was perhaps the more effective medium of expression. But neither as a dancer nor as a gambler nor as a writer was he fully accepted by those he sought to entertain. Just as he had been tossed out of parlors and boardinghouses and even a public reception for Thomas Jefferson, he was scorned by those he tried to get to buy his book. The same kinds of men who had refused to play with him as a professional gambler labeled him a liar and slanderer. Bailey quoted one critic who swore he would never "subscribe to the life of a man who had been instrumental in ruining so many young men."[4]

The lessons Bailey learned (or refused to learn) all revolved around the differences between the style and the substance of class expression. "I prided much," as he put it, "in dress, riding fine horses, &c. which pride seems not to have forsaken me even now." He was also proud that he had tried to run for Congress, and he returned time and again to his brief and futile campaign as a mark of social legitimacy. The legitimacy Bailey sought was indeed elusive, for he could not turn the leisure of the rich into a successful commercial enterprise, and pride and bearing would not suffice to turn a professional gamester into a gentleman. Bailey acknowledged that he was dubbed "a libertine and not a fit associate for the virtuous and genteel part of society."[5]

Bailey was a professional, rather than a "professed," gamester, a man who made money by rational calculation from the impassioned and irrational habits of others. The professed gamester may from time to time have employed a skillful cheat or ruse, but such occasional ruses were far from the constant manipulations of men who depended on gambling to support themselves. The line between professed and professional, however, was never clear, and Bailey leaped on the ambiguities to point out the hypocrisy of those who played among themselves while they accused him of criminal gambling. In one notable instance he lured a traveler into betting on the contents of a needle case. The trick was a popular one involving a false-bottomed case and an elaborate ruse that implicated victims in a gaming plot. When the victims tried to have Bailey prosecuted as a cheat he turned on them, saying, "Gentlemen, you are caught in your own snare."[6]

Bailey was not simply the wandering stranger who passed through town with a dishonest game. He presented himself to strangers as a well-known citizen who came well recommended. Even if his taverns and boardinghouses in Berkeley Springs, Virginia, and Washington, D.C., were short-lived commercial enterprises where he hosted gambling games, Bailey held himself as an upstanding member of the community. He depended on a network of kin and acquaintances to bail him out of jail, to get him out of debt, and to attest to his character and credit. Yet testimony seems as often to have been fraudulent as honest. Bailey used the checks and promissory notes that had well served a closed world of social gambling, but in a shifting world of strangers checks and notes merely delayed the welching, fraud, and cheating that assured Bailey's profits. Still Bailey never gave up his quest for respectability. He peppered his book with affidavits from various respectable citizens and announced that he played with only the "best of company": members of Congress and the state legislature, "attornies, judges, doctors & merchants."

The social and cultural contradictions in Bailey's career as a sometimes threadbare professional gambler reappeared in his second career when he became, as he styled himself, an "illiterate" writer. He worked as a gambler in the public world of taverns where men told stories and played cards, billiards, and dice. He returned to this largely oral world to sell a book he had written for literate audiences. He sold his book by word of mouth, by reading aloud from a prospectus in "crowded taverns," but when he described himself in print he moved out of the closed world of tavern storytellers into a world of silent reading individuals. Several times Bailey questioned his own credentials for entry into the literate world of books and writers, describing himself as "an illiterate, obscure man" and suggesting that people buy his book as much out of charity as "from any calculations about [its] intrinsic worth." Bailey also carried his obsession with the appearance of the right company into his career as an "illiterate author." When he was attacked as a "blackguard" by a man who said that he wanted to be left in peace to drink, and furthermore that he would not read so unworthy a life, Bailey countered with his desire to be read only by "gentlemen" and by young men who might heed his counsel. "If my work was not of equal merit with Franklin's and Henry's," he went on modestly, "I hoped to God it might produce some good to the human family, more especially to youth, if they would be admonished by powerful example; it was my earnest prayer to make a useful book, and no exertion on my part shall be wanting to further this laudable purpose."[7]

Bailey spent his gambling career searching for wealthy bettors in taverns and boardinghouses mostly in rural Virginia and in Washington, D.C., but when he set out to sell his book on the evils of gaming he made the rounds of many of the same taverns. Because he straddled two cultural worlds, a world of bettors and a world of readers, and tried simultaneously to appeal to the expectations of both, he was never fully accepted by either. He produced, however, a curious commentary on money and social class in early nineteenth-century Virginia. He mingled his admonitions on the evils of gaming with descriptions of his sexual conquests, scatological jokes, and attacks on the hypocrisy of those who had imprisoned him for debt. Although he dressed like a gentleman and bragged that he danced and carried himself with more grace than his social superiors, Bailey knew that when he was rebuffed and rejected he had encountered the limits of his social aspirations. He was a poor boy who became a gambler because he wanted to be a gentleman and gentlemen gambled. But Bailey professionalized what was a consummate leisure activity for those who lived off wealth others had produced for them, and the gentlemen whose patronage he sought shunned his company.

Bailey's sense of the gentlemen among his potential readers reflected what he had learned of gentlemen customers as a gambler. A gentleman was usually a working professional capable of paying debts, not necessarily a member of the landed gentry who had been famous for their love of gambling a century before. In the early nineteenth century

Bailey described a world of gambling that lay somewhere between the high-stakes public betting of wealthy Virginia planters and the commercial recreation of northern cities. When Timothy Breen studied the high-stakes betting of the Virginia gentry during the middle years of the eighteenth century, he found that its seeming irrationality served to enforce class cohesion and to assert social power. While Breen's conclusions seem to rest on a functionalist rationality that itself undermines his premise that gambling was irrational, he does offer a rich reading of how gambling represented social structure of Virginia to Virginians. Gamblers grouped themselves according to family and estate, along the lines of what Rhys Isaac has referred to as Virginia's "rank-structured" society, and not by profession. Great risk, as well as great gains and great losses, served as symbolic affirmations of gentry power. Breen turned to Clifford Geertz's study of Balinese cockfights and argued that high-stakes betting, especially on horses, was a dramatic expression of who wealthy Virginians thought they were and what they thought they stood for. Gambling was a "device by which the participants transform[ed] abstract cultural values into observable social behavior," a "mechanism for expressing a loose but deeply felt bundle of ideas and assumptions about the nature of society." That "deeply felt bundle" included the competitiveness, individualism, and materialism that were on display when the gentry wagered and matched horses.[8] It also included the direct and immediate display of the power of wealth which separated the richest men from everyone else. In Bali, Geertz studied the elaborate structure of side bets that expressed various village animosities and loyalties. The betting Breen examined was related more to isolation than to allegiance, to hierarchy established by exclusion rather than by willing participation.

Bailey objected to exclusion and hierarchy and complained about the persistence of class lines in the altered social world of postrevolutionary Virginia. He found that class divisions were based on a hypocritical assertion of difference rather than on cultural merit, and he took it upon himself to expose hypocrisy whenever it suited him. His success as a gambling entrepreneur depended on his ability to evoke, even if only in parody, that "deeply felt bundle of ideas and assumptions" which had characterized gentry culture. When he could afford to, he went about "powdered and elegantly dressed," sporting a "gold corded cloak," carrying a "gold headed cane," attended by various

FAMILY SCENE.

Major Robert Bailey, Lucy Harris and twin children, Esau, and Jacob, in the Cabin.

There my dear Lucy is my prospectus, which is now all my dependence—I must endeavour to get as many subscribers as possible and finish my book; which will be a handsome support for us.

From *The Life and Adventures of Robert Bailey* (Richmond, 1821). Courtesy of the New-York Historical Society, New York City.

slaves and servants, and driving a coach and four. In his establishment at Berkeley Springs he provided "the best accommodations" and all sorts of the fancy food and fine drink that divorced money from any need that it be earned or spent on necessities.[9]

Bailey's evocation of gentry culture was a complex self-advertisement designed to promote his gambling business. He wanted to live in a world of risk, of close personal relationships, of combative, independent white men. One by one Bailey acquired the habits, traits, and baggage that would have marked a gentleman seventy-five years his senior. But when he danced, wore a powdered wig, rode on a high horse, and bet more than he could afford, he turned the trappings of an old gentry culture to the commercial ends of the postrevolutionary economy. The project was rich in contradiction. Bailey created a persona who rejected the rational accumulation of early nineteenth-century capitalism and most of the cultural apparatus that went along with it, but his persona was directly designed to reap the commercial profits that were the badge of social success. He refused to subscribe to the orderliness, rationality, and privacy now deemed cardinal social virtues, but like an orderly, rational, and private citizen he bent his energies to making money. He rejected the abstinence and refinement of postrevolutionary culture, but twisted rejection to produce postrevolutionary profits. For instance, when a doctor suggested that his survival depended on abstinence from alcohol Bailey bragged that he cured himself by drinking champagne. Even Bailey's sexual adventures and salacious stories can be read as criticism of a world newly inclined to privacy, civility, and refinement.[10] Bailey's display was advertisement, symbolic theater perhaps, but drained of the deep meaning that had bound together earlier generations of rich Virginians.

As a child Bailey may have witnessed high-stakes betting by rich gentlemen, but his own introduction into gaming took place at the hands of sharpers operating in Philadelphia. Bailey had gone north from Virginia, or so he said, to sell cattle. A "distant relation and pretended friend" seduced him into playing loo with the delicate challenge: "I never saw a Virginian but could play some."[11] A naive Bailey quickly lost all his money and sank into a suicidal despair. A loyal servant saved him, and on the way home he won at the races in Annapolis all that he had lost in Philadelphia. He won on the horses and at dice, but the six hundred dollars he won at faro made a "sportsman" of him.[12]

Faro was the preeminent banking game of the early nineteenth century. It is rarely played today, but in the gambling literature of the nineteenth century it is the backbone of the professional gambler's repertoire and the prime vehicle for the seduction of moneyed innocents. The name faro was a corruption of the French *pharaon,* and writing in the 1930s, Herbert Asbury speculated that the game appeared along with French colonists in the early eighteenth century in Louisiana and Alabama. Faro was a commercial game designed solely for winning and losing money, and it worked well for itinerant professionals because "any number of persons" could play against the bank. Players placed bets on a cloth layout illustrated with the cards of a deck. They bet on individual cards or on various combinations of cards. The dealer, assisted by croupiers, who collected and paid bets, turned through the deck. The first card would win for the players, the second for the bank. When a dealer turned two cards of the same denomination, a "split," the bank took half the money bet on that card. Except "splits," which won for the bank, and bets placed on the last four cards remaining in the deck, all bets paid even money. Hoyle calculated the odds in favor of the house of an honestly played game at no more than 3 percent.[13]

The appeal of faro for players lay both in its simplicity and in the relatively close odds; for bankers, in its speed, simple commercialization, and, if nineteenth-century chroniclers are to be believed, in the ample opportunities it afforded for creating crooked games. One former gambler doubted an honest faro game had ever existed and admonished that a man "would act more rationally and correctly to burn his money than to bet it on faro."[14] By the middle of the twentieth century faro had become largely a confidence scam, and one student of gambling slang writing in the early 1940s found that "although faro is not dead, it has withdrawn from popular patronage to such an extent that many persons who consider themselves gamblers have never seen it played." It was, he argued, culturally important as a source for American criminal argot and for such popular phrases as "both ends against the middle" and "buck the tiger."[15]

Faro made Bailey's career in a number of ways. He played faro and won. He dealt faro and backed others who dealt faro. He ran taverns and boardinghouses where faro was played, and he invented and patented a special spring box—his "Fair Dealer of Chartae Lusoriae"—designed to guarantee that faro was cleanly dealt. Bailey's dealing box, supposed insurance for players against the sleights-of-hand of able dealers and for dealers against the players' ability to read the backs of marked cards, merely created the occasion for more elaborate technical tricks. Explanations of the various complicated means of cheating at faro dominate the nineteenth-century literature on gambling to a surprising extent. Crooked dealers rounded, roughed, trimmed, sanded, marked, or altered cards in ways that made it possible to pull or to bury a card, depending on how the players had bet. They made honest-looking boxes that hid all sorts of springs and levers allowing them to pull particular cards. Hoyle's nineteenth-century American editors all amended the master's rules for the game of faro with disclaimers that such honest games could no longer be found.[16]

Obviously many of faro's ruses could have been performed as well from a deck held in the hand, but Bailey played off an incipient faith in the fairness of technology and tried to persuade dealers and players to insist on his box. The pretense of a fair game only made schemes worse, but Bailey's concern for honest faro play fitted well with the ambivalence that structured his narrative. Bailey's many self-reformations were short-lived; perhaps he recognized that the real interest in his story was in the description of the sin rather than the pious account of contrition. Several times Bailey swore off both women and betting only to find himself commissioning one more gilded miniature for his latest conquest, supporting one more bastard child, and backing one more gentlemanly gaming enterprise. Even at the close of his autobiography, after a long passage of contrition, he could not resist one last advertisement for his box: "If you are determined to indulge make sure you play out of *Bailey's patent box*."[17]

Bailey's self-interest in the success of gambling enterprises reflected a peculiarly southern ambivalence in the critique of gambling. While northern ministers, reformers, and employers attacked gambling as a form of theft, an individual vice based on the hope of return without labor and exchange without consumption, gambling southerners accepted the possibility of idleness and relished the pleasures of gaming. They did see danger in excess, and acknowledged that while gambling was not a vice in itself, it might become one when the inordinate pursuit of play led to a neglect of business or to losses greater than one could afford. Doubts about gambling reflected class divisions. Because gambling was recognized as the privilege of gentlemen, it became a vice for all those who were supposed to be producing wealth for others or earning their money in slow and steady accumulation.[18] Bailey clearly understood that as long as a gentlemen's adventurous deportment was celebrated as the pinnacle of social achievement, it would be hard to produce an unambivalent critique of gambling.

Throughout the nineteenth century northerners encountered similar ambiguities when they tried to delineate the differences between gambling and speculation. Proponents of gambling were fond of attacking the hypocrisy of those who gambled in stocks yet condemned gaming with cards. As we shall see, the northern reformers' critique of gambling can be read both as a legitimation of speculation and as a validation of the slow gains of wage labor. By the same token, the southern celebration of gambling must be seen against the backdrop of slave labor and as part of the cultural celebration of "unearned" wealth.

Two Southern Sermons

The colonial South did not criminalize gambling per se; the earliest attempts at control were aimed at curbing abuses and avoiding excessive losses rather than overt prohibition. In 1727 the Virginia House of Burgesses adopted the Statute of Anne, a law first passed by the House of Commons in 1710. The statute barred the collection of gambling debts through the courts but allowed losers of more than small amounts to sue for recovery.[19] In effect, by making gaming debts unenforceable, the law freed the legal system from complicity in large gaming losses. It did little to prohibit gaming in a closed society of peers where gambling obligations were policed by ample informal social sanctions. Virginia law on gambling continued to mirror the divisions of a rigidly ranked society. In 1744 the House of Burgesses adopted a law that prohibited gaming and betting in public, but once again enforcement seems to have been sporadic at best, occurring only when gaming was accompanied by other disorders or, as in Bailey's case, by financial chicanery.[20]

At various times there were also more informal but perhaps more effective voices that protested the dangers of gambling. In the middle of the eighteenth century at least two clergymen saw gambling as one of the abiding sins that threatened to bring ruin on Virginia. Once again protest followed the lines of social rank. William Stith, an

Episcopal minister, addressed prominent Virginians and warned them, for their own sake, that their vices might undermine their power. Samuel Davies, a dissenting New Light Presbyterian, offered a more stinging description of the social corruption implicit in a society given to high-stakes betting.[21]

In "The Sinful and Pernicious Nature of Gaming," an address delivered before the House of Burgesses in 1752, William Stith tried to make clear just why gambling might be wrong for Virginians. Stith implored politicians to enforce laws against gambling, for gambling threatened to turn from innocent amusement to sinful habit. Stith warned legislators that if they had the good of the country at heart they would enforce the law by example, by deed as well as by word. Gentlemen, he said, should stop throwing their money away: "Instead of defiling themselves with so foul a Practice, and setting Fashions to the lower People in vice, they ought by their Example to lead them on to everything that is virtuous and honest, and with the utmost Severity to restrain and punish this execrable custom."[22]

Stith recognized that the custom of gaming was enriching "tavern keepers and other panderers to vice" and that neither individuals nor their families nor society as a whole profited from the indulgences of the gaming table. Gambling drew men from useful labor, and its practice promoted no useful art. It robbed families not just of the money to meet their expenses but of the "gentler passions of Tenderness and Humanity." It turned individuals into drunken maniacs who, if they did not take their own lives, were destined to live in "continual Confusion and Perturbation." It also turned men against God. "Cursing and Swearing," they blamed the almighty for their losses; yet mired in the oaths and blasphemies of their defeats, they never credited God with their victories.[23]

Stith painted a society heading toward riot and ruin, but he was sure vice, however widespread, could be corrected if leaders recognized the social costs of indulgence and mended their ways. Four years later Samuel Davies, a New Light Presbyterian preacher, added up the moral costs of indulgence and attacked gambling as a sign of the corruption that infected men in high places. For him the sins of the gaming table had not simply led to dangerous dishonesty and a passion for gain but were part of a collection of vices which had prompted the Lord to punish Virginians with drought and military defeat. Virginians, he said, "*will* drink, and game, and swear, and whore; they *will* pursue the world with Eagerness and Avarice," and such pursuit had turned them from God to a world of "criminal diversions."[24] Although Davies found sin throughout society, he recognized gaming as the besetting sin of "People of high Life, and affluent Fortunes" who abused and wasted the "blessings of Providence."[25]

Davies, the evangelical outsider, attacked gaming as one of the nasty expressions of an indulgent society. Stith's was a more sympathetic and more secular critique. He entertained the possibility that gaming, even for money, might begin in innocent amusement. It became evil only when it engrossed "too much thought and Affection or too much time." Stith warned fellow Virginians, especially the wealthy and prominent, that they had reached that point of danger. He appealed to established authority imploring the members of the House of Burgesses to act as exemplary men and to reform their own ways on behalf of the people. Davies, on the other hand, dismissed the very idea of innocent gaming and offered a strict and stern condemnation of the vice that characterized the waste and extravagance of gentry culture. It is Davies's intolerance that suggests the power of the cultural critique he offered. Virginians may have been one people in the eyes of the Lord, but Davies reproached the rich for the vices he associated with an irreligious and corrupt society. In effect, by turning gambling into a moral issue and labeling it as one of the vices which threatened to bring ruin on society, he allowed himself to criticize wealthy Virginians and the culture they had made. Gambling turned class issues into moral issues and made it possible for moralists to see the dangers in certain kind of gain.

As Rhys Isaac has argued, such evangelical moralism was based on a renunciation of certain social practices labeled evil, and such renunciation embodied the deep cultural changes that led directly to the political and cultural transformations of the Revolution. Gambling was one of a complex of cultural vices which, if not abandoned, had at least to be denounced in the new political and economic order. Certain forms of gambling, especially the races and card games of the very rich, smacked of an aristocratic indulgence that was anathema to newborn republicans. In the 1770s the Continental Congress promoted revolutionary virtue, which entailed giving up "every species of extravagance and dissipation, especially all horse-racing, and all kinds of gaming, cock-fighting . . . and other expensive diversions and entertainments."[26] But gaming also represented a dangerous form of irrational waste which threatened the tenets of economic liberalism. By the early nineteenth century gambling represented an anachronistic expression of aristocratic pretensions, as well as a dangerous flirtation with unstable passion, and a serious violation of the steady accumulation and delayed gratification designed to control a wild enthusiasm for gain and to turn selfish profit seekers into a capitalist community.

The Anti-Gambling Society of Transylvania University

Nearly sixty years after the Revolution, Charles Caldwell, a displaced Philadelphia physician turned southern educator, addressed the students at Transylvania University in Lexington, Kentucky, on the dangers of their hereditary tendency to gamble. He argued that they should give up gambling because it was an addictive vice that would render them mad. The threat of gambling was not, as it had been in Virginia, to the order of a closely rank-structured community nor, as it had been to Davies and other evangelical reformers, to the divine intentions for a properly pious society on earth. Rather, addiction to gambling threatened to undermine the economic values now internalized in each of the individual students Caldwell had come to teach. Caldwell argued that his phrenological investigations of the properly balanced human mind had convinced him that those who grew addicted to gambling gave in to animal passions and grew mad.

Caldwell, an irascible, egotistical, contentious man who formed opinions and wrote on most of the major social and scientific issues of the day, joined the Transylvania University medical faculty in 1819. In the fall of 1834 he formed the students into an antigambling association, warning them in two long sermons about the dangers of the "nefarious" vice.[27] He shied away from religious issues, leaving the "*impiety*" of gambling to clergymen, and turned instead to the distortions created in the individual psyches of those who based gain on "the *fraudulent intention* . . . of one person to deprive another of his means of subsistence, contrary to his wishes, without giving him an equivalent for them." This fraudulent or felonious intention made gambling kin to theft, robbery, and pickpocketing, and few, he was sure, would object to the assertion that robbery was wrong. His students had been deceived by those "falsely styled the *best society,*" by "*gentlemen gamblers, who assume the mask* of some other calling, *by day,* and consort with the *Black-leg* and ruffian, by night. And," Caldwell added, "grieved I am to say, that there are multitudes of these day-maskers and night-revellers, in every section of our country."[28] Like Bailey, Caldwell objected to the masks of the rich, but what he read in gambling in his speech of 1834 was more an individual than a social danger.

While Stith had found gambling a dangerous misuse of productive time and energy, and Davies had found it offensive to God's plan for Virginia, Caldwell found it violated the proper balance of the well-ordered brain. It elevated the "Animal Faculties" of "Covetousness," "Secretiveness," "Destructiveness," and "Combativeness" over the "Intellectual and Moral Faculties" that were the seat of all that was good in human nature: "No man with moral and reflective organs preponderating in power, over his animal organs, has ever been a gambler or a robber, a thief or a pick-pocket." Caldwell contended that one witnessed on the sporting field a "revolting carnival of the grosser passions," "a spectacle of brutishness, tricked off by some of the gaudy trappings of humanity."[29]

Not surprisingly, Caldwell's phrenological delineation of the gambling vice within the individual followed particular lines of class and gender. Rich men, who derived their money from the labor of others, particularly slaves, risked at the gaming table a monomaniacal madness, no different in Caldwell's argument from the madness that afflicted "the invalid [who] believes himself haunted by ghosts and goblins, visited by angels, or favoured by an intercourse with the apostles and prophets." Gentlemen gamblers who did not go mad became desperate for cash and were inclined to take up "swindling, or some other sort of sinister employment, less dangerous than theft or robbery—though equally disreputable and immoral." Professional gamblers whose social origins were less exalted turned to "*positive and technical*" felonies. Poorer men caught up in the snares of professionals reflected the asymmetrical economy and turned to undisguised robbery. Gambling induced the apprentice to steal from his master, the shop boy and clerk from employers, the ward from the guardian, and the son from his parents. "Lady gamblers," in spite of their addiction to play, fell into verbal rather than economic vice and gave themselves over to "tattling, slander, and *unlady-like language.*"[30]

Gambling (and how people responded to it) served to position individuals within society and the economy. Caldwell urged his students, lest they be revealed as madmen or felons, to begin the move against gambling in all its forms. He exhorted them to stand as examples to the citizens of Lexington and then to come forward as witnesses against those who continued to gamble.

A year later he addressed the students again and congratulated those who had held to their pledges not to gamble. "As far as could be ascertained, not a card nor a die was thrown, nor a game of hazard of any kind indulged in, during the session of last winter, by a single pupil belonging to this school." And their good influence had spread to the firesides of Lexington, where Caldwell noted a decline in family gambling, and throughout the Mississippi Valley, where he sensed a turn against professional gamblers.[31] He read these as signs that the time was ripe for the extirpation of vice.

Caldwell's tactics in the second speech differed from the first, as he turned more explicitly to the social dangers of gambling. In 1834 he had avoided moral issues and turned to a loosely phrenological description of gambling's dangers. He had addressed neither the intricacies of play nor its physical setting. In 1835 he explained his abstractions as evidence of his innocence, insisting that his "language is wanting in power" to describe "the flagitious scenes of a GAMING HOUSE." Instead he ventured to comment on the future of Lexington and on professional gamblers' role in the riot and disorder of the summer of 1835. He found gamblers conspiring with "horse-thieves, robbers and rebellious slaves to spread conflagration and havock through the south." Slaveholding states, he argued, had a particular interest in precautions against gambling. "To their injury and disgrace, they are the principal hotbeds of gamblers; and, from the character of their population, such felons and vagabonds are dangerous to their peace."[32]

Caldwell did not touch on the economic and cultural circumstances that might explain just why the slave states should have been "hotbeds of gamblers," but he knew precisely why gambling had proved "dangerous to their peace." Caldwell referred to specific events that had been much in the recent news: to rumors of conspiracies and slave revolts to be led by the criminal comrades of the notorious land pirate John Murrell; to pamphlets describing Murrell's plots; to the execution in Madison County, Mississippi, of several men, white and black, who under the lash had confessed that they were members of Murrell's

Clan of the Mystic Confederacy and announced that a bloody slave uprising planned for Christmas 1835 had been moved up to July 4; and to the hanging, on July 6, of five so-called gamblers who were the friends of a man who had caused a ruckus at a Fourth of July barbecue in Vicksburg.[33]

Caldwell read the violence through the lens of gambling and argued that professional gamblers, along with all outsiders who proposed abolishing slavery, posed a real threat to the good order to southern society. A gambler's disregard for accumulated property extended to a disregard for property in human beings, and gamblers thus joined the loose conspiracy of blacklegs and slave stealers. He then worked through a series of equations that implicated gamblers in the rumored slave revolts of the summer of 1835. He made them kin to the "slave stealers" and horse thieves who had no respect for the property of others and linked them to the northern abolitionists he saw meddling in southern society and trying to alter that particularly southern idea that human beings might be property to be stolen. Describing a motley collection of villains, he engineered a subtle defense of much of the racial and antiabolitionist violence of the summer of 1835. Murrell, the slave stealer who lured slaves away from masters with promises of freedom only to murder them when they were no longer useful to him, stood in Caldwell's discourse as the perfect representation of a criminalized abolitionist. Murrell, the land pirate, harbored precisely those abominable motives slaveholders would have liked to have found in northern abolitionists.

Caldwell drew lessons for Lexington from the bloody events in Mississippi and encouraged his students not to be afraid to become "informers and witnesses" as they led the community against gamblers. Again indirectly defending the lynch mob at Vicksburg, he attacked those who might hold secret knowledge of criminal conspiracies; he chastised jurors who failed to convict gamblers, lawyers who defended them, and judges who gave lenient sentences to those few unfortunates who were convicted. He attacked landlords who tolerated gamblers and tradesmen and mechanics who defended them because they profited from their generous custom. He warned families who continued to gamble that they were the "fatal source of the entire evil" and that by allowing their children to gamble at home they incubated victims for "satanical" professionals. Caldwell also turned on "gentlemen gamblers" who hid their vices in the successes of their public lives or who passed laws against gaming which they then "flagitiously violate(d)."[34]

But Caldwell continued to insist that the main risk in gambling lay in flirtation with an "ungovernable spirit of adventure" which made men willing to abandon all for the sensation of risk. Vicksburg was only an extreme example of habits already present in Lexington. During racing season he observed the worst excesses: "During this unbridled explosion of the vices, neither servants, apprentices, journeymen, clerks, nor any other description of labourers, or hired men of business can be held to their duty. In defiance of advice, remonstrance, and command, they abandon their employments, rush to the carnival, gamble, drink, quarrel, blaspheme, and perpetrate all other sorts of enormity. Or if authoritatively withheld from the intoxicating revel, they become sullen, dissatisfied, and useless at home."[35] Gambling hurt the commercial prospects of Lexington, but Caldwell entertained a greater vision. He encouraged his listeners to imagine a community redeemed, reformed, and rid of its gamblers, inhabited by rational, controlled individuals protected from their animal vices by proper hierarchical ordering of their psyches and freed from the corruptions of monarchy and aristocracy to live in "*genuine republicanism.*" Caldwell never stressed the sobriety, industry, and frugality so central to northern renunciations of gambling, but he did base his call to shun gamblers on particular constructions of what it meant to be American and on what it meant to be a doctor trained at Transylvania. "A spirit of enlightened and manly Americanism would rid us of all these outlandish appendages, which create in us such a mongrel, piebald character, and bestow on us, in lieu of them, *substantial nationality.*"[36]

He had found just such "manliness" and "substantial nationality" in the citizens of Vicksburg who had risen, he said, to exterminate their professional gamblers. In this he seemed to have sided with his adopted South against "eastern writers and other noisy medlars," whom he labeled "shallow and censorious news-mongers." He argued that the peace of Vicksburg had been genuinely threatened by a conspiracy among gamblers, slaves, traveling "steam doctors" who treated slaves with herbs and heat, itinerant preachers, and abolitionists who were "to lead the slaves to pillage and massacre." Citizens had acted in their own self-defense following assumptions that, even if proved mistaken, had appeared to them to be genuine and therefore justified their behavior. And furthermore, as Caldwell's study of the corrupt bar and bench amply proved, the formal workings of the law were but feeble safeguards for a community truly threatened. Lexington, he warned, should act now before it too needed such a bloody purge.[37]

Vicksburg, Mississippi, July 1835

Caldwell was not the only writer to comment on the gamblers hanged on July 6, 1835, at Vicksburg, and it is possible to reconstruct something of the bloody days from accounts in the contemporary press. There is no consensus on why some white men in Vicksburg killed gamblers—or on whether the hangings revealed, as Caldwell believed, the health of the community or, as northern abolitionists believed, its pathology.

At a Fourth of July barbecue, a drunken gambler (or variously, a blacksmith turned pugilist who happened to fraternize with gamblers) named Francis Cabler climbed on the tables and interrupted the official toasts. His behavior offended some members of the recently organized militia company, the Vicksburg Volunteers, who tossed him out of the barbecue. A few hours later Cabler showed up at the militia's public drill armed and reportedly ready to kill the militiamen who had thrown him out of the barbecue. A crowd of "respectable" people seized Cabler, took him into a nearby wood, tied him to a tree, and "lynched him"—a punishment which might stop short of hanging. They whipped him, coated him with tar, and rolled him in feathers.[38]

That night citizens of Vicksburg called a meeting at which they passed a resolution giving all "professional GAMBLERS" twenty-four hours to leave town. They warned "all persons permitting faro dealing in their houses . . . that they will be prosecuted therefor," and they ordered printed one hundred copies of the broadside warning and posted them at street corners."[39] One witness asserted that "a majority of the gang, terrified by the threats of the citizens, dispersed in different directions without making any opposition." On the morning of July 6, he continued, citizens and militiamen "marched to each suspected house, and, sending in an examining committee, dragged out every faro table and other gambling apparatus that could be found." In their search they happened on one group of armed men, holed up in a "low groggery," who had refused to leave. The mob surrounded the shack and exchanged shots with the men inside. Dr. Hugh Bodley, "a citizen universally beloved and respected" was shot and killed as he broke down the back door. Bodley's friends in the mob then grabbed the five "gamblers," marched them to the center of town, conducted them to the scaffold, and hanged them without ceremony and without blindfolds. "All sympathy for the wretches," the witness concluded, "was completely merged in detestation and horror of their crime." After watching the men die on gallows the "whole procession then returned to the city, collected all the faro tables into a pile and burnt them."[40]

By blaming gamblers for the violence in Vicksburg, Caldwell brought his lesson home to his students. He described the lynchers not as a wild mob but as citizens who had acted with "decision and promptitude" and "weighed" the blood of a few felons against the innocent blood of hundreds of women and children. Caldwell found in Vicksburg a laudable expression of American democracy, but he also found an excuse for the violence against slaves and abolitionists that was far more common than violence against gamblers. The citizens had rid themselves of a "blood-thirsty gang" who "had made beggars first, and gamblers afterward, of many respectable young men," but in so doing they had also acted against the abolitionists who threatened their social order. Caldwell was convinced that their prompt action had prevented the riot and pillage which that same summer plagued Baltimore, Philadelphia, Charleston, and New York.[41]

In 1840, Thomas Brothers, an antichartist Englishman, ignored gambling and found the lynchings ample illustration of democracy's crashing failure. Brothers wrote to repudiate the Painite tendencies of his own youth, and he gathered copious evidence of social evil and financial corruption in the United States. He compiled the excesses of the 1830s, listing all manner of "murders, riots, and other outrages," including flour riots, race riots, election riots, antiabolitionist riots, dueling, and piracy—all to illustrate the "fallacy of self-government." The men who were hanged in Vicksburg, ropes pulled tight around their necks, had asked for "the last privilege of *American citizens,* the trial by jury." The trial was denied, and Brothers found a society so divorced from the principles of civilization ("Such conduct would disgrace Algiers, and could hardly have occurred in a barbarous state.") that even in a sentence of death it refused victims their rights. He found a society lacking not only in justice but in sentiment. Warm tar dripped into a gambler's eyes and a young wife who was denied permission to bury her husband was forced "to fly, with her orphan child, in an open skiff."[42]

Brothers did not find universal accord on the hangings, describing citizens moved to tears at the spectacle, but like Caldwell, he quickly buried discord and individual tragedy in a heap of political meaning. That the men hanged were gamblers was entirely incidental. "I mention this case of *Lynching*," Brothers concluded, "for two reasons; first because the Lynchers were the first men in those parts, headed by a captain in the United States army; secondly, because the most bloodthirsty among them was a cashier of the planters' bank and the planters are the leading men of the state. If we find such conduct in them, what can we expect from the mass?"[43] In effect Brothers asked the same question about social order and social example that had troubled the Reverend Stith when he addressed the House of Burgesses in the 1750s, but here the troublesome example had moved from the gaming table to its violent repudiation. Brothers also used Vicksburg as an example of the banking disorders he so detested in the 1830s. What he saw behind the Vicksburg hangings was not so much the agitation of northern abolitionists as the disorder caused by the rampant speculation that followed Jackson's veto of the charter of the Second Bank of the United States. He blamed state banks for inflation and for the heady climate of speculative profits which drew adventurers into the Mississippi Valley and encouraged gamblers and their excesses.

Writing in 1844, the geologist George Featherstonhaugh also read the "repudiation" of the Vicksburg gamblers as a harbinger of the financial difficulties that plagued the state after the Panic of 1837. After a detailed description of the hangings he turned from the moral order of the community to the financial order of the state. He pointed out that Mississippi was the first state to repudiate its debts in the face of fiscal crisis. He deemed "repudiation . . . a mode of fiscal purification of their exchequer, almost as serious in its effects to the many confiding creditors it has ruined, as the storms with which they are accustomed to purify their moral condition are to the objects of their vengeance." The state purified its debts with the same unthinking zeal that had characterized the impassioned violence at Vicksburg.[44]

Caldwell, Brothers, and Featherstonhaugh all thought the panic that followed Cabler's drunken irreverence indicated that something more was going on in Vicksburg than the elimination of a few crooked faro dealers. A punishment so severe in a society that had long tolerated most forms of gaming would seem to suggest, as the journalist Hezekiah Niles editorialized late in the summer of 1835, "a *society* . . . *unhinged.*"[45] Although historians of gambling would like to think that society had become unhinged over gambling, gambling seems a merely incidental, if perhaps an apt, representation of the changes about to finish off the "flush times" in the Mississippi Valley.

One lawyer turned writer relished the heady opportunities and the combined literary, financial, and legal chaos of the "flush times" of the early 1830s. In 1854 Joseph Baldwin remembered Mississippi in the 1830s as a society "wholly unorganized," standing "on its head with its heels in the air." Paper currency inflated cotton prices and speculators raised land prices. "Money, got without work, by those unaccustomed to it, turned the heads of its possessors, and they spent it with a recklessness like that with which they gained it. The pursuit of industry neglected, riot and coarse debauchery filled up the vacant hours." Baldwin's "riotous carnival" during the land boom in the Southwest was a perfect setting for all manner of gambling, lying, and swindling. But the frolic ended with a resounding crash in 1837, and the Mississippi banks that had underwritten the speculative boom were now as poor as any in the country. When John Peters, a young Brooklyn dry-goods merchant, arrived in Vicksburg in 1837 he found little sign of Baldwin's revels. In fact, he found the very antitype of flush times, and throughout the late 1830s and early 1840s he repeated in his diary the refrain "times dull, money scarce." It was during these "flat times" of the 1840s that gamblers who had run the "low groggeries" along the river took to the steamboats. The source of wealth was to be commercial travelers or their agents operating between New Orleans and the Northeast.[46]

In the 1830s and 1840s, travelers grew fond of describing corrupt gamblers who induced bored passengers to play. James Silk Buckingham remembered cards and dominoes as the passengers' constant occupation, "from immediately after breakfast till near midnight, with the intervention of meals only." The strict social separations that helped assure games between financial equals on land dissolved on the river. One gambler bragged he could get into any game after treating wealthy passengers to drinks. He stole a trick from *Puss in Boots* and made wealthy travelers believe him the proprietor of an immense domain by paying slaves all along the river to call him master. Tales of great gain by scheming professionals tend to be highly exaggerated, but gamblers were well placed on river boats, where cash carried by travelers appeared to be divorced from social safeguards and from the circumstances in which it was made. Descriptions all play the relatively easy wealth of the Mississippi Valley in the 1830s off against the social dangers of commerce with strangers and the forced leisure or boredom of long river voyages.[47]

Economic changes do help explain why men called gamblers got hanged, left the river towns, and began to deal to wealthy travelers on steamboats. As Bailey's career amply illustrated, gambling was flush with symbolic power. Gamblers in the Mississippi Valley operated in a commercial economy. Yet in dress, manner, and style they quoted from gamblers of the past, and they played with the trappings of authority still holding sway among the slaveholders of the South. Their evocation of gentry culture, however, had very different consequences from Bailey's. When low-life, crooked card sharps appropriated the airs and habits of a gambling gentry, they threatened a hierarchical slaveholding society in ways Bailey had never done. For all his commercial goals, Bailey embraced gentry values. He may have projected a bad example and reveled in blasphemy and self-indulgence, and in his efforts to make a living by winning money from the "best of men" he may have been insulted, jailed, persecuted, mocked by stone-throwing youths, and had his possessions sold to pay his debts, but his was a reactionary celebration of cultural forms and not a direct challenge to the cultural authority of rich gambling planters. He wore fancy clothes, owned slaves when he could afford them, and celebrated just those forms of cultural expression which represented the power and privilege of the rich. He posed no profound or unsettling challenge and, unlike the next generation of professional gamblers, he was never whipped, tarred, feathered, or hanged.[48]

One historian of American gambling, John Findlay, has argued that in the 1830s Vicksburg had moved away from a frontier economy of rowdy transients to one with more settled and diversified markets and that, as the economy grew more complex, "respectable" citizens no longer felt compelled to tolerate the vices they had once indulged. Vicksburg levied a tax on flatboatmen and closed riverside gambling resorts. Findlay concluded that vigilante justice "heralded the closing of the frontier." "While vigilantism still belonged to western societies, it often constituted the first step in a sometimes rapid process of transition that ultimately asserted eastern culture over western ways."[49] The incident in Vicksburg is perhaps better understood as a contrast between the economies of the North and the South than between the cultures of the East and the West. Even if the hangings represented economic development for Vicksburg, the town was moving into the future by embracing cultural symbols of a southern past. Slaveholders were defending their interests against the threat posed by escalating abolitionist attacks and by increasingly effective abolitionist propaganda.

Gamblers might be hanged along with slaves who wanted to revolt, and with steam doctors who used their profession to befriend slave families, and with abolitionists whose tracts might inspire rebels because, like them all, they challenged the power of the slaveholding elite. What was the professional gamblers' challenge? The grubby professional gamblers who ran low dives on Vicksburg landing made a mockery of the cultural symbols of a planter aristocracy and they made it just at a moment when the slaveholders of the South felt themselves most threatened both by the intensified abolitionist campaigns and by the increasing commercial economy of the lower Mississippi Valley. It appeared to one inhabitant of Vicksburg in the 1830s that nasty gamblers had taken over the town. "Our streets everywhere resounded with the echoes of their drunken and obscene mirth, and no citizen was secure from their villainy."[50] The panic paranoia of white slaveholders, however, meant that "obscene mirth" led to death rather than laughter.

Leonard Richards's study of the "respectable men" who made up northern antiabolitionist mobs helps us understand why mockery might turn bloody. Richards concluded that mob violence against abolitionists in the North could be understood only as a reaction to "larger forces that were drastically dislocating northern society." Violence grew out of racism, fear of miscegenation, but, as well, out of the manner in which organized antislavery challenged traditional structures of authority. "New organizations invariably disrupted established forms of social control and social organization. They competed with both traditional leaders and other organizations for funds, for cadre, and for loyal followers. They cut across traditional boundaries of kinship and loyal community, intruded upon prerogatives of pastors and local gentry, and drew members of the local community into their orbit."[51]

The abolitionist threat in the South was still more immediate. Many years ago the historian Clement Eaton suggested that mob violence in the Old South grew out of "the popular excitement that was engendered by the antislavery controversy." Although he dismissed the Vicksburg hangings as frontier vigilante justice, a popular response to "the lack of adequate courts and jails" at a time of controversies over authority and property, it is not possible to separate what he labeled vigilante violence against gamblers from violence against slaves and abolitionists.[52] Although there was no proof that plots were intertwined, Caldwell perhaps expressed something of what the "respectable citizens" of Vicksburg were thinking when he associated gamblers, blacklegs, horse thieves, abolitionists, and revolutionary plotters. Gamblers may not have directly conspired with "slave stealers," but low-life rowdies who mocked the pretenses of gentry culture did conspire in undermining the symbolic presentation of authority that supported a threatened world run by slaveholders.[53]

There was little genteel or gentrified in the gambling dives' that catered to transient flatboatmen and river workers and local dockhands. One witness described them as low "tippling houses" where innocent (and not so innocent) men lost their money. Caldwell was glad to have found in Vicksburg gamblers who were anything but respectable. By the 1830s gamblers were smalltime criminals, figures allied with "murderers and swindlers," with a "banditti of blacklegs," or with "itinerant preachers, steam doctors, and clock pedlars."[54] These lists are important, for in the antebellum South gambling alone rarely troubled observers. For gambling to appear wrong it had to be grouped with other vices, and for gamblers to appear menacing they had to be associated with other villains. At the same time the label "best of men," the men Bailey had cultivated with his fine dancing and genteel airs, had to be stripped from any who would gamble to make a living. For the "best of men" were professionals, doctors, bankers and militiamen, who had little to do with gaming. In the summer of 1835, after the bloody purge, the inhabitants of Vicksburg published a statement in their own defense defining just who were the best citizens and asserting that "the *revolution* has been conducted here *by the most respectable citizens, heads of families, members of all classes, professions, and pursuits.*"[55]

Moves against gambling, then, whether offered by evangelical preachers as moral admonition or by a professor who organized student societies or by militiamen who became vigilante mobs, suggest how communities might divide over moral and economic issues. Gambling offered a means to represent the cultural prerogatives that accompanied the economic privileges of class. But gambling also allowed the poor to challenge the rich. Controversies over gambling frequently broke out at moments of cultural and economic change. As Isaac has argued, when New Light evangelical ministers began their attack on gentry culture and its vices they laid the groundwork for the cultural transformations of the Revolution. When Caldwell's students renounced gambling they embraced the beginnings of a cultural code of professional physicians. And when the so-called respectable citizens of Vicksburg turned on the gamblers, they announced not only that their economy no longer depended on adventurers, speculators, fortune seekers, and transient laborers whose vices they had indulged, but that they had drawn lines that made outsiders expendable. "Bullying insolence" and social parody that mocked the trappings of authority were to be met with violence. When professional gamblers reappeared on steamboats in the late 1830s and 1840s, writers and preachers who told stories about them testified that the cultural center of unearned and easy wealth had shifted from the river banks to the floating palaces of trade and credit that plowed the rivers.[56]

Gambling in New York

When northern communities moved against gambling they did so in a less dramatic fashion. It proved very difficult, as we shall see, either to make gambling the center of a constructive reform crusade or the means of separating a community damned from a community saved. In the 1820s and 1830s the gambling that had been part of working-class recreation began to trouble economic reformers. As production and finance changed, so too did the cultural significance of gambling. Gambling's status as recreation as well as its nature as vice changed as the economy shifted from one of limited gain to the open and endless commercial markets of the early nineteenth century. It was one thing to bet with friends or with peers; it was quite another to wager in a commercial setting against professional gamblers who made a living off their customers' losses. People who bet in a fair game within a close a community of friends could be assured that as the game continued money would eventually return. Early nineteenth-century reformers feared that strange "professional" gamblers waiting on the edges of the market would break into the community of friends and drain away money, especially cash carried by undisciplined clerks who worked for large mercantile houses. Financial reformers also worried that gamblers eyed the miniscule accumulations of superstitious wage laborers and that the professionals, who appeared and disappeared with tides of prosperity, fell under no structural constraints to return their winnings. As strangers they felt no social obligations to continue the game another day. The possibility of money lost to gamblers haunted a middle class insecure about the origins and future of its own wealth yet determined to reinvest the wages of the laboring poor. These anxieties determined the complicated representations of gambling and shaped efforts to describe the motives of those who continued to wager.

Gambling continued to appear in the various catalogues of the vices of the very poor, in lists of the troubling habits of workers, in outlines of the pleasures of the very rich, and in descriptions of the temptations of the young, foolish, and recently moneyed. A few northern ministers and moral advisers looked on gambling as a problem that might afflict their charges. While southern reformers had imagined the social disorders the bad example of a gambling gentry might encourage, northern reformers worried that slow and steady gains of labor might pale and turn insipid beside the allures of gambling. To guard against such dangers, northern legislatures abolished state-supported lotteries and banned gambling in public—on streets, in inns and taverns.

Reformers saw personal ills of gambling as well. When gamblers, especially working-class gamblers, won, they ceased to labor and quickly adopted the airs of decayed aristocrats. Winning undermined the character of true and steady workers; winners grew distracted, lazy, and useless. By the 1840s reformers produced sermons and advice books detailing the sad fates of young ambitious clerks who had lost money gambling and begun to steal from their employers. In these highly stylized portraits, when their thefts were about to be exposed, clerks committed suicide. All who would gamble, however, the rich and the poor, flirted with a dangerous passion that threatened to explode psyches built for measured gain and to destroy the communities built to turn the passion for gain into a mutual interest in accumulation.

In the North, as in the South, to gamble or not to gamble was to comment on social class. Robert Bailey had hoped to use his gambling to rise in the world and to use opposition to gambling to sell his book to the literate citizens of the new republic. Caldwell hoped to use opposition to gambling to mark his Transylvania students as trained physicians. And members of the Vicksburg militia, whatever they did in private and whatever their private motives, announced to the world that "respectable citizens" would no longer permit professional faro dealing in their town. Both gambling and its representation differed in northern cities. Even if members of the early industrial working class gambled in neighborhood taverns and groceries and bet among themselves, reformers never turned to gambling as their besetting vice. In efforts to inculcate that great trio of early industrial virtues—industry, sobriety, and frugality—it appeared that excessive expenditure on drink more often accounted for violations of frugality than gambling. A few reformers made gambling the parent of all other vices but most preferred to concentrate on drink. Drink opened on a richly symbolic universe that made it possible for reformers to alter working-class worlds of work and play while talking and thinking about temperance.[57] Gambling was never so fertile. To have stopped gambling was by no means so easy to construct as a culturally worthy act as to have stopped drinking: gambling's symbolic connotations were full of disquieting contradictions. Gamblers had experienced life in a world of unearned wealth. Could someone who once gambled be trusted to carry out commissions or to feed his family? Could a former gambler be reconstructed as a trusted employee?

Nevertheless to give up drink and to renounce tavern fellowship might also mean to give up gambling, and to give up gambling might well mean abandoning certain traditional forms of recreation and traditional companions who might propose a friendly wager. In conjunction with other reforms, to renounce gambling might then lead individuals who were so inclined to the rational recreations and careful accumulations of ambitious employees or even to the enlightened fellowship of republican workers. Reformers hoped it would lead them from the tables of taverns to the lines of savings banks. And for reformers the very act of opening a savings account separated the virtuous workers from their gambling comrades. Those who promoted savings banks designed them to preserve the small surpluses of wages for times of economic distress and old age and to protect savers from temptation to pleasurable indulgence. As the historian Brian Harrison discovered in his study of temperance in Victorian England, virtuous independence was open to a variety of interpretations; it served the interests of employees as well as employers. The man with a savings account might stand as adversary to an employer. He "need not care whether he sold his labour one day or another, but could wait and sell it to an eager purchaser instead of being a needy seller."[58] Promoters of savings banks were willing to risk such independence.

Much of the evidence on northern gambling is highly anecdotal, but historians have found that at the beginning of the nineteenth century urban artisans and mechanics gambled in grog shops, groceries, and taverns. They played cards, billiards, shuffleboard, and dice, bought chances and fractions of chances in lotteries, and bet on contests between bulls, bears, cocks, badgers, horses, men, and dogs; but they did not write about what they were doing. Most evidence on urban gambling comes from sensational descriptions, reformers' complaints, and a few confrontations with the law. It appears, however, that gambling (particularly the lottery) was widespread and a part of daily life.[59] Urban historians, like early nineteenth-century reformers, mention gambling most often in passing either as one item on a list of pleasures available to city dwellers and visitors or as part of a male world of play. Likewise, professional gamblers appeared at the edges of northern crowds, joining pickpockets, prostitutes, and drunks along the grand boulevards of cities and setting up their games at fairs, public festivals, races, and militia musters.[60]

At its best, working-class gambling in the North served to reinforce traditions of reciprocity and mutuality, perhaps offering poor laborers an escape from depressing prospects in crowded cities and from the increasingly pervasive controls of the early industrial workshop. Limited wagers on games and contests can be seen as part of "traditional" patterns of working-class recreation and exchange. But such traditions, Sean Wilentz reminds us, were not the heritage of a distant past; rather they were a distinct creation of the urban workers' world of the early nineteenth century.[61] As long as poor people gambled among themselves in honest games money would return, just as it had done for the aristocrats in Virginia. Professional gambling was a different matter. Purveyors of vice and their customers became visible as reformers and philanthropists worried about how the poor spent their money and about how young men on whom they were forced to rely in an expanding commercial economy might spend theirs.

The continuing popularity of northern urban gambling can be understood only as part of this world of employers, wage earners, and young clerks and not as some timeless remnant of a superstitious past. Reformers designed a two-pronged attack on gambling: they turned attention to the young clerks who ran financial errands in a mercantile city and to the laboring poor who seemed to spend a portion of their modest accumulations on vices like gambling. The first raised doubts about financial integrity in an economy of strangers; the second about the cultural independence of a working class who chose to spend in ways offensive to the sensibilities of employers, philanthropists, and reformers. The battle for the salvation of gaming clerks was fought by ministers and moralists and by writers who argued that gamblers were cheaters who pretended to offer a fair game. Their main worries were about justifying speculative gain and securing the coffers against the folly of employees. We will meet them in the next chapter. The battle to wrest the small surpluses of the urban poor from the grasp of gamblers and tavern keepers was led by those who changed the structures of New York philanthropy from charity to self-help and promoted thrift with institutions like savings banks. They realized that for wage workers the temptation to gamble had to be eliminated, not only because the workers might be tempted to steal but because gambling gains offered an attractive alternative to the small hourly, daily, or weekly wage. To abolish gambling would thus help to legitimate wage labor; it would also help to secure the gains of those who speculated in lands, stocks, and merchandise.

The most detailed descriptions of gambling in the antebellum North center on New York. All descriptions emphasize the danger and the glamour of easy wealth, suggesting, as they had in the Mississippi Valley of the 1830s, that money made in ways other than slow and steady gain was money that might readily be gambled. And in descriptive literature on New York the thirst for great gain touched the very rich and the very poor alike. Gambling followed distinctly marked class lines, and reporters described varieties of gambling in a sort of descent from the honest sporting palaces of the wealthy to the dingy, but perhaps honest, dives of the very poor. In between were the markedly dishonest houses designed to attract clerks who had access to their employers' coffers.

Reporters' descriptions began with professional gamblers who operated what were called "first-class hells," clubs where rich card players dealt faro to wealthy merchants who played in luxurious surroundings and dined on fine food. Because the amount of money staked allowed a profit even on the slight odds in favor of the house, the first-class establishments were described as honest, and they isolated those who could afford to lose from those who might turn to crime. As Bailey had done in Berkeley Springs, proprietors used decor as bait and created settings that evoked the boundless wealth of European aristocrats. Rooms were decorated with an "exquisite refinement of taste," with tapestries, antiques, and portraits—all made to evoke eighteenth-century France, where aristocrats had gambled with no regard to the poverty around them. Players drank fine wine, ate fresh fruit and "delicate paté." When these highly rational players lost all they were willing to lose, they turned "first-class hells" into gentlemen's clubs and sat down to discuss business, politics, and wine.

For critics such seamless transitions obviously suggested that business and gaming were, in the last analysis, near kin, but descriptions served other purposes as well. Settings conjured a world where wealth and capital lay buried in land, and in so doing they helped to sever what, for a wage economy, was a necessary connection between money and the necessity to earn it and to spend it in a rational manner and, as important, the connection between money and measured time. Gamblers played late into the night, and victims, especially in sensational fiction, always staggered into the dawn wondering just how they had lost all their money and an entire night at the gaming table. Reformers worried that the presence of these fancy gambling halls proved dangerous for poor souls who depended on their own labor to amass a meager fortune. As one minister warned, "The gayly-illuminated halls for eating and the haunts of gaming hold out strange colors of delight. The half-intoxicated rustic sees fairy-land in the common saloons of merriment."[62]

New York reporters also found a group of houses, mostly along Broadway, that looked like first-class houses but were, in effect, "skinning houses," where play was not always honest. Here dishonest professional gamesters fleeced innocent, but infinitely corruptible, victims in a style worthy of melodrama. These houses introduced a whole new set of urban figures known as "ropers" and "steerers" who earned their keep by charming foolish young men and luring them into gambling halls. Their likely suckers included anyone new to New York, but also firemen from rival fire companies and members of rival political parties. The houses were the home of the male "sporting fraternity"—professional pugilists, card sharps, and Tammany "shoulder hitters." These same types also patronized the "wolf traps" on Ann Street where anyone with a small stake could open a game. "Wolf traps" provided cards, tables, and layouts, and the proprietor took 10 percent of a dealer's winnings. Reporters and reformers also found gamblers who had congregated on the edges of Wall Street, where they pocketed the profits of young merchants and brokers unable to give up their daily speculations.[63]

In New York there were also "skin" games in the back rooms of saloons and "penny-poker dens," especially in poor neighborhoods like in Five Points. The gambling dens were described in rather formulaic fashion as the "small, dimly lit and meanly furnished" resorts of smalltime thieves and randomly idle men and women, black and white. Reporters condemned the dangerous social mix. One brave type was distressed to find "men and women . . . indiscriminately mingled" playing with "greasy cards." Such descriptions of penny-poker dens served as local color in reporters' sensational portraits of New York. They illustrated just how far reporters had actually ventured beyond the boundaries of the respectable, and sinister descriptions of smalltime filth and dishonesty served once more to naturalize bourgeois definitions of honest wealth and worthy labor and to equate the habits of the poor (especially immigrants and African Americans) with sin and vice.[64]

Gambling appeared in the popular press aimed at northern audiences as an exotic vice of the very rich, a dangerous vice of the very poor, and a dangerous inclination of those newly moneyed clerks who might be called middle class. In popular fiction gambling appeared as one of the hidden vices of the corrupted aristocrats who threatened the republic of honest producers. But, as we shall see, the complicated class lines of gambling produced problems for writers of fiction just as they did for reformers.

In the early part of the century, one of the men who dominated New York's financial and philanthropic communities, John Pintard, wrote to his daughter in New Orleans telling her of young men, bankers and bookkeepers, who had been led by gambling to defalcation, desperation, and suicide. He reassured her that although he and his friends raced horses, "as very respectable gentlemen belong to the Club, Gambling and the usual concomitant of race grounds are suppressed." Not that they were entirely successful, for he found that "the black leg gentry and all sorts of pickpockets &c will evade the strictest laws." But his prohibitions on gambling were by no means global and he happily forwarded to her her portion of a one-hundred-dollar lottery prize.[65]

Pintard's inconsistencies were mirrored in the sporadic enforcement of New York's laws against gambling. From time to time gamblers and gambling-house proprietors, the poorer ones, were brought before the New York Common Council, but they were rarely convicted. Although laws passed in 1801 and in 1811 made it illegal to gamble in inns and taverns, and in parks and "public places," it was rarely for gambling alone that tavern keepers or bettors were brought before the bench. And tavern and boardinghouse keepers, at least, usually escaped punishment by appealing to the logic of commerce and arguing that they kept tables only at the request of customers and professing ignorance of any betting.[66]

The council looked upon gambling by the poor with a combined moral and financial stewardship and worried that the poor ventured small sums on the lottery and that whether they won or lost they became enthralled by "a spirit of gambling." The spirit touched not only the "labouring poor, but even Mendicants, children and servants who do not scruple to make Crime the instrument to enable them to become Adventurers." In 1811 the Common Council constructed a system of fines for gambling and dice playing and enjoined the public to police play, especially on holidays because "gambling is a practice highly injurious to the morals of the young and rising generation." It was also injurious to economic dependents, and they determined that if a "minor, an apprentice, a servant, or a slave" were caught playing, then parent, guardian, master, mistress, or owner would pay the fine.[67]

In March 1812 the members of the Common Council heard the "Report of the Committee for Suppressing Immorality." The committee worried that Sabbath breaking, gaming, and drunkenness were "increasing to an alarming degree," but they admitted to only "a limited knowledge of the real state" of the gambling vice. They had no doubt, however, about its fatal effects. It is known, they said, "that among the higher circles are to be found those who can lament the loss (at the fascinating and deceptive game of Brag) of from one to thirty thousand Dollars at one sitting, while many of the humble poor who to imitate as much as possible the examples of what they deem the accomplished Gentlemen will sacrifice at a Raffle the small pittance obtained for a day's labor, and thereby leave their children in a State of Starvation." In their efforts to curb gambling the committee skirted the issue of emulation (as they did the issue of a day's wages deemed but a "small pittance") and recommended that the council pass an act authorizing aldermen or their assistants to enter taverns to seize gambling equipment, to sell the useful parts, and to "use the residue thereof as fuel."[68]

In one well-publicized incident, zealous member of the Police Watch entered a house where they suspected people were gambling. But their zeal led to a scandal that suggests the problems of suppressing gaming in a commercial metropolis, where it might well have been a practice of the rich as well as the poor. Late in March 1826 the watch, responding to a complaint "made by a credible witness," entered the house of a Joseph Collett at 42 Broad Street. Eighteen watchmen, armed with clubs, secured the doors and windows of Collett's boardinghouse and gathered up about thirty people—foreigners and citizens—whom they took to the watch house and held for the night. They caught a journeyman baker who had been playing keno, but they also took in a Spanish merchant who was looking for lodging for his friends and a "French gentlemen." A committee called to investigate the conduct of the watch concluded that the watchmen possessing only a warrant for the arrest of Mr. Collett had violated the Fourth Amendment of the constitution of the State of New York. Their unlawful entry violated as well the hospitality of a commercial city whose business depended on the custom of "respectable strangers." The committee did not discount the "importance and necessity of suppressing gambling," especially on the Sabbath, but even such a laudable end did not justify the conduct of the watch, whose "summary mode of proceeding," they concluded, was the cause of greater evil than the abuses it was intended to remedy.[69]

The Society for the Prevention of Pauperism and the New York Bank for Savings

The vague fears about dangerous gambling habits which had been raised before the Common Council fueled the philanthropy of the

Society for the Prevention of Pauperism. The society was organized in December 1817 by a group of prominent New Yorkers, largely merchants or "members of the commercial and professional middle class," who had long been active in humanitarian endeavors. They began at once to investigate the prevailing causes of pauperism (or chronic poverty) in New York City, and they looked to habits of the poor (which they labeled vices), that they were convinced made it hard for the laboring poor to accumulate enough to stave off the menace of hard times. "The indirect causes of poverty," they began, "are as numerous as the frailties and vices of men. . . . Some of them be so deeply entrenched in the weakness and depravity of human nature as to be altogether unassailable by mere practical regulation. They can be reached in no other way, than by awakening the dormant and secret energies of moral feeling."

The society's gentlemen organizers turned directly against the older forms of public relief which had approached poverty not as moral failing but as a necessary condition of the uneven distribution of wealth. By making poverty in part, at least, a moral issue they turned the habits of the laboring poor into moral failings and approached them as sins to be corrected. The benevolent humanitarianism that had characterized poor relief in the eighteenth century began to falter with the dislocations of the War of 1812. Urban growth and increasing immigration in the early part of the century also accentuated the poverty of city dwellers. In her recent study of poor women in New York, Christine Stansell argued that changing survival strategies of poor people themselves also induced changes in the relief system. Poor people, she found, came "to see relief as their prerogative." As the contemporary John Pintard complained, "indigent foreigners" worked for high wages in the summer but squandered their earnings and passed the winter as public charges. The able-bodied, it seemed, spent a season of unemployment in the Almshouse and then accepted outdoor relief without changing habits or customs. To the distress of reformers those habits included drinking and gambling and all with the largesse of taxpayers.[70]

Vice did not go unremarked. In December 1817, as P. W. Engs noted, "a number of philanthropic gentlemen" met at New York Hospital to consider causes of pauperism. Neither public relief nor humanitarian benevolence solved what these active philanthropists had come to consider the problem of urban poverty. The Society for the Prevention of Pauperism, by encouraging habits of industry and frugality, would help the worthy poor to help themselves, and would do so by adopting the latest English innovations, including savings banks, in philanthropic relief.[71]

The society's founders set out to enumerate the vices that bound the poor in chronic poverty and that resisted the "secret energies of moral feeling." The prevailing causes of pauperism included ignorance, idleness, intemperance ("the most prolific source of mischief and misery"), "want of economy," "impudent and hasty marriages," lotteries, pawnbrokers, "houses of ill fame," charitable organizations that taught the poor to expect their aid in times of crisis, and war. Over the next few years they lengthened the list to include "want of cleanliness," "disregard of religious worship and religious institutions," "emigration," and "conditions in the prisons." With the exception of war, as Stansell pointed out, all were habits, solutions, remedies, or conditions that had long been "familiar aspects of poor people's lives." They became vices only against the backdrop of "emerging bourgeois values of industry, sobriety, thrift and sexual restraint." Efforts at extirpation included personal moral reform as well as legal prohibition: "Every exertion should be made to exterminate these dangerous vices by inculcating religion, morality, sobriety and industry, and by diffusing useful knowledge among the indigent and labouring people."[72]

The Society for the Prevention of Pauperism objected to the generally loose ways the poor had of handling their money. Not surprisingly, public gambling in New York City figured in their objections. "Prodigality is comparative," they had written in their founding documents. "Among the poor, it prevails to a great extent, in an inattention to those small, but infrequent savings when labour is plentiful, which may go to meet privations in unfavourable seasons." The poor squandered these small savings on lottery tickets, or portions of them, and in despair over their losses they squandered the rest "to seek a refuge in the temporary, but fatal oblivion of intoxicants."[73] In 1818 the society appointed nine standing committees to gather information on the interconnected vices that they determined to be the vicious causes of pauperism and instructed them to report on both lotteries and gambling houses and on the "best mode of diminishing or suppressing them."[74]

Gambling proved an elusive and intractable problem. Although the

S.P.P. claimed some success in encouraging official regulation of public and private lotteries, informal or private gambling proved more difficult to attack. In 1821, nearly three years after the S.P.P. had called for a catalogue of all gambling houses in New York City, they were still unable to state the exact number of gambling resorts. They were more numerous, they were sure, than one would believe. "The consequences of gambling must always be apparent. It leads to poverty and crime, in countless ways. It creates an excitement in the mind that dissolves the strongest obligations to a virtuous course of life and obliterates the last trace and vestige of moral feeling."[75]

Despairing of devising the means to calculate the extent of gambling, they declared it so odious a vice that even its practitioners hid in shame. Gambling houses were secret places because gamblers wished "to avoid the odium which the moral sense of the community attaches to the character of a gambler. And why is the night selected as the most favourable time for gamblers to seek these by-places of wickedness and amusement? Because the consciousness of their own dissipation cannot bear the light of day."[76] Or so they said. They thus read their own views on the shame of gambling into the difficulties they encountered when they set out to discover the haunts of gamblers. They transformed their inability to calculate the precise extent of vice into a declaration of moral victory. Judging from gambling's diminishing importance in their reports, they clearly turned their attention elsewhere. The best way to combat the relative prodigality of the urban poor was not to close gambling houses, it turned out, but rather to divert their small surpluses to other ends. The society advocated a few draconian measures—an innovative treadmill, for instance—for the incorrigible, "unworthy," or criminal poor, but for the worthy poor, it took its campaign against the moral causes of pauperism straight into the realm of finance and opened institutions to encourage frugal savings by poor people.[77]

Historians of the New York savings-bank movement have found its inspiration in a letter written by Patrick Colquhoun, a London magistrate and philanthropist, to Thomas Eddy, a wealthy insurance broker who served as one of the managers of the S.P.P. In 1816 the Englishman described saving banks as a most useful means "to assist the laboring poor to preserve a portion of their earnings for old age, and to give them provident habits." Late that year Eddy called a meeting to establish a savings bank in New York City, and in the spring of 1819 he wrote to Colquhoun telling him he knew of no other philanthropic institution so "admirably calculated to be beneficial to the poor, by promoting among them a spirit of independence, economy and industry."[78]

Several of the men who managed the Society for the Prevention of Pauperism also served as directors of the New York Bank for Savings. Eddy, Engs, Pintard, Brockholst Livingston, John Griscom, and James Eastburn shared their philanthropic talents between the two organizations. Their concerns shaped the moral and financial discourse over vice and poverty. It was Engs who had signed the investigation on the police watch that had invaded the boardinghouse, and it was Eddy, the prominent insurance broker, who appeared before the Common Council in 1819 asking to house a savings bank in the basement of the old Almshouse. Eddy and Pintard compiled the documents on savings banks for the S.P.P. They took on this rather indirect campaign against gambling as part of their benevolent rule of the city and its poor, but Eddy's plea for a savings bank in the Almshouse is an apt geographic symbol of the replacement of the social obligations of humanitarian relief with the independence to be instilled by moral injunction.[79]

Savings banks were to be agents of philanthropy rather than either charitable or business institutions, and they were to deal with the causes rather than the effects of poverty. "Philanthropy, with further sight and broader reach, aims to avert the conditions of need which demand the ministrations of charity." A few members of legislature objected to chartering what appeared to be another bank, but promoters managed to use the power of philanthropy to keep savings banks outside the world of business. They were not to be banks of issue, and deposits were surely to be too small to interest commercial banks. They were designed to compete instead with purveyors of vice, with tavern keepers, with lottery and policy dealers, with gambling-house proprietors, and with friends and relations who lent and borrowed among themselves.[80]

In 1819 the S.P.P. compiled a report on savings banks. In it they celebrated the poor who had begun to save their money in official institutions. They found white women and African Americans in Baltimore "who during this whole summer deposited a dollar per week. This is the most desirable kind of depositor, for all this is saved from luxury and dress." Once they had discovered the luxuries of the poor, savings-bank promoters eyed the little savings of the sailors, tailors, and men out of jail, the women, children, laborers, and apprentices who might have bought lottery tickets or wasted their small accumulations (that they had perhaps gleaned from public relief) with wandering gamblers. Witnesses wrote to the S.P.P. explaining just how the very existence of savings institutions might help to separate the worthy from the unworthy poor. They found savings banks peculiarly designed to benefit the "mixed and destitute species of population, who earn a livelihood by various precarious callings in our large cities." "Humble journeymen, coachmen, chamber-maids, and all kinds of domestic servants and inferior artisans who constitute two-thirds of our population" could be encouraged in habits of "industry, sobriety and *frugality*."[81]

Economic historians have recognized that savings banks stood in direct competition with the lottery. "Savings banks, lotteries, and insurance companies, served as means by which small savings of large numbers of people were collected into sizeable pools of capital," one of them has written.[82] Even the directors of early savings banks recognized that to move the small surplus from the lottery or the tavern to the savings bank meant cultural change; it meant breaking into an informal system of loans and bets that dramatized for the urban poor that economic ties were also cultural ties, ties of kin, class, and friendship rather than business. Savings banks provided capital for the wealthy by offering the urban poor "a secure disposal of their little earnings, which would otherwise be squandered, or unwisely lent to petty fraudulent dealers, on a promise of usurious interest. . . . More than a *hundred* instances have occurred, in our experience, of such losses by lending to neighbors or cousins."

By construing such loans as losses and as social dangers, savings-bank promoters tried to redraw the family and class loyalties that were cemented by debt. Savings banks, they argued further, would reduce the temptations of those who had saved a little at home to brag to a "less prosperous neighbor" and be led by them into foolish speculations. Squirreled away in a savings institution sums too small to interest a bank would be saved from unsecured, spontaneous loans "to friends" as well as from "pernicious modes of spending money." If one man would save he would make "his friends and acquaintances pursue the same plan." For good or ill he would be unable to lend on impulse his small accumulation, and the sick and the unemployed would be forced back on their own meager resources, independent of the charity both of the city and of their friends. Savings institutions would also provide a convenient pool of capital for rich men's schemes, offering the rich the added return of the stake of the poor (who were now turned into creditors) in the successful completion of wealthy capitalists' projects.

Saving would change the social pattern of expenditure. In 1819, after six months, the trustees were gratified to report to the legislature that though it had been expected that those who began to save "would necessarily withdraw . . . from places of public resort, and thus excite the enmity of those whose emolument was the fruit of prodigal expenditure," such cultural conflict had not occurred. Savers had indeed withdrawn from taverns, but tavern keepers had joined "industrious and thrifty toilers," seamen, destitute widows, orphans, clergymen, minors, and servants at the savings bank.[83]

Economists may have accepted money as a fungible commodity, but as long as the S.P.P. held to moral rather than financial distinctions, how money was saved or spent was all-important. By encouraging the poor to lend their money to the rich rather than to one another, the S.P.P. took up the battle against pauperism with a strategy that, like many of the altruistic projects of the early nineteenth century, well served their own self-interest. By promoting savings banks as charitable institutions they made capital accumulation into a moral issue and addressed themselves to vice and virtue (although their use of phrases like "scant wages" and "meager accumulations" would suggest they knew what they were doing) rather than to economics. Like temperance reformers, the bank's promoters devised a moral language to talk about financial issues.

Gambling was not central to their concerns, but when wages had to be saved for self-help in hard times, gambling could still be a problem. As class worlds diverged in northern cities, gambling could be construed as an assertion of working-class independence: wages earned in an anonymous world of free labor to be freely spent. Cultural independence was not what the promoters of savings banks had in mind. Recreational and professional gambling suggested to them that there might be competition (both cultural and economic) for the small accumulations of poor people. They argued that to enter the savings bank was a cultural as well as an economic act, and they hoped that savings curtailed expenditure on certain pleasures. To save was the act that elicited their praise, and gamblers who refused to participate in the cultural project that turned all gain into careful accumulations were unworthy of either aid or sympathy.

Passions and Interests/Wages and Wagering

Despite ample injunctions to the contrary, evidence suggests that people continued to gamble, and their persistence raised the troubling possibility that the "instinct" for accumulation that bank promoters had discovered and on which they depended for the social and economic power of their institutions was not quite universal. Gamblers, as Bailey tried to explain, had trouble with accumulation; they lost money as readily as they had won it. His slaves, his coaches, his gold-headed canes, even his lands and boardinghouses, appeared and disappeared in a life shaped by intervals of poverty and prosperity. Bailey shared an interest in property with ambitious savers, but he did not share a stabilizing interest in the process of accumulation, and for him property carried no social obligations. Wealth was evanescent; property was liquid. Bailey's experience with liquid property was typical of nineteenth-century gamblers, and their disregard for the social obligations of property, whatever their airs and pretensions, separated gamblers from the aristocrats they liked to ape.[84] Their proof that the sense of accumulation was neither instinctual nor universal was also the origin of their vague cultural challenge to the celebration of rational gain. Gamblers made most money where the supposed instinct for accumulation had not quite blossomed. Bailey was a professional gambler who understood that he could make a profit if he could find in others weaknesses similar to his own. And he did.

In the early nineteenth century, reformers, especially in the North, tried to identify this weakness as a destabilizing passion that lurked behind what they identified as the common social interest in accumulation. In gamblers such passion took one form, in their victims another. Gambling was dangerous, especially in a commercial economy, because professional gamblers had learned to manipulate the passions of their victims without themselves losing control. In 1854, when the Rev. E. H. Chapin set about to advise young men on the moral aspects of city life, he described Bailey's gambling descendants: "In other men, the indulgence of vice blends with the play of the emotional nature; passion swamps the brain. But this man trains himself to restrain passion with all the solicitude of a stoic." Gambling began in play but, ceasing to be "an amusement," wrote another who was likewise concerned about the future of young clerks, "it becomes a passion, a frenzy, it absorbs the thought and scorches the brain."[85] For both workers and clerks such passion paled the discipline and ardor needed for steady gain.

The political scientist Albert O. Hirschman has argued that by the late eighteenth century one set of deadly passions—those associated with avarice, greed, and money-making—had been intellectually transformed from dangerous and destabilizing forces into innocent "interests" and "given the task of holding back those passions that had long been thought to be much less reprehensible." Because of its "constancy and persistence" the "passion of accumulation" was deemed the basis of social and political stability, and an interest in gain was promoted, not because of a self-interest in religious salvation, as Weber would have it, but because it kept people out of trouble.[86] Gamblers—especially professionals and those they cultivated as victims—revealed, perhaps as cultural models, perhaps as real historical figures, that early in the nineteenth century the transformation of a passion for gain into an interest in accumulation was not complete. Unstable gamblers revealed how close, in fact, an interest in accumulation still lay to the passion of covetousness. At the gaming table, Eliphalet Nott warned the graduates of Union College in 1814, "Every man's interest clashes with every man's interest, and every man's hand is literally against every man."[87]

Dr. Caldwell had also thought about the scorching covetousness that perverted gamblers' brains. As he warned Transylvania students about the passion lurking in a world of seemingly innocent play, he described a human mind in which the "covetousness" unleashed by gaming was not the seat of a rational interest in gain but rather that of an animal passion. Let loose, it led men to "theft, pickpocketing and robbery." Indulgence had physiological consequences. "By being constantly and intensely exercised, the cerebral organs concerned in gambling attain a size and a degree of vigor, and are thrown into a state of excitement so inordinate as to become ungovernable." In gamblers, covetousness failed to police the lesser passions, and they became consumed by maniacal or criminal compulsions. To cure a gambler's monomania it was necessary to develop the "moral and

reflective organs of the brain." To this end Caldwell proposed sooth-
ing measures: he would hospitalize gamblers, isolate them from other
patients, dress them in "cooling clay caps" of his own devising, and
feed them a "low diet."[88]

In the 1840s and 1850s a small group of northern clergymen and
reformers, including Henry Ward Beecher and William Alcott, added
gamblers to the pantheon of dangerous types waiting to seduce country youths new to the city. They used them, as Karen Halttunen has
argued, to express their doubts about the origin and future of the often
speculative earnings of merchants and city dwellers and about the
structures of authority in a world of unrelated and anonymous employers and employees. Their gamblers were financial villains because
they produced no wealth, offered no fair exchange, and discouraged
industry with the false hope of rapid gain.[89] Popular reformers also
tried to isolate the dangerous tendency that made gamblers dissent
from the social goal of accumulation. They described gamblers' de-
scents through addiction and madness into crime. Instability crossed
class lines to the very core of what was being called human nature,
although the exact expression of instability certainly followed class
lines. If you were a poor man you neglected home and family and
finally died in prison. If you were a young clerk in a bank or a
mercantile house and your frauds were discovered you took your own
life. Sermons and advice tracts helped separate the venality and greed
of gamblers from the greed at the core of all excess profit, but they
also praised the steady gains of wage labor and made a working man's
earnings one form of money a gambler would rarely touch.

In the early part of the nineteenth century Mason Weems published
a series of sermons describing God's revenge on those who abandoned
themselves to any one of several vices. God plotted certain and dramatic revenge against drunkards, murderers, duelers, adulterers, and
gamblers. In this world of damned villains Weems's gamblers were
both "useless" and "savage." They offered nothing to society, kicked
and cuffed their fellow men, and finally found themselves, winners or
losers, unmanned by the search for gain. "Yes, I *am* a Man," a gambler
reassured Weems, "a rather *mad-man*. I am the thing, sir, they call a
Gambler."[90] Gamblers risked madness, later preachers and reformers
argued, in large part because they did not accumulate their wealth in
wages paid for steady work. "Man is so constituted," William Alcott
wrote, "as to be unable to bear, with safety, a rapid accumulation of

property." Rapid accumulations, however, affected the constitution in different ways, and a gambler's madness might run in one of two directions. Either it turned to a dispassionate social pathology that permitted cold-blooded robbery or to a desperate passion for the excitement of gaming. "The best of men are endangered by it. As in knowledge, so in the present case, what is gained by hard digging is usually retained and what is gained *easily* usually goes quickly."[91]

The minister E. H. Chapin, turning to biblical injunctions to toil, expressed a similar sentiment. Gamblers had no right to live without labor, and in their "haste to be rich" they lost all innocence. "That which is lightly gotten will be lightly spent. The value of that possession only, which has been toiled for, is truly felt. The hands which have ached with labor only know how to dispense the fruits of that labor with prudence." He supported his assertions on the nature of wealth by telling gambling tales in which the money wagered and lost at the gaming table was money loaned, inherited, or carried in trust, but never money earned in wages.[92]

If the essence of recreational gambling was social equality and reciprocity, commercial gambling shattered equality by introducing a hierarchy of profits which transformed participants into merchants and customers at their best, or into purveyors of vice and their victims at their worst. As Robert Bailey's career in and out of Virginia illustrated, the need for profits changed the nature of betting. When gambling became work, became the way a gambler earned his living, gamblers had to cheat to assure their profits. Since they themselves produced no wealth, offered no service, their only sources of gain were the earnings of others. They had to attract a never-ending supply of victims to furnish them with cash, and they did so by disguising their work as a part of the play of others. This disguise made them seem especially dangerous to those who wondered just what was to be the recreation of those obliged to labor for a living. Gamblers would not only lure them into losing their money, they would make them lose all sense of the measured time essential for a wage laborer.

As all men became rational creatures of the market, something else made gambling dangerous as well. Like those who owned the means of production in a capitalist economy, gamblers now bent their energies to the systematic extraction of profits, and the rational search for profits eliminated pure chance as surely as it had eliminated exchanges based on a balanced reciprocity. Gamblers, like employers who pretended to share their enterprise with employees, seemed to do one thing while doing another. They seemed to gamble, to share risks, but they rigged the game, turning gaming into mere semblance and proving once more that all men were rational economic actors bent on gain, even those who appeared to be votaries of irrational fortune.

Middle-class proprietors, determined to imagine their world as rational and just, could not see themselves as kin to venal gamblers. Gambling completely distorted what was emerging, especially in the North, as the dominant social vision based on the stability of accumulation and the proper relations between work and leisure. Gambling denied the perfect dyad of work and leisure and mixed them in an unseemly and dangerous fashion. In the hands of professionals gambling was changing to resemble the work of rational capitalists, and professionals helped promote a commercial leisure that was to become common by the end of the century.

In the 1840s it was not possible to see them offering a service. For workers in northern cities it was their work itself that was changing to resemble gambling, and not in the high-flown metaphoric sense of great profits and great risks. Rather, in Walter Benjamin's phrase, it was prosaic, repetitious, futility that made the "drudgery of the laborer . . . a counterpart to the drudgery of the gambler." Even the gambler's repeating gestures with cards and dice mirrored the repeating gestures of a man tending a machine. Gambling was not just a "negative analogue" for the profits of speculators and capitalists, but a negative analogue for the automatic operations of factory labor. The work of unskilled factory labor, the "mere mechanical members" of society, "lacks any touch of adventure, of the mirage that lures the gambler. But it certainly does not lack the futility, the emptiness, the inability to complete something which is inherent in the activity of a wage slave in a factory."[93]

Eliphalet Nott, president of Union College, had seen mindless gamblers feeding machines as early as 1814. Nott's worry about gambling did not extend to the lottery, and he is often best remembered for his suits against the firm that ran New York's last lottery for his Union College. But when he addressed students he turned his attention to the evils of card playing with money at stake. Like factory work, gaming required only the most basic intellection, and like wage labor, gaming offered little hope of extensive gain and only the most ephemeral satisfaction. Nott's social metaphors were perhaps unconscious, but he seemed to touch on the fate of routinized labor. To engage in either gambling or factory labor ended in numbing degradation. "The intellectual condition of the gamester, so far as his occupation is concerned, is but one degree removed from that of the dray-horse buckled to his harness, and treading over from day to day, and from night to night, the same dull track, as he turns a machine which some mind of a higher order has invented." Parents who played cards with their children helped to "extinguish their intellect, and convert them into automatons, living mummies; the mere mechanical members of a domestic gambling machine, which though but little soul is necessary, requires a number of human hands to work it."[94] Had Nott fully envisioned the factories that were to transform the northern landscape, he might have found gambling better preparation for a life of repetitive labor than pious instruction in delayed gratification and measured gain.

The Mind of Economic Man

All types of society are limited by economic factors. Nineteenth century civilization alone was economic in a different and distinctive sense, for it chose to base itself on a motive only rarely acknowledged as valid in the history of human societies and certainly never before raised to the level of a justification of action and behavior in everyday life, namely, *gain.*

—Karl Polanyi, 1944

The capitalist process of rationalisation based on private economic calculation requires that every manifestation of life shall exhibit this very interaction between details which are subject to law and a totality ruled by chance.

—Georg Lukács, 1923

In February 1845 the reformed gambler Jonathan Harrington Green, who was seeking publicity for his fledgling antigambling crusade, presented himself for a phrenological reading before Orson Squire Fowler. Fowler, the great American promoter of phrenology, analyzed the bumps on Green's head and pronounced him well suited to a gambler's career. He reported that Green had a head "calculated to make money very fast, yet illy calculated to keep it, because he had the *back* portion of Acquisitiveness, which *gets* money, yet not the fore part which keeps it."[1] When Fowler bisected Green's Acquisitive Bump (the phrenological locus, if ever there was one, of economic man's natural "propensity to truck, barter, and exchange"), he not only found economic man in the human bone structure, he also revealed why gambling might still be a problem for the middle class of the 1840s. It was not just a vice of the idle rich and idling poor. In Green, Fowler found a middle-class nightmare, an economic freak: a man who had joined the cultural celebration of acquisition but who

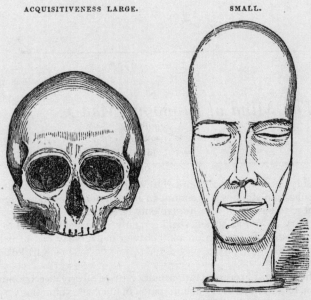

ACQUISITIVENESS LARGE. SMALL.

No. 40. TELLER. No. 41. GOSSE.

LARGE Acquisitiveness saves for future use whatever is of any value ; is pained by the waste or destruction of any thing which can be turned to a good account ; loves to lay up the means of procuring subsequent comforts and luxuries ; desires to acquire and possess property ; and is industrious and frugal.

From *The American Phrenological Journal and Miscellany*, ed. O. S. Fowler (1847), vol. 9. Courtesy Yale University Library.

had not followed a proper course of development and been led by rational self-interest in accumulation back to the community of acquisitive individuals. Gamblers, like misers, represented the antisocial possibilities in the celebration of gain. The gambler was an economic man in whom the natural magic of Adam Smith's invisible hand had been perverted by the unnatural deceptions of sleight-of-hand and in whom the individual search for gain never served the collective interest of the community.[2]

The figure of the socially isolated, parasitic, and destructive gambler appeared in reform literature, in sentimental fiction, in financial guides for young boys, and in the pantheon of social types constructed by phrenologists like Fowler. It is not surprising that a phrenologist working in the middle of the nineteenth century would find acquisitiveness to be part of human physical development, but in gamblers something in the evolution of economic man had gone awry.[3] Distortions followed class lines. Working-class gambling stood in direct defiance of the industry and sobriety employers deemed necessary for a productive labor force and the frugality that would assure working-class independence in hard times. Those who managed savings institutions saw gambling games as direct competitors for the small surplus of the laboring poor, and as we have seen they argued that such surpluses could serve the interests of society either by augmenting the pool of capital available for investment or by purchasing necessities.

A few reformers took up a campaign against the gambling that might linger as an imaginative possibility in the middle-class world of speculation. They used gaming to illustrate dangers in financial worlds shaped by exchanges between strangers and rife with occasions for easy speculative profit. Like Bailey, they labeled gambling gains vicious, dangerous, and destabilizing, but they also helped make a virtue of speculative gains by marking gambling as a vice. Gambling and speculation shared elements of risk and hunger for gain, but gambling was money made without working, profit without fair exchange, and it promised nothing to advance society. For the speculation to stay, the gambling had to go.[4]

Green, the man whose career interests me here, addressed the gambling entertained in the imaginations of literate city dwellers. Like Bailey, he fancied himself a gambler, a reformer, and a writer, but the clients for his games and the readers for his books differed from those of the Virginian. Green touched lingering doubts about the capitalist celebration of gain and described the dangers of gambling, especially professional gambling, in a commercial economy. He cultivated an audience of wealthy merchants and their young clerks.

As Bailey knew so well, reciprocal, recreational gambling, whether of the rich or the poor, was fraught with personal drama and social symbolism, but it did not directly threaten the accumulated capital of the middle class and their concern for an internalized sense of economic order. The gambling that threatened careful accumulations and undercut injunctions to save and to acquire was a carefully constructed, but largely imaginary, horror that reformers located on the edges of the northern marketplace. Reformers told stories of young men who ventured too far, financially, socially, or geographically. They used gambling as a parable to warn young clerks that when they traveled beyond class, family, and home they risked purse, sanity, family fortune, and finally their lives. A few writers and reformers used a discussion of gambling to characterize the moral and psychological dangers of the market world the middle class had made.[5]

Just as labels like "panics" and "revulsions" served to isolate and label as extraordinary the disorder endemic to nineteenth-century capitalism, so gambling served to isolate what might be a pathological version of characteristics, like acquisitiveness, deemed natural to "economic man."[6] Because, as we shall see, the pathology appeared only at the extremes or in extraordinary cases, the stories were as reassuring as they were accusatory. Discussions of gambling were the means of warning the middle class about the dangers of certain kinds of gain, but to an audience of readers safe at home in eastern parlors they simultaneously offered the reassurance that danger lay in remote social, racial, geographic, and economic areas. Readers could be safe from gambling by accepting measured gain, by avoiding economic frontiers, and by exercising caution in commerce with strangers. Gambling provided an anecdotal structure for gain and loss, and a convenient way to turn economic processes into moral problems without ever touching the structures of wealth and power.

The literature on gambling reform had a second, largely imaginative aim. Time after time, gamblers were revealed as cunning cheaters who only feigned a belief in luck. This denial of the very possibility of gambling suggests that those few who wrote on gambling helped extend and universalize the rational search for gain. The cultural work they performed involved a transformation in the imagination, in the ways people thought, more than in the ways they behaved. They sought to eliminate belief in the possibility of gain without work or gain by lucky chance. In so doing they helped turn all transactions into market transactions. But when they described market relations that extended through all of human society they cut themselves off from the support of moral reformers who looked to an area of home and heart free of even the most rational of market motives and safe from the endless calculations that shaped the world of business.

The Northern Middle Class and Gambling Reform

In the 1830s and 1840s slick urban gamblers who used polish and sophistication to seduce unworldly young men became stock figures in advice books written for young male clerks. In her study of Victorian mores, Karen Halttunen explained gamblers' presence as an implicit expression of middle-class concerns about "major social, political, and economic forces transforming the American nation." The gambler/speculator along with the "urban companion" and the political demagogue appeared as incarnations of confidence men waiting to seduce youths new to cities and new to a world of party politics and speculative markets. For Halttunen the multifaceted figure embodies fears about wide-ranging changes in early nineteenth-century middle-class life. Transformations included

a high rate of geographical mobility and particularly migration to the city, the decline of social deference and a loosening of ties between family generations, the breakdown of traditional restraints over single workingmen, and in general a replacement of traditional social relationships with modern peer relations. In the image of the demagogue, they expressed anxieties regarding the political changes of their time: the growing dominance of party politics, and techniques of mass politics, the new tyranny of the majority, the nationalization of public opinion, and the decline of 'natural' local leadership in the face of the manipulative, charismatic leadership of new professional politicians. Finally, in the spectre of the gambler/speculator, they embodied their fears of the economic forces shaping the young American republic: the rapid expansion of the national market and of speculative economic activity.[7]

Halttunen finally read middle-class obsessions as evidence of insecurity about their social position in a society in flux.

But the gambler/speculator was by no means a simple figure, and those who tried to use gamblers and gambling to talk about the economic dangers of early nineteenth-century market society found the figures full of contradiction. Ministers delivered a few sermons on the hazards of sudden wealth and the folly of wagering, and a few reformers tried to start crusades with gambling reform as an object. Jonathan Harrington Green spent his life gambling and trying not to gamble, writing about gambling, and trying to stop others from gambling.[8]

Card Sharps, Dream Books, and Bucket Shops

Green had a brief public career as an antigambling reformer in the 1840s. He wrote five books on gambling that were published by popular presses, and he started reform associations in the Midwest and throughout the Northeast. He published a brief series of antigambling papers for children and wrote reports for the *New York Times* on gambling in the West. He told stories that he presented as autobiography but that read like the tall tales of the Mississippi Valley then circulating as popular fiction. His books were part personal narrative, part melodrama, and part technical manual on card playing. In them he created a whole category of seducers who won the purses of careless young men who were carrying money entrusted to them by parents and employers. Green was not content to leave his villains and victims in fiction, and inspired by his sensational fictions, he wrote strict antigambling laws designed to punish professional gamblers and their associates who induced young men to bet. He then lobbied eastern and midwestern legislatures to pass the laws he had written. Still pushing his fictional designs in the real world, he abandoned his small midwestern antigambling societies for New York City, the capital of gambling vice. In 1850 he gained brief fame in New York, where he started an Association for the Suppression of Gambling designed to spy on gambling clerks for their employers. In the late 1850s and 1860s his books were republished in cheap popular editions, but after the Civil War he disappeared.

Time and again Green described the course of a gambler's career from innocent parlor play to vile professionalism. In his mind those who gambled were caught in a relentless sort of logic: they began in innocent play, but gained in skill only to be consumed by vice and to end their days in ruin and degradation, playing ever simpler and ever stupider games. Gamblers moved from dominoes and checkers to games of "all-fours and eucre" and then on to "the great and scientific game of whist." No gamblers stopped with whist, however, and they were soon drawn on to the "attractive games of boston, brag, and poker." Poker brought the ill-fated gamblers into the company of genteel sportsmen, but once there they began a gradual downward course through faro, roulette, "chucker-luck and twenty-one," and finally in the last throes of hopeless addiction they were to be found playing the "despicable game of thimbles."[9]

Green chastised ministers, reformers, legislators, and editors for failing to "check this mighty evil," and he proposed to cure gambling by attacking gaming among the young. Gambling was a social and not a solitary vice and was therefore spread like infection by social intercourse. The social sin of gambling would disappear, he thought, if he could stay the "passion for gaming" in the rising generation. "For if we can succeed in restraining the young, the aged votaries will soon have run their race, and, passing away from the stage of action will leave us free from this evil."[10] Green set for himself the task of saving society from its gamblers. First he had to find the right audience for the crusade he wanted to begin and to make it clear just why it might be a sin to gamble in a society he found otherwise so happily bent on gain. He doubted he could redeem the fallen gamester or that anyone would care if he did, so he directed his initial efforts at young men who might be tempted to gamble.

He aimed his work at boys new to the ranks of merchant clerks and at their parents. He offered them advice on the proper forms of recreation, suggested ways they might protect their wealth from the greed of traveling gamesters, and exposed the ways gamblers drew them into games to rob them. He framed all his descriptions and all his advice with discussions of the dangers of unearned wealth. Gamblers' gains were characterized as products of pathological greed that led to destruction and loss. By contrast, all other gain appeared normal, natural, and socially salubrious. He described, as had Beecher and Alcott, a world in which the only safe money was money earned in slow and steady wages. But he also described gamblers themselves swept up in the rational search for profits, using a pretense of irrational or lucky gain to separate men, and sometimes women, from their money. As aspects of everyday life, especially the speculative profits of the middle class and the repetition and futility of factory labor, came to resemble gambling, what was called gambling in sentimental fiction and reform literature became more sensational, more venal, more corrupt, less subject to chance, and therefore less like gambling. The gambling that served as a negative analogue for speculative gain and repetitious labor was in fact nasty robbery.[11] Complicity of victims added to the ambiguity of gambling as a vice, for in their victims gamblers seemed able to turn to vice the search for accumulation, the love of risk, and longing for commercial expansion which had made the virtuous middle class. This confusion made it difficult to sustain a reform crusade based solely on the elimination of gambling.

Green based his representation of gambling and his attacks on gambling as a vice on several strains present in the northern middle-class imagination. He and his few allies (the few ministers and reporters who expressed an interest in his crusade) paid homage to a morality based on production and argued that gamblers who "produced nothing" were the antithesis of a productive economy. He combined the language and values of producerism with the language of exchange and attacked gamblers who took "without rendering an equivalent."[12] Gamblers violated injunctions to save, they ignored pleas for measured accumulation, they scoffed at equitable exchange, and they engaged in "speculation" that had no social utility. Gamblers also embodied corruption, particularly the corruption of excess or irrational wealth, and here Green and his followers entered the remnants of a discourse about men and money which had been shaped by a republican emphasis on the worth of labor. Still, in their relentless search for profits, in their love of risk, gamblers resembled the capitalists who were determined to extend their markets and to establish the search for gain as normal, natural, and proper behavior.

Popular writers, including Green, depicted gamblers as men whose tastes ran toward the aristocratic, useless, and frequently imported luxuries that threatened to upset the delicate balance of self-interests that maintained the middle-class republic. "The gambling loafer," as one witness put it, is "noticeable from his general 'get up,' regardless of expense—snow white shirts, elegantly-fitting dress and fine jewelry." Worse, in a gambler's hands even these luxuries were liquid. They assumed the airs of aristocrats but accepted none of the social responsibility that the possession of even an aristocrat's property should have implied. Clothing, jewelry, wigs, canes, and slaves were, as Bailey's experience amply illustrated, liquid: things that could be easily wagered or pawned. Possessions also served as bait. Gamblers used their appearances to lure victims into betting because they carried objects that were themselves imbued with special social significance. Gamblers carried possessions as portable wealth, but in their hands portable wealth was designed to deny any connections between money and necessity.[13] They cultivated a frivolous luxury but at the same time they refused what Weber identified as a "man's duty to his possessions." Worldly goods were neither a "light cloak" nor "an iron cage," rather they were infinitely mutable wealth that served as a lure to attract deluded victims. Property imposed no obligations.[14]

For popular writers, gambling stories also illustrated exactly how selfish individuals would fall prey to the temptations of idleness and luxury, and, once in the clutches of luxury, how they might violate the political principles of the republic. When Karen Halttunen studied the middle-class construction of republican ideology in early Victorian America she found that northern advice writers were concerned that youths who fell into a "riotous life of luxury and sin" would fail to become virtuous citizens and would bring about the destruction of the liberty their fathers had so carefully constructed. The literature on gambling constantly acknowledged the possibility of individual corruption and the delicate interconnection and interdependence of market relations and republican politics. Such acknowledgments had both literal and symbolic components. Gamblers undermined an independent electorate drawing voters into foolish bets and grand wagers. George Combe, the English phrenologist who visited the United States in the late 1830s, marveled at the American passion for wagering on elections and warned that "a people is preparing for despotism when it turns the elective franchise of its highest offices into a mere subject of pecuniary speculation." Green tried to capitalize on whatever dangers might have been present in election betting, and speaking in grand abstractions, he announced that gambling reform was "a work of *patriotism*" because it helped to ensure the "morality and virtue of the people" who were faced with the serious obligation to choose their leaders.[15]

There was something more at stake in Green's crusade. For all his portraits of the dangers and evils of gambling, his stories all concluded that it was not really possible to gamble in the economy of the early nineteenth century. People looked as if they were gambling, playing a fair game with an uncertain outcome, but one of them was invariably cheating. Rational economic actors who eschewed the irrational and uncertain gains of gambling and who dominated the political, economic, and cultural discourse of the early nineteenth century had made it impossible to gamble and therefore dangerous to assume that money could be won in gambling games. Green described gamblers as rational men of the market using the ruse of irrationality to draw others to their ruin. By making the irrational dependence on luck, fortune, superstition, mutuality, and chance appear impossible, Green helped extend the domain of rational economic gain. Those who appeared to gamble were venal purveyors of vice who robbed their victims and led them to their ruin by unleashing in them an uncontrollable passion for gain.

Green led fights to eradicate gambling on many fronts, but his own suspect character set off against the class divisions of the urban North made victory in his battles impossible. He took up the campaign begun by middle-class moralists and bankers who in their quest for rational recreation, thrift, and measured gain fought the gambling associated with working-class leisure. In his battle against working-class gambling, however, Green became an employer's spy on one of the few remaining realms of freedom and independence for workers in the urban Northeast. At the same time he picked up the materials of a popular working-class critique of the degenerate corruption of hypocritical capitalists who preached measured gain and hard work to their employees while reveling in their own speculative fortunes. If the working class rejected Green as an informer, the middle class rejected him as a corrupt swindler who presumed to define those worthy of trust and credit and who tried to sell a reform that he should have provided out of disinterested benevolence.

Nor did Green have much success on a practical level. He tried to persuade preachers to join his crusade and attack gambling with moral injunction. He also tried to persuade state legislatures to suppress gambling by legal injunction. A few ministers wrote sermons on the moral problems of gambling and a few state legislatures passed harsh antigambling statutes, but to little lasting effect.

Green's great personal work was a cultural crusade to eliminate gambling by fictional "injunction." The dramatic unmaskings of cheating gamblers made his stories more than simple cautionary tales designed to warn middle-class youth about the dangers of money. His stories were active agents in the extension of market relations to all human encounters: they exposed irrational gamblers as rational, economic men, and they thus lost the powerful and dark appeal so important to stories of drink and sexual license.

The stories warned people not to gamble, not just because gambling was morally wrong, but because in a world of rational, self-interested profit seekers no one was a true devotee of chance. "I know of no crime," Green wrote, "even of the blackest hue, that the gambler will not stoop to commit, when to obtain money is his object; and what better can we expect of men, whose lives are spent in defrauding and cheating their fellow-men, by artifices so base, so vile, that every honest mind shudders to contemplate them?"[16] Instability, irrationality, and passion were revealed in gamblers' victims, but Green's victims could not be read as pathological outsiders. They were the most normal of young northern white men, and if they could not be said to possess by nature the economic rationality that was the foundation of the liberal republic, then who could? Gambling stories, in other words, did not work in the same ways as other stories of vice.

Green's discussion of the moral issues of gambling gain brought him into contact with major cultural issues and cultural figures of the early nineteenth century. His failures also reveal important divisions in the imaginative labor of cultural production. He violated the rules that structured popular sentimental reform. In the course of his brief public career Green flirted with evangelical reform, wrote juvenile literature, and performed card tricks. He taught ministers and editors how to read marked cards and showed audiences how gamblers, posing as traveling gentlemen, would try to cheat them. He shared Edgar Allan Poe's fascination with cryptography and with the emotions of gambling, and he shared something of Poe's literary ambitions. He wrote popular stories and manuals on card tricks and parlor magic and participated in exactly that commercial leisure he was trying to reform. When he was not writing and crusading against gambling, he worked as a detective and bounty hunter. But he never quite freed himself from the crimes and criminals he pursued, and he once spent twelve days in the Tombs for passing counterfeit Treasury notes. Like his contemporary, P. T. Barnum, he tried to be a self-promoter and a creator and exposer of humbugs, but he could not enter into Barnum's world of advertising publicity and mass entertainment. He tried to talk about economic reform *and* moral reform; to be a stage performer, an evangelist *and* a contrite, repentant sinner; to present the hard facts needed to generate a reform crusade *and* to create the tropes needed to make it feel right and necessary.

None of this makes him unusual. But when he talked about gambling, he ventured beyond the psychological and spiritual taboos that the critic David Reynolds found so immensely creative for those, like Green, whom he labels "immoral reformers." Green ventured, I argue, onto a terrain of economic taboos, and there he encountered both the limits of the sensational literature he wrote for a northern working class and the sentimental reforms he proposed to the northern middle class.[17] He fell victim to the contradictions of a market culture expanding on fictional foundations of character, heart, and home outside the market and he disappeared in the gaps opening between the cultural worlds of wage laborers and middle-class clerks. Green was a petty working-class criminal, a sleight-of-hand artist, an aspiring author who presumed to address the middle class about economic danger and who tried to tell them, quite against their will, that there was no safe sanctuary from the relations of the market. Green's portrait of expanded market relations was perhaps closer to the truth than their own, but his truth violated the great fiction of his reform-minded audiences and they ignored his pleas for gambling reform. By relying on a monstrous picture of the expanded market, he offended a middle class who might have heard his pleas for benevolent reform. By setting out to reform the public recreation of northern cities he offended a working class who might have responded to his sensational revelations of venality and corruption. He not only presumed to invade the traditional working-class pastimes of northern cities and to offer rational parlor card tricks in the place of reciprocal, recreational gambling but, worse, to tell employers when their workers were gambling.[18]

The Life and Work of J. H. Green, the Reformed Gambler

Jonathan Harrington Green was born in Lawrenceburg, Indiana, around 1814, the son of a pious mother and a drunken father. His mother died when he was seven, but not before eliciting from her son a deathbed promise that he would never drink. It never occurred to the mother that her sober son might become a gambler and card sharp. The father bound him out to an "unkind master" and left for Cincinnati. Green went through a series of apprenticeships, mainly in the carpentry trades, and for one reason or another he found them all unsatisfactory. He kept running away to Cincinnati to find his dissipated father. In the sort of mismanagement of interests and passions that was to emerge as thematic in his portraits of gamblers and victims, Green confessed that "the deep and abiding anxiety which I felt to see my father, and to enjoy his society once more, made me lose all control over myself, and sacrifice my interest to my passion."[19]

The passion, here briefly directed to family ties, was soon to turn in another direction. In Cincinnati, Green found work as a joiner, but following a path of urban corruption, he fell in with a "bad set of boys" who took him to visit a ten-pin alley. The proprietor of the bowling alley turned out to be a thimble rigger, and Green, along with his bad companions, was implicated in a plot to fleece a rich-looking gentleman. The conspirators were caught and Green was arrested and held in jail because he was unable to pay his fine. In jail he began his actual apprenticeship in crime. He learned how to play cards and he began to develop the bad character that was to follow him throughout his public life.[20]

He also began to get a sense of the social and imaginary geography of antebellum vice. For the next decade he traveled around the Mississippi Valley tending bar in hotels and on steamboats, running errands for a gang of counterfeiters, selling cards, and gambling. He spent some time in New Orleans and more time in jail for more crimes he said he did not commit. He ran into counterfeiting corrupters of youths, young men seduced into gambling, and their grieving parents. In preparation for his career as a reformer, he worked briefly as a police informant. But in preparation for his career as a author of sensational books for northern audiences, the counterfeiters he was hired to follow led him not to minor outlaws but to the already legendary gangs of robbers who haunted the banks of the Mississippi from plunder-filled dens at "Ford's Ferry" and "Cave-in-Rock."[21]

Green spent twelve years gambling. On occasion he tried to quit the criminal life and to finish his trade as a joiner. But as he mastered the arts of dealing he said he "came to the conclusion to become a gambler, till fortune should prove enough in my favor to enable me to settle down at my ease."[22] Although he did marry a woman who figured largely as a victim of plots to rob and discredit him, Green never did settle down. Nor did he have much to do with either fortune or rational ambition. If he is to be believed, he spent most of his time perfecting and performing various crooked deals and sleights-of-hand. He was finally drawn away from gambling by an elderly Methodist minister he met on board a steamboat. The Rev. George Light appealed to Green's gambler's superstitions and conjured up images of a dead mother mourning her lost son. Green was saved and resolved to make a career out of his salvation.[23]

Green's early career gave him the material for his books, and he recognized that tastes in popular fiction made a market for his adventures. Green, however, played a peculiar part in his tales. He was not

Eng.ᵈ by W. Warner Philad.ᵉ

From J. H. Green, *Gambling Unmasked! or, The personal experiences of the reformed gambler* (Philadelphia, 1847), frontispiece. Courtesy Yale University Library.

at all like the nasty gamblers or the newly wealthy gamblers' victims who peopled his tales of reform. Green's own background was one of working-class marginality which merged easily with a world of smalltime vice. Green worked in physically, but not socially, mobile trades—he was a carpenter, he worked on flatboats and steamboats, he was a sort of salesman—that made economic development in the Mississippi Valley possible. When he set about to write books he addressed as large an audience as he could imagine. He wrote for working-class boys, like himself, who might have delighted in what Twain's Huck Finn would later call "robber books," but he also turned to middle-class parents and employers who might buy books with a moral message and finance his crusade as a traveling economic evangelist.[24] Green's contradictory audiences would prove his undoing.

Green was not the only young man growing up in the 1830s to find himself unable to finish his trade. In one sense, he was a failed journeyman, but his failure has to be set within an artisan world that was failing around him. What choices were open to Green? He did not fall into the deskilled working class of northern cities, nor did he become one of its radical spokesmen. Nor did he rise into the nonmanual world of the middle-class proprietors and clerks.[25] He followed artisan failure, instead, into the world of the imagination and became an author. At times he wrote the sensational fictions that were part of a northern working-class world, but he used his fictional musings on the horrors of gambling as an excuse to investigate the habits of young men who might gamble. He often wrote about young boys who were making it into the world of merchants and clerks, and he peddled his books to their parents who might worry about children they had been unable to apprentice to an accommodating neighbor or relative and who were now operating on their own in a world of anonymous wealth.

Green was a relatively successful author. He complained about being poor, but his books went through numerous editions. In authorship his social and literary ambitions met in a brief and uneasy collaboration. He could imagine an audience made up of people worried about money and he could write about them, but when he tried to pass as an economic adviser, to pass judgment on the respectable and ambitious, he met with accusation, character assassination, and laughter. Like a good bourgeois man he made money by handling money, but Green was a working-class gambler and he could never get the middle-class equation between money and character quite right. He had transgressed a rigid, if unacknowledged, boundary that divided those who might speculate economically and philosophically from those who must live in a concrete world of getting and spending.

The same barrier divided those who might offer economic counsel from those who must accept it.[26]

Green's Crusade against Gambling

Green gave up gambling in 1841 or 1842 and tried to make money by writing books and peddling them and by lecturing on gamblers' tricks with cards and demonstrating them. In 1844 and 1845, he traveled through the Northeast and Midwest and tried to add antigambling societies to a landscape already amply covered with reform societies and voluntary associations. Although he never made it very clear what the actual tasks of his associations would be, other than to espouse a general disapproval of gambling, he used a well-tested approach. He arrived in town, arranged for a hall, and paid a call on a local editor or a Methodist or Baptist minister. In the privacy of an office or study, Green demonstrated the card tricks gamblers used to cheat victims. He used these private demonstrations to generate publicity for evening lecture-performances open to the general public. When the audience seemed enthusiastic he would form the locals into antigambling societies and then he would pass the hat, usually, he said, with little success. Not only was gambling rarely the reformer's vice of choice, but it seemed in Green's case, at least, that any money in a gambler's hands, even those of a reformed gambler, remained suspect.[27]

Green finally wound up in New York City, where with the help of Horace Greeley he started the more formal and more businesslike Association for the Suppression of Gambling. Like many of the reform associations of the 1840s, Green's was a short-lived and controversial affair, and like other reformers he tried to use a shell of evangelical reform to "alter everyday secular behavior." The phrase is from Mary Ryan's study of Utica County, New York. She found that both in their composition and in their ends "evangelical reforms created major social conflicts and spawned opposing associations that split the community into competing interest groups."[28]

It would be going too far to argue that Green and his crusade divided communities, but he does provide us with one of the few occasions in the early nineteenth century when the language of moral reform was brought to bear directly on the personal economic relations of the market. Green's discussions of gambling were not filtered through the moral or salutary ends of temperance, and he made none of the humanitarian claims of abolitionists. His crusades were aimed directly at how men earned, held, and spent their money. For Green it was not fragile human souls or even fragile human bodies that were in danger, but the fragile credit relations of an extended market. Green started out with more modest claims about vulnerable young men, but as he gained confidence or as he saw opportunities to create bigger markets for his services, he saw the possible depredations of gamblers as ever more widespread and ever more destructive. For his New York mercantile clientele, Green described a world in which gamblers threatened the credit relations that had become the real network of social interdependence.

To explain the threats of gamblers and to generate support for his crusade to wipe them out, Green tried to combine two modes of discourse—the discourse of the market and the discourse of sentiment. But their very logic depended on mutual exclusion, and Green's anti-gambling crusade did not work out quite as he had planned. When Green used the sentimental tools of the 1830s to talk about the economic relations of the 1840s and 1850s, he produced as much laughter and controversy as he did moral resolve and contrition. The controversies he inspired turned into investigations of his own character and not into fervent crusades to eliminate gambling. The moral cadences he used to talk about gambling had a hollow ring, and his crusade began to look like a parody of earlier evangelical reforms.

Although Green announced that he was part of the "great work of moral reform" and claimed inspiration from temperance reformers, especially those involved with the working-class Washingtonians, the thrust of his work lay elsewhere. The historian Paul Johnson, among others, has explored the ways Protestant evangelism, in general, and temperance crusades, in particular, helped transform the social and labor relations of early nineteenth-century capitalism. As Johnson pointed out, however, if ministers, moralists, and reformers were talking about capitalism, they were talking about it in religious ways.[29] Green did not, could not engineer such an imaginative transformation. Money was at the heart of his crusade, as it had been at the heart of his stories. His commercialism was undisguised and without a benevolent disguise, his reforms were too blunt, too economic, and too self-serving to inspire those men and women, especially women, who had become the sources of reformers' support. Specifically, when he went about constructing an audience for his reform movement, Green moved through self-interest rather than disinterest. And the self-interest appeared to be primarily his own, for he could not transform his own interests into those of the community at large. Nor could he create the disinterested selflessness, or the appearance of disinterested selflessness, which helped fuel crusades for both temperance and abolition.

The failure of the crusade against gambling helps us understand the ways moral reform helped define a sphere, as John Ashworth has recently put it, "in which self-interest did not operate." Ashworth argued that abolitionists and temperance reformers, however unintentionally, helped legitimate market relations and wage labor by creating a "rigid separation between those areas of life where the market could rule those where it was forbidden." Ashworth included home, family, and conscience in areas outside the market.[30] Green's failures seem to substantiate Ashworth's claims. He stumbled into contradictions between the sentimental assertions that fueled reform crusades and his own implicit claims that there were no human relations outside the market, and his crusades drew little support.

His pitch was fated to miss its audience. Leonore Davidoff's and Catherine Hall's study of the English middle class perhaps suggests why. They have argued that middle-class self-definition was "premised on the separation between market and family."[31] Green's reform was based on the contention that men had neither character nor conscience free of the market, and when he raised the spectre of the monstrously expanded market he lost the audience that might have heard his appeal to benevolence. He created a private imaginary world in which the delicate dialectic of market and family did not quite apply. But this violation of cultural logic was not his only error. He also erred in his choice of examples. His corrupted victims were neither degraded poor nor dissipated aristocrats, but sons of the middle class itself, and once they had given themselves over to the greed that lurked beneath the driven search for wealth they were hardly sympathetic objects for reform. Their falls provided ample evidence of the failures of parental training.

It took Green a few years of crusading in the hinterlands to earn the attention of the New York merchants who proved, at least briefly, the best customers for his peculiar services. He campaigned in Pennsylvania, Ohio, Kentucky, Indiana, and upstate New York, where he tried to persuade audiences that gamblers' threats warranted their funding his crusades. He started antigambling associations in Lexington, Louisville, St. Louis, Columbus, and Cleveland, but he had trouble raising money to meet his expenses. His fourteen-month campaign was not, as he put, it a "profitable tour." The "Lady Washingtonians" in Rochester gave him some silver spoons, but at Columbus, Ohio, he complained that he was able to only raise $7.80 from an audience of fifteen hundred people. He also wrote antigambling laws for Ohio and New York, but he never managed to get the legislatures to pass them.[32]

Green attributed his failures to organized plots by gamblers, but there are other ways to read him as well. He may have exaggerated his poverty in order to emphasize the personal sacrifices he had made to become a reformer; but even with such assertions of sacrifice, he had trouble establishing his sincerity. Like the members of the Magdalen Society who had tried to save prostitutes in the 1830s, Green was accused of fostering an unseemly interest in the vice he attacked.[33] He was also accused of fraud, called a "humbug," and compared to traveling magicians rather than to wandering ministers. Green claimed that gamblers generated these criticisms, and he used the "plots" to feed a vision of the world divided into honest wage earners and dishonest gamblers. One who witnessed a demonstration of tricks by "special invitation" confessed that he could not, "of course, describe the manner of these frauds." Reports on the emotional content of Green's meetings varied. Sometimes witnesses found that he conducted his meetings with "utmost solemnity"; sometimes that he delivered "heart rending and blood chilling narrations"; sometimes that he created a "sensation"; and sometimes that he "was truly amusing."[34]

But it was not theatricality alone that got Green into trouble. Evangelical reformers had long been theatrical. Theirs, however, was a theater of the emotions which seemed genuine compared to Green's rational card tricks. Green, perhaps, tried to play upon a widespread Jacksonian interest in exposures, but questions remained about Green's status as an exposer. Although Green might have claimed the authority of experience to certify his right and ability to expose card tricks, he had no moral authority to interpret their meaning. "If he were a man of proper sensibilities and had the right sort of mind and conscience for a successful reformer," the New Haven *Palladium* reminded him, "he would appreciate the difference which he does not comprehend between a reformed Inebriate and a reformed Swindler, such as he professes himself to be": "A reformed swindler . . . wanted constant watching and should 'don' the sackcloth of the anchorite rather than the plumes and epaullettes of the haughty leader. . . . When such men attempt to regulate public authorities, rebuke the press and misrepresent it, and to degrade themselves to the condition of hired spies and informers, which are deemed odious in every civilized land, they deserve public rebuke instead of public confidence." The editors "shunned him as a humbug whose career as a pretended reformer is full of mischief." The proper stance for the swindler was penitent humility, not leadership.[35]

When he stopped gambling Green said he chose to be a reformer because he could do nothing else. He admitted that he "had no education, and was entirely unacquainted with the usual business pursuits of men." Green's choice to make a "livelihood out of agitation" was not unusual, and reform did give Green a way to make a market for what knowledge he had. He could also use his taste for a nomadic life and his tolerance for irregular earnings. But gambling proved to be something less than an ideal subject. It offered no spiritual redemption, no saved souls, no vision of a world transformed, perfected and made ready for the millennium. Green's reform also provoked the wrath of his former friends. Green used their opposition, as he had used his poverty, to establish his reformer's credentials. But when he announced, with great drama, that he knew he "must encounter the fiercest opposition and hostility of my former associates," he moved away from the market and into his fictional world of evil plots and plotters.[36]

When Green addressed the New York phrenologists in 1845, he told them a sad tale of a youth who had been led astray and destroyed by gambling, and he began most of his antigambling meetings with a personal confession followed by the same story. In the beginning he said he was inspired by the Washingtonians, and like them he offered combinations of personal narrative and entertainment. He even led audiences in singing the "Gambler's Wife." In his reformer's persona, he considered himself a simple, truthful man putting himself in the hands of his peers and trusting in their sentiment and sympathy. Inspiration and ends, however, were two different things, and Green was not saving gamblers the way the Washingtonians were saving drunks. He could hardly call out to an audience to join him on the mourner's bench. And he did not offer much in the way of alternative recreation. His performances inspired neither sentimental release nor group activities and he failed to attract those who might have been interested in revelations of capitalist corruption. When Dick and Fitzgerald reissued a condensed version of his books in 1868 and called it *A Gambler's Tricks with Cards Exposed and Explained,* they presented Green, the erstwhile gambler, as a tutor for parlor magicians who wanted to amuse their friends. Gamblers' tricks had been fully domesticated, stripped of financial exchange and freed from the dangers of intercourse with strangers.[37]

Green had set himself up for reduction to the scale of the parlor by attacking card playing. Green, as had Charles Caldwell at Transylvania in the 1830s, tried to persuade audiences that in the world of impersonal markets innocent amusements were no longer so innocent as they had once been. The threat was purely hypothetical, but he tried to argue that in the context of the market, improper social preparation was economically dangerous. Fluid class relations also made putting money on the table a risky business. A closed social world might have ensured the eventual return of any money bet as well as the relative parity of money wagered. In an open social world, however, a young boy challenged to bet by a gambler of great wealth would be sure to lose his little all, and his money was sure to be dispersed.

Again Green addressed himself to families whom he assumed were trying to train children to economize, to succeed, or to survive. "Reader, you may be standing upon the edge of a precipice, though you know it not. Fathers, your sons may frequent these haunts of vice, and be entangled in the snares of the destroyer. Wives, mothers, sisters, daughters, lend us your aid to save those you love from destruction." Green revealed the economic ties that ran from the countinghouse straight back to the hearth. When he did so he reversed a key premise in the cultural foundation of the antebellum middle class: that home and hearth stood as citadels unaffected by the venality and greed of the market. However accurate Green's description of the open relations between home and countinghouse, it was not what middle-class audiences wanted to hear.[38]

He also tried to make parents his customers by explaining to them that playing cards, like reading *Sinbad the Sailor* instead of the *Bible,* was likely to leave their children unable to recognize the social and economic risks they were taking or, worse, to inspire in them a dangerous thirst for adventure. Again Green was not far from writers of popular advice books who saw dangers in unsupervised reading of the wrong sorts of books, but again he misplayed his hand. Sinbad was not pornography, and card playing did not loom on the cultural horizon as a monstrous threat.[39]

By attacking parlor card playing Green tried to thrust his gamblers into middle-class homes. He tried to make family card playing the source of evil, implying that boys who played at home would never hesitate to play abroad. Charles Caldwell, of course, had taken up gambling reform in the 1830s at Transylvania, making the same point, and Rev. John Richards at Dartmouth in 1852 recognized that he was moving young men from their parents' parlors into the world and that he had a role to play in instilling economic discipline. College reform organizations were generally short-lived, but they acknowledge a particular moment of economic transition between childhood and adulthood. College boys were open to the temptations of gambling for the very structural reasons Green described. "There is no safety," Richards warned, adopting the rhetoric of temperance reformers, "but in total abstinence." His young scholars were not yet full participants in the market; they had not entered into the fully measured time of industrial work relations; and what money they carried was rarely the result of their own slow and steady labor. Caldwell had added another caveat to his southern boys who had come to Transylvania to study medicine. While they may have gambled at the family card tables, if they continued "at the academies and colleges" they would end their gaming careers in the "Pandemonium of BLACKLEGS."[40]

Green's own crusade did very little to promote the self-discipline that temperance reformers considered part of their great work. During his midwestern campaign the high point of his nightly program was a demonstration of his prowess with cards. Green turned the tables on his own demonstration, however, not flaunting his skill in legerdemain but announcing that his tricks depended on marked cards. Like temperance reformers who attacked liquor dealers as profiteers from vice, Green attacked card manufacturers who were in cahoots with gamblers and made enormous profits from the sale of cards, especially marked cards. Gamblers were not free agents: they worked for card manufacturers, creating profits so great that even journeymen card printers "average thirty dollars per day clear money."[41] To prove that all cards were marked, Green would ask a member of the audience to provide him with a deck of cards. If no one offered him a deck, he would send a volunteer off with a quarter to buy one. Green would then read the cards from their backs, claiming that any skilled gambler could read faces from blank backs. Printed backs, however, were becoming more common and not, as the manufacturers claimed, because they stayed cleaner longer but because they were easier to read.[42] Whether or not cards were marked, Green's skill sometimes earned him the plaudits of the local press and comparison with great magicians. He demonstrated, one paper said, the "skill of a Poller, or Signor Blitz." One of Green's nineteenth-century critics, however, asserted that he had worked with henchmen and with a small mirror inserted under the podium.[43]

Green asserted that he could read human motives as well as cards. He used his descriptions of gambling to claim that human relations, especially those involving exchange, had become unintelligible to all but those initiates in the fraternity of gamblers. His portrait of the mysteries of commerce along the Mississippi and in the corrupt metropolis is one of the themes which ties together his career as a reformer and his career as a writer. In the cultural world in which he operated, however, it was one thing to describe gamblers and victims in sentimental tales, it was another for him to catch gambling clerks, to chastise them, and to reform them in the real world. When Green became a spy for employers, in other words, he isolated himself from a working-class audience that might have delighted in his revelations of greed and corruption among those who thought themselves respectable. But he worried the rich with portraits of corruptible employees and with illustrations of the immense dishonesty hidden beneath a shell of respectability.

Like such popular writers and reformers as George Lippard, Ned Buntline, and T. S. Arthur, Green moved from self-exposure to revelations of corruption, from wildly imagined fictions to appeals for reform. In the process he stumbled onto contradictions that doomed his career. In a recent study of dime novels Michael Denning explored the imaginary worlds of northern mechanics and described the ways a writer like Lippard represented labor, both fictionally and politically. In Denning's reading Lippard clearly felt the politics of class in Philadelphia, and he knew his loyalties, however varied his career. Green abandoned the working-class allegiance he had invoked in his stories and turned against workingmen's vice in New York.[44]

Green tried to become a respectable figure, a writer and reformer, but such a move required that he establish an authoritative voice. If distance from plots and victims served to establish his fictional innocence, it did not serve to heighten the authority of Green's narration, and he began most of his books and lectures with an apology for his lack of literary polish. His books were not displays of "fine writing," but one of his editors argued that he professed "to speak nothing but the plain truth. He does not aspire to an elegant style of writing adorned with the ornaments of the orator and the scholar; but to one quality may lay claim, without being thought a vain or immodest man. He speaks with earnest sincerity."[45]

Green used his sincerity, his naiveté, and his embarrassment to create an innocent literary persona as a foil to the hypocritical sophisticate who had perpetrated his gambling schemes. The gambler's double was humble and apologetic. Like Bailey, Green described himself as an author unacquainted with the writer's arts. "It is taken into consideration that there are many in the field who are immeasurably my superiors both in literary acquirements and abilities as speakers," but few, he would add, so well acquainted with the gambler's arts.[46] Green further acknowledged his distance from the literary profession by choosing a "literary friend" to revise his first book, *An Exposure of the Arts and Miseries of Gambling.* The friend corrected "grammatical errors" and "verbal inaccuracies," and, he added with literary flourish, "If the reader should take up this volume with the expectation of being fascinated by a display of fine writing, his anticipations will not be realized; he will nevertheless, it is believed, meet with an *intelligible* presentation of such revolting and astounding *facts,* in reference to one of the most abominable evils that ever cursed the civilized world."[47]

The Fictions of Gambling Reform

In 1843 Green presented his first book, *An Exposure of the Arts and Miseries of Gambling,* as a text inspired not by writers but by the raw narratives of reformed drunks: "Reflecting on the well-known fact, that the simple narratives of reformed inebriates have, in general, a far more extensive influence than the most polished and eloquent discourses of others, it occurred to him, that the adoption of a like course in reference to the formidable vice of gambling, might be productive of equally gratifying consequences."[48] The search for "gratifying consequences" began with the predictable tale of a young man who ruined himself and his family when he fell in with gamblers. He then amplified this tale with other examples, but each tale served as the occasion for an interlinear commentary on Hoyle's rules of card games. Green presented a simplified version of Hoyle, because although it was not his stated purpose to teach games, he needed to explain the rules before he could explain how they were broken by cheating gamblers.[49] In writing about mere rules, however, he could not evoke the power that lay in others' tales of murder and drunkenness, the great darkness of the human psyche. He tried not to teach sleight-of-hand but to explain how to handle a deck already marked or stacked. He also listed the cards to palm or "steal out" to gain an advantage in particular games. He showed his readers how partners could sign or signal the contents of their hands, how a partner could change decks, and how a dealer could give one player a very good betting hand and give himself or his partner one ever so slightly better.[50]

Green addressed his *Arts and Miseries* to parents of young boys, and he followed it with a short-lived tabloid series published in Baltimore in 1844. He launched *The Gambler's Mirror* at young readers. He intended to use it to expose gamblers, but the first three issues were built around a serialized drama of an unhappy family fated to produce gambling children.[51] As he gained confidence in his publications, Green included more autobiographical material and stopped apologizing for his writing, but in *Gambling Unmasked! or, The personal experience of the reformed gambler, J. H. Green, designed as a warning to young men of this country*, he began to worry that his narrative might create excitement rather than alarm. Nevertheless, he felt assured of an audience. The excitement probably would have pleased the Philadelphia publisher G. B. Zeiber, who in 1847 reprinted *Gambling Unmasked!* with illustrations by F. O. C. Darley.[52] Two years earlier Green had had the book stereotyped by Burgess, Stringer and Co., a New York publisher, and he had sold it himself "at the low price of 50 cents per copy, and $4.00 per dozen." In two years, however, Green had become a professional author and was approvingly reviewed in a Lutheran newspaper: "His pen is his only source of support, while, for the cause of good morals, he has turned his back upon the prospects of princely wealth."[53]

Even as a member of the antebellum "literary proletariat," Green saw possibilities in his new profession, and his next literary endeavor was an attempt to create the fictional universe that would expand his field of reform. *The Secret Band of Brothers; or, The American Outlaws,* Green's attempt at just the kind of "robber book" that inspired Tom Sawyer's wild schemes, was published by G. B. Zeiber in 1847. Green announced: "There is not a line of fiction in these pages. The solemn truth is told, in all its strange and horrible interest." The book contains wild caricatures of his version of the financial concerns of the popular culture of the antebellum North and tells a tale of thrilling intrigue, blood oaths, purloined letters, and secret parchments. He revealed the workings of a widespread gang of gamblers who set out to steal money from business travelers. The story is a full-blown conspiratorial fantasy, combining elements of Masonic ritual with fantastic tales of bandits who led slave insurrections. But here the conspirators met to undermine the foundations of commerce and the personal and technical networks of communication that supported it, not to overthrow the government or to lead slave rebellions.[54]

In most of his autobiographical tales Green painted himself as a victim of plots by gamblers and a victim of a fate he could not avoid. In *The Secret Band of Brothers,* however, Green, the narrator, took a direct and active role. By dressing as a woman, disguising his voice, and befriending a dying colonel, he had managed to obtain the secret parchments of a band of gamblers. In the parchments he discovered the designs of a group who had sworn loyalty to one another and pledged to rob the rich. Green, a tireless, moralizing Dupin, made invisible ink visible, cracked codes, interrupted plots, and told readers that the band robbed because they had rejected the Bible as priestcraft, respected only the god of nature, and swore to fight against hypocritical Christian morality. If a member were arrested, the brothers would free him from jail; if they failed and he were forced to stand trial, the brothers agreed to bribe judge and jury. Like other fraternal organizations, Green's organized banditry served practical purposes. The secret constitution specified an allocation for the "Secret band of Brothers Mutual Insurance." A member who paid dues of twenty-five cents each month was entitled to thirty-three cents a day if he were confined by sickness or imprisoned while about the band's business.[55]

The band's business was the perversion of the relations of commerce and the diversion of its channels. Their "work" consisted in confusing the communications necessary for far-flung mercantile dealings. They wrote fake letters and intercepted men of business with artful conversation and vile flattery. Hardly the stuff of nightmares, but like his more famous contemporary, the abolitionist merchant Lewis Tappan, Green saw that the systems of credit and communication lagged behind the ambitions of urban merchants. Tappan's solutions were postal reform and a commercial credit rating scheme, the Mercantile Agency. Local contacts provided him with physical and fiscal descriptions of possible credit risks. Green's band had the same idea. They passed along physical descriptions of men carrying money. But, in fact, they acted out the worst fears of Tappan's detractors, who were sure that the Mercantile Agency was full of spies and informers.[56]

Members of Green's band pretended to be respectable gentlemen, ingratiated themselves with young men traveling on business, and used an elaborate system of secret mail drops—in hollow logs, behind boulders—and a code language, or "flash," which described a man's appearance and his habits and how much money he might be carrying, to get information to their friends around the country. To know where a man came from, to know whether he drank or played cards and whether he suffered from a disease or enjoyed perfect health was enough to give a band member an advantage in the adversarial relations of Green's imaginary commerce.[57]

Green laced the whole mercantile world with fraud. He resurrected his assertions of outward respectability and inner pollution, and he expanded the definition of a gambler to include any member of a "wide-spread organization—pledged to gambling, theft, and villany of all kinds." The organization also conveniently included all Green's enemies and detractors; all the editors, former friends, and skeptics who had denounced Green's crusades had fallen under the band's influence. They had been swallowed by a fiction.[58] And a slightly outdated one at that. The Secret Band of Brothers was a rather primitive band of confidence men. They were not smooth manipulators of fraudulent stock sales or sophisticated entertainers. They were men who undermined old-fashioned mercantile contacts by offering a false handshake and writing a false letter.

Green ended his seven years of literary production with a distillation of his arguments, *Gambling in its Infancy and Progress; or, A Dissuasive to the Young against Games of Chance,* and a revision of his autobiography, *Twelve Days in the Tombs; or, A Sketch of the Last Eight Years of the Reformed Gambler's Life.*[59] In *Twelve Days,* Green attempted to account for his life in the realms of fiction and the realms of fact. He offered accounts of his midwestern crusades and descriptions of the persecutions, trials, misunderstandings, betrayals, and illnesses that had plagued him since he abandoned vice. All his suffering was an imaginative atonement that Green hoped would preempt critics who accused him of profiting from his reform.[60]

He was still hoping, however, to profit from his stories, and he compiled a number of repetitious gambling tales in *Twelve Days in the Tombs.* Like treasure seekers, who a generation earlier had entertained people in taverns with tales of mystery and adventure, Green tried to gain recognition as a man of words with accounts of cunning and greed in the search for wealth. He had what Walter Benjamin described as a storyteller's traditional sympathy for rascals and crooks, but in Green's case the end was not the story itself. Because he could not admit to sympathy any more than he could admit to direct complicity in the fleecings he described, Green presented his tales in a frame and redirected them to the ends of reform. Yet he found that his protective shield did not serve him quite the way it did even the most controversial temperance reformers.[61]

Green the storyteller was, and remained, Green the ex-gambler, a man with a very high tolerance for repetition and, by his own confession, a man whose desire for money held him at an emotional distance from victims and audiences. In the best tradition of tales told by repentant sinners and "dark reformers," Green was far more interesting in the midst of the turmoil of sin than in the repose of salvation. His autobiographical tales, while building to dramatic moments of reform and repentance, depended for their content on a past filled with adventure and corruption. That past implied considerable repetition and futility. Like a series of coin tosses, his stories unfolded without reference to past experience, and like innocents saved only to be seduced again Green's victims never escaped the snares of gamblers. Once seduced, their fates were sealed.

Early in 1845, Green attracted the attention of Edgar Allan Poe, who reviewed his books in the March 1 issue of the *Broadway Journal.* Poe defended Green against critics in the press and dismissed those who worried that "Mr. Green's object is merely to make money."

"And what then?" asked Poe. "We have nothing to do with his private object; nor will the public object be one iota the less attained because, in attaining it, the public puts money in the pocket of Mr. Green."[62] According to Poe, Green's particular strength as a gambling reformer lay in his literal portrait of gambling's consequences. He compared him to temperance reformers who exposed the "costs of a drunkard's stomach." But Poe quickly moved beyond scientific "facts" and beyond Green's portrait of vice to a "gambling principle" that infected politicians, merchants, stock speculators, and land speculators. The deeper vice, according to Poe, would require "exposure by some stronger hand." Green's books nevertheless had their virtues: "They bear within them distinct internal evidence of their truth. The volumes have often, too, a less painful interest, and are sometimes exceedingly amusing."[63]

Poe's sympathy with Green is not surprising, and we can add Green to such popular cultural figures as John Lofland and T. S. Arthur, whose moralizings Poe refashioned into deep and inspired explorations of the mysteries of the human mind. In August 1845, when Poe published a revised version of "William Wilson," his story of a haunted gamester, it was not Green's amusing gambling tales he had in mind.[64] Green's readers would have recognized Wilson's cheating techniques—the rounded cards, the hidden honors—revealed at the end of Poe's gambling sequence. And Poe's dark portraits of a venomous double and of conscience murdered for gambling gain contain powerful versions of the cursed solitude and dark anonymity that Green had tried to describe as characteristic of gamblers. Poe went far beyond Green's revelations of cheating, however, and described the pathological isolation of the professed gambler and the financial schemes that perpetuated isolation.

Green knew that the gambler was, as he put it, "without sympathy; and when he loses his property, he has none to care for him; and when he dies, his name rots with his loathsome body."[65] But Poe had personal experience of gambling losses, as well. He also understood just how a gambler's lack of sympathy for victims might stand for the problems faced by a writer trying to reach an audience. Several times in the story of "William Wilson," Poe suggested that the patterns of honest economic exchange, the patterns gambling destroyed, stood for all human exchange, both verbal and monetary. We learn in "William Wilson" that readers of stories told by gambling narrators were to be as wary as victims who sat down to play, for both the narrator and the gambler depended on the naive good faith and gullibility of their audiences. Poe sensed the ties between a gambling author's deceived audience and a gambling villain's deluded victims. Like the gambler who had cut himself off from fellow men because he had murdered his social conscience for the sake of gain, Poe's narrator confessed at the outset that he had committed an "unpardonable crime" and was confined to "unspeakable misery," without any to care for him. "It could hardly be credited, however, that I had, even here, so utterly fallen from the gentlemanly estate, as to seek acquaintance with the vilest arts of the gambler by profession, and, having become an adept in his despicable science, to practice it habitually as a means of increasing my already enormous income at the expense of the weak-minded among my fellow collegians. Such, nevertheless, was the fact." Weak-minded collegians, fodder for the gambler, and weak-minded readers, fodder for the writer, shared a common sense of the credible. Neither audience nor victim could read "William Wilson" with the assurance that their interpretations were correct. In these two sentences the narrator, making amends in telling his tale, exposes to his audience what Wilson's double, the good and noble William Wilson, exposed to his fellow collegians. A sequence rendered complicated, like a game, by plays, feints, and asides, by short blows and rhythmic commas, is broken by a simple revelation: "Such, nevertheless, was the fact."

Wilson also asked readers to accord him a refuge of chance, "some little oasis of fatality amid a wilderness of error," for it was only by removing himself from willed evil that the narrator would be able to evoke the solace of human community. But Green set out to prove that there was no longer such an oasis of fatality. The narrator's request for sympathy in fatality also runs against the rest of the tale, which Wilson tells with verbs of will, agency, and intent—"planned," "contrived," "had long been plotting," and "induced by my artifices." Will implicated the gambler in the rational search for gain and severed him from the sympathetic bonds of shared human fate.

What the Gambler Knew

Green's intended audience as well as the intended victims of his gamblers were profit-minded individuals, young men and their parents and employers, who were trying to take advantage of the economic developments Green described. Boys working for New York merchants or young men sent on errands by their fathers carried money they had not earned. An earlier generation of highwaymen and dishonest rivermen had preyed on the flatboatmen who returned north over the Natchez Trace, their pockets full of profits from their produce sales. The "land pirates" needed only the force of arms and physical isolation to work their schemes. By the 1840s flatboatmen, although they still carried agricultural produce downstream, no longer dominated the imaginative portraits of the river trade, and those traveling with cash in hand took steamboats. Green redesigned victims, villains, and plots to suit the technology of the steam generation. The gamblers' schemes he described were based on several elements: on technical skill with cards, on deception, disguise, and wit, and on the opportunities produced by social isolation, by extension of the commercial markets into the West, and by possibilities of economic intercourse among strangers. Green asserted that merchants flirted with financial disaster when they hired clerks they did not know or when they depended on boys who had not learned to scorn the kindness of strangers. Green warned young travelers against placing "confidence" in "those despicable rogues who skulk about under the specious garb of gentlemen and useful citizens."[66]

Green's personal history and his knowledge of plots and schemes made his position as narrator a difficult one. He did not hesitate to advertise his technical skills, describing games of chance, their rules and how to break them, in great detail. Technical knowledge was morally neutral, and Green readily admitted to a gambler's technical skills but not to the moral and ethical indifference that allowed gamblers to take other people's money without giving them something in return. He had to be careful, therefore, to keep himself on the emotional periphery of most gambling scenes.

Despite his detailed descriptions, Green claimed that he did not intend to teach readers to cheat at cards. Some read him as a Hoyle for crooked card players, but he preferred to present himself as a narrator who merely witnessed the destructions of gambling schemes. His experience, he contended, made him the better detective, the man best able to comprehend the sinister logic of gambler's plots and to apprehend the gambling deceivers who preyed upon the innocent. Such knowledge could prove socially useful. Experience also made

Green an interpreter; sad young men and grieving parents approached him with their stories, and when Green retold them he turned the expertise that had served him at the gaming table into the skills of narration. He was a patient listener and an experienced guide. He understood the greed of gamblers and the weaknesses of their victims. Green's complex position was a safe one for a future reformer because it allowed him to emphasize the innocence of others rather than his own past guilt. It also permitted him to present his stories as in keeping with popular sentimental portraits of suffering and death.[67] When Green heard the stories he retold it was always already too late for him to save the gamblers' victims. Such tardiness served him well, turning him from venal expert into perfect sentimental witness. As Philip Fisher recently put it: "Only a witness who cannot effect action will experience suffering as deeply as the victim."[68] Had Green been able to save his victims, he would have been forced to reveal the ways expertise implicated him in gamblers' plots. He would also have left readers with a portrait of human greed at odds with sentimental beliefs.

Green's portraits were thus far more complicated than those of the gamblers who sometimes appeared as seducers in the popular sentimental fiction of the 1840s and 1850s. Gambling seducers shared a common biography. Most had been inducted into vice in a refined and corrupted Europe, and they appeared in the innocent United States as "roués" and "unprincipled libertines," as evil agents determined to seduce the innocent clerks of the young republic.[69] Like other sentimental villains, gamblers seduced young maidens, cheated the husbands of young matrons, and duped the clerks of aged merchants. Gambling plots, however, were built around finance, and the tales occupy a curious space between sentimental tales of seduction and betrayal and detective tales of mystery and revelation.

Charles Burdett's 1848 novel *The Gambler; or, The Policeman's Story* is a good example of popular gambling fiction. Green perhaps read Burdett's story before he set off for New York, but there are crucial differences between Green and Burdett. Burdett was never implicated in the gambler's plots he described. In fact, Burdett made several moves to distance himself from a gambler's knowledge of the weakness for greed buried within all human hearts. First he named a policeman to share the title page with the gambler and then he asserted that he had intentionally "deprived himself of much of the credit which might be accorded to him had he permitted the work" to appear without acknowledging its source. But Burdett's acknowledgment served as a disclaimer that shielded him from implication in gamblers' plots and allowed him to maintain the sentimental fiction of a human heart free from the venal motives of the market. The policeman, not the author, had knowledge of gamblers' evil ways, and Burdett the wise and distanced author is able to entertain both sentimental identification with a suffering wife and instrumental curiosity about mercantile losses.[70]

A contradiction between sentiment and technical knowledge was not all that was at work here. Green's slightly distanced narration in his gambling scenes also allowed him to emphasize the two most important points of his stories. In the first place, titles notwithstanding, his stories were not about gambling in the strict sense, for Green revealed all winning gamblers to be rational thieves and confidence men. Green transformed his gamblers into men of the market and helped make every economic encounter follow the laws of the market, not chance. Gamblers may have appeared to be outsiders, old-fashioned superstitious characters worshiping a fickle goddess of fortune, but appearances were deceiving and a belief in luck was dangerous.

In the 1840s Green's gamblers liked to imitate eighteenth-century Virginia planters, planters who themselves had imitated English aristocrats. They imitated games and styles of play, but imitation was designed to evoke the particular economic and social relations of worlds in which labor that produced wealth had been most successfully hidden. For Green, indeed for all those who wrote on nineteenth-century-American gambling, there were no economic relations outside the market. Nor were there—and this is important to understanding the ways opposition to gambling helped promote a particular version of economic rationality—imaginary economic relations outside the market.[71]

Green's gambling stories were all based on property loosely held. He tried to cultivate the concern that young men, carrying someone else's money, had not gone through the long processes of earning and saving that wed men to their wealth. Clerks and young heirs had not learned the industry and frugality that provided a cultural framework for the accumulated wages of their fathers and employers. Like postrevolutionary politicians who risked corrupting the republic because they had not experienced the hard lessons of their revolutionary forefathers, a generation of young men coming of age in the late 1830s and

1840s had not been through the shops, mills, and factories where their fathers had learned to save. Green worked within a very old literary tradition of foolish young men who lost inherited wealth, but he gave the stories a particularly American turn by setting them in the Mississippi Valley and in eastern cities and by playing representations of a gambling South off against representations of an industrious North.

Green's stories took place on particular economic and cultural frontiers. He opened his first book with the story of a boy who was educated in Philadelphia but who, on his return to Virginia after five years in the North, fell victim to an elaborate gaming scheme that eventually led to the ruin of his poor parents. The boy's education had not prepared him for his encounter with the "vile destroyer," and he finally blew his brains out in New Orleans, the last stop of so many a doomed gambler.[72] This boy was very close kin to the young men sent into the South, either on steamboats or overland, by northern merchants and to boys sent from New England farms to northern cities. They were as little prepared as the innocent son, and like him they lost money to smooth gambling strangers. Educated for one set of economic circumstances, they lost money in another. All of them also revealed the extent to which money was still connected to kin relations and how moral weakness might bring down family and business. Middle-class fathers may have provided for their sons, but economic provision did not ensure their sons the moral competence to guard their treasures. Green emphasized uneasiness over the future of middle-class wealth. Middle-class property, by its nature liquid, was subject not only to natural disasters but to market fluctuations and to individual moral failure.[73]

Green's gambling youths had not learned the delicate art of turning their passion for gain into the enlightened self-interest that magically manufactured harmonious social relations. The further they were from the actual labor that had produced the wealth they carried, the more likely they were to be carried away by passion and to lose their money. Because Green's cautionary tales were intended to support the logic of wage relations, they gestured both backward toward the kin and commercial relations that had given young men their money and forward toward the future dangers of a nation gone over to passion when they would lose it. To enter into a gambling relation was to wager family and fortune, self and sanity. It was to risk all that had become "natural" and "human": "There is no reality in his wealth or his pleasure; nothing substantial, nothing to satisfy the cravings of human nature. All is unnatural, and therefore unsatisfying. A man never, never can promote his own present actual enjoyment by becoming a pirate upon all the best interests of society: and such is the gambler. His hand is against every man, and every good man's hand ought to be against him, not to injure him as an individual, but to keep him from destroying others."[74] In one tale, the young gambler's desperation stopped with his sister's legacy, but in a purer version of the story, the young victim (the son of a farmer who had accumulated a small amount of capital) finally wagered his family's farm, and his parents were turned out by heartless gamblers.[75] If the gambler's lack of social feeling lets him rob the aged parents, a boy infected with vice has only one recourse. He must commit suicide. Whether they wagered money that belonged to their parents or to New York mercantile houses, Green's gambling young men had to die. By putting so much at stake, Green once again made his gambling stories express a popular version of lingering doubts about how people living in a world devoted to the self-interested pursuit of gain might form themselves into a cohesive society. If audiences supported Green's crusades gamblers might curb their perverted passion for gain and be brought back into the fold.

By describing young men who brought down their houses and then killed themselves, Green described a world in which there were no alternatives to the emotions of the market. Self, not just social standing, had become co-equal with the purse. Mothers and sisters wept, but their prodigal sons and wayward brothers did not return. The evil market Green painted seemed unconvincing to reform-minded audiences who liked to believe that there was still a world of the heart untouched by the rational calculations of the market.[76]

Green recognized that carefully accumulated middle-class treasures were vulnerable to gambling because young men had not learned the lessons of their fathers. He reasserted cautions the moral philosopher Orville Dewey had drawn from the speculative mania of the 1830s. "A man trained in the school of industry and frugality," Dewey wrote, "acquires a large estate. His children possibly keep it. But the third generation almost inevitably goes down the rolling wheel of fortune, and there learns the energy necessary to rise again."[77] Green knew that the danger of vice spread beyond the individual because kin relations were still intimately connected to the market. Personal financial relations were subject to a sort of structural imbalance that made self, sanity, and family all vulnerable to the folly of those who handled cash. In similar fashion the stories of gambling on Mississippi steamboats seemed to describe the imbalance generic to a commercial world that had been extended beyond the established world of financial services. Green set his fictions at these points of personal and financial disorder, and he tried to fashion a career for himself by peddling protections against the excesses of the passion for gain.

He told youths, who may have learned to play cards in the family parlor, that out of the house a game with strangers was dangerous. He told them that they could not believe in luck, in wealth that came without long, hard work. Green argued that youths who did not repeat their fathers' travails were a threat to their fathers' fortunes. But the threat was professional opportunity, and Green, along with those who wrote etiquette books, tried to provide a literary substitute for the experiences that accompanied a family's first fortune. In his own peculiar way, Green was a mother's ally, part of the early nineteenth-century cultural project in which education aimed, as Barbara Epstein put it, "to inculcate a certain personality type—rational, controlled, competitive, ambitious, and rigidly honest—and a set of attitudes—contempt or pity for poverty and the poor; desire for respectability, material achievement, and social status."[78] The lessons frequently revolved around work, or more precisely around gambling's remove from the world of work.

Except in very rare instances, workingmen did not bet wages in gambling stories.[79] Also, stories took place in settings physically and temporally removed from work: during the forced leisure of long voyages, at resorts of the rich or at retreats for those too old or too ill to work, or very late at night long after working hours. In these settings gamblers were especially dangerous because they hid their work in play, perverting both work and leisure. Reformers described practiced card sharps, men who possessed both the skills of craftsmen and the wit of actors, ministers, or speculators, but they applied their gifts to the wrong ends. As one reporter put it: "It is true he toils— it is true he expends upon his unholy pursuit labor which would win for him, if virtuously applied, honor and respectability."[80] But gamblers inhabited an unseemly territory that lay between work and play, and they used an aura of not working to attract customers. Just as they used the physical trappings of aristocracy to make money seem unnecessary, so they turned the leisure of others to their own greedy ends. In so doing, professional gamblers extended the market to areas of nonwork, and in particularly onerous ways.

In his books and in his demonstrations Green tried to take advantage of commercialized leisure, but the gamblers he described offered nothing to their clients, victims, and customers. Green himself produced the melodramas and popular literature that were part of the reorganized leisure of the early nineteenth century.[81] His gamblers, however, offered only a false version of the aristocratic idleness that was directly opposed to the industry and sobriety characteristic of both the work and leisure of the northern middle class. No one in the 1840s and 1850s defended professional commercial gambling on the utilitarian grounds that one had a right to purchase pleasure in risk taking.[82] Green's highly moral language made such utilitarian notions inconceivable. Victims were trapped not through pleasure in risk taking but through venality and greed. Gamblers were either villains or moral weaklings, and their penchant for vice made it difficult to build a sentimental reform crusade around them. When Green tried to use gambling as a vehicle for evangelical reform he encountered the limits of what a crusade based on the sentimental separation of home and the market could sustain.

The Audience Laughed at the Reformed Gambler

Green's literary career and his early reform career were preparations for an assault on New York, the citadel of the gambling vice. If he lost his middle-class audience by exposing the endless greed behind their search for gain, in New York he lost his working-class audience by setting himself up as a would-be informer on gambling houses and gambling habits. In the course of his travels Green discovered that, while temperance may have been a crusade begun in small towns as well as big cities, the crusade against gambling would have to be an urban one alone. The vice, as Green defined it, was highly commercial.

After his unsuccessful tour of the Midwest, Green returned to the Northeast in the mid 1840s and settled down in New Haven, where he lectured to Yale students, attacked billiard parlors and ten-pin alleys, and worked as a bookseller, stationer, and bounty hunter. He went to Canada looking for a murderer, but when he tried to return to the United States he was arrested because he was carrying canceled Treasury notes. According to Green he had the notes because he was tracking counterfeiters as a special agent of the Treasury Department. He complained that charges against him were trumped up by his enemies in New Haven and by gamblers in New York who were determined to defeat an antigambling bill he had pending before the state legislature. He was taken to New York, and after some debate about his exact classification as a criminal he was confined to the Tombs. He spent twelve days in the famous jail, one for each of the years he had spent gambling.[83]

While confined to the Tombs, Green attracted Horace Greeley's attention, and with the editor's help he emerged from jail with a new mission. Greeley, ever catholic in his reform tastes but perhaps by the late 1840s looking for something new in the reform repertoire, commented on Green's arrest and release in the *New York Tribune* and called him to do battle with metropolitan vice. Green was needed, Greeley said, "to watch the operations and defeat the snares of gamblers, who are here numerous, daring and most pernicious." Greeley asserted that gamblers stole "not less than five millions of dollars . . . annually" and destroyed "one thousand young men."[84] Since Green had incurred the wrath of New Haven journalists, he readily moved to New York, where he set himself up as a part-time stationer and full-timer reformer. For at least two years Green worked as the executive agent and promoter of the New York Association for the Suppression of Gambling. The job with the A.S.G. turned Green away from fantastic tales of the Mississippi Valley, and in May, June, and July 1850 he devoted himself to "collecting facts and statistics regarding the matter of gambling in New York."[85]

Green asserted that the vice of gambling was a "colossal abomination." He detailed the colossus and revealed that there were no less than 6,126 gambling houses in New York. Green's definition of a gambling house was quite generous, and his enumeration included places where games were "played for rum, turkeys and money—ten pin alleys and billiard rooms, lottery and policy offices, faro rooms and cock pits, arenas where dogs are fought and badgers baited, and a few of the shooting galleries and fashionable club rooms." The class lines that tripped up earlier gambling reformers were to be no obstacle to Green. He would go after all gamblers no matter their social positions, although surely he recognized that the gambling citadels of the rich were harder of access than the dives of the poor. He trumpeted his special expertise on professional gamblers, and he estimated that gambling supported some thirty thousand individuals who had lured at least another thirty thousand to ruin.[86]

Green also went through the history of New York arrests for gambling, and considering his immense claims for the extent of the vice, his findings were distressing. The city was commercial corruption incarnate, yet arrests were rare, even for gambling misdemeanors, and convictions for gambling crimes by juries, who often admitted to holding illegal lottery tickets themselves, were even rarer. Green found that in six years between 1845 and 1851 only fifty-nine individuals had been indicted for "keeping gambling houses and winning money at play." The only gamblers found guilty had been convicted on their own guilty pleas, and since two individuals accounted for eleven indictments, it would appear that the police bent on gambling raids just rounded up the usual suspects. Between November 1, 1849, and March 31, 1850, when in the course of his careful calculations Green estimated that over sixty thousand people had gambled in New York City, only seventeen individuals had been arrested for gambling. In 1851 the New York City delegation to the state legislature voted, to a man, against Green's antigambling law. Such official indifference illustrated all the more clearly to Green the need for an unofficial organization to do battle against organized vice.[87]

At its most benevolent the A.S.G. promised to save the thirty thousand victims of vice, but Green shifted his tone for his New York audience and offered to supplement the work of an overburdened police force and keep an eye on the establishments that catered to young men. Green turned practical and offered to sell his expertise on gambling to any who might be concerned about what their employees did at their leisure. The A.S.G. was especially designed for the city merchants who employed young men they did not know. In Green's impeccable logic of unearned wealth, such young men were likely to gamble away money they held in trust. Gambling was not simply a moral problem, it had become dangerous in a commercial economy dependent on credit, trust, and deals between strangers. Just as temperance reform suggests changes in the nature and discipline of a work force rather than a simple increase in consumption of alcohol, and moral reform charts the changing sexual demography of the urban

97

work force rather than a simple increase in male licentiousness, so efforts at gambling reform tell us more about concerns over market transactions than the actual spread of vice. Like Lewis Tappan, the abolitionist merchant, Green sensed the growing distance between exchanges policed by intimate ties of kin and acquaintance and the wide-open exchanges of urban markets.

The New York Association for the Suppression of Gambling was organized in the spring of 1850. Its president was an elderly merchant and insurance executive named Rensselaer N. Havens. The officers also included the educators Albert Gilbert, "Clerk Board of Education," and Joseph M'Keon, "Supt of Common Schools," and two men well known for the great range of their reform interests, Horace Greeley and Lorenzo Niles Fowler, a phrenologist, publisher, and younger brother of Orson.[88]

By garnering the support of New Yorkers prominent in the business community Green hoped to generate a larger following for his gambling crusade and to make a living for himself. He criticized ministers and reformers who concentrated on temperance and reminded them that dishonest clerks could do more harm than drunken hands. He would convince the wealthy of the real danger around them, he said, by exposing hidden patterns of vice and by publishing statistics on gambling losses. He had already located the gambling houses in New York, and he could now watch them for the presence of merchants' clerks. The association was also to encourage the passage of antigambling laws and to fight for the suppression of lotteries in states where they were still legal. None of this provoked much comment or controversy.[89] But the A.S.G.'s real objects were the urban leisure of office workers and employees and the fragile relations of credit and trust. When Green proposed that the A.S.G. actually apprehend gambling clerks, he created a dilemma for the men and women who had wanted to see reform as a benevolent enterprise free of any direct market aims. When he proposed a private police force to supervise all sorts of small gambling dens, he offended those who might have delighted in his exposures of greed and dishonesty.

In Green's fictional tales gamblers threatened to undermine the delicate emotional relations of kin and family, relations still contained in the money carried by young men. Kin relations were made vulnerable by wealth, and Green at his most sentimental proposed that boys who left the safety of home opened a channel of destruction. Their ruin spread like an infection and destroyed all who had supported them in the past. In New York, as in most big cities, it was rather the absence of kin that created fragile wealth. Once Green moved to New York, he abandoned his weeping sisters and widowed mothers and entered an economic world of strangers where employees, precisely because they came without recommendation of kin and community, were likely to fleece their employers. Green recognized that the problem was both demographic and moral. "The population of our larger villages is rapidly increasing; and the influx consists largely of young men, unsettled in character, inexperienced, and in far too many cases—wanting alike in just parental instruction and a deep-toned sense of obligation."[90]

A great deal has been written about the unsettled young men who bore the brunt of the economic changes of the early nineteenth century, and Green had them in mind when he proposed an association to act in loco parentis. The historian Allan Stanley Horlick argued that the A.S.G., along with the YMCA and the Mechanics Institute, was a temporary institutional solution to the urban social problems created by an influx of unsupervised young men. Such associations were backed by merchants, who, like manufacturers, needed tractable, dependable workers who had learned to share their employers' expectations and aspirations. But beyond this openly hegemonic function, the associations also served the needs of their participants by providing a place for socialization and relaxation. Horlick's point is an important one, but I also think it is necessary to examine the failure of the A.S.G. beside the success of such organizations as the Mechanics Institute and the YMCA. Green's association failed both as a reform organization and as an association designed to fill a social need.[91]

Green failed because his symbolic construction of gambling offended both the middle class and the working class. Gambling tales would not resonate with the symbolic power of tales of drink, sexual license, or even slaveholding. The villains caught drinking, whoring, or engaged in sadomasochistic violence had all been consumed by the dark and compelling irrationalities lurking in the human psyche. Flirtation with irrationality gave these tales their popular cultural power, but irrationality worked differently in gambling tales. The gamblers Green described stood exposed not as wild irrational devotees of chance, but as consummately rational figures—the capitalist refigured as thief. These figures might have pleased working-class members of Green's audience, but he turned against just such audiences by promoting himself as a spy on their leisure, and spies and informers had little potential as culture heroes.[92]

Gamblers resembled both businessmen and thieves, and such resemblance made it very hard to admit to having gambled. Green admitted that gambling reform was a challenge. "Other vices may be, and often are, abandoned by their votaries, upon cool reflection, and a conviction of their ruinous consequences; but it is seldom, indeed, that the professed gambler is restrained in his infamous career, either by the still small voice of conscience, or the admonitions of those who take an interest in his welfare."[93] Gamblers were hard to reach, and any effort to help them was likely to be met with scorn. And any money, especially money offered in charity, was likely to be wagered. When Green passed his reformer's hat and tried to appeal to charitable impulses in his audiences, he ran directly into his own assertions that it was dangerous to provide gamblers with money.

Nor did Green's crusade provide any of the intellectual services of an organization like the Mechanics Institute; nor did it serve the social functions of temperance crusades. He did not provide his followers with libraries, or with occasions for political discussion, or self-improvement, or with a social substitute for the casino or the friendly game of cards. He may have taught card tricks, and parlor magic may have played a part in middle-class socials, but it hardly provided a substitute for the mutuality and pleasure of a working-class card game in the backroom. Green was also a dubious figure of authority. Merchants could speak about their careers, and reformed drinkers could speak about harrowing experiences with the bottle and, however facetiously and theatrically, about the rewards of a temperate life, but what kind of authority was a reformed gambler, an admitted swindler, and professed card sharp? Even Green's entertainments turned from the dark exuberance of working-class theater to card tricks for the middle-class parlor. He was not a savory character, but he tried to construct alliances with respectable ministers and merchants, with exactly those people who wanted to turn making money into the most natural and moral of activities. They depended on the assurance that character formed outside the market, in the church and at home, provided the best insurance within the market. Green's whole fictional argument was designed to illustrate that there were no areas outside the market. This assertion hardly appealed to reformers who wanted, or needed, to believe that there were areas still ruled by the human heart.

Once again, with the A.S.G., Green determined to find a market for his gambler's skills, but in New York he was inspired not by the entertainments of the Washingtonians or by tales of bandits and murderers, but by no less a benevolent figure than Lewis Tappan. Green had used Tappan once in his fiction of a criminal underground, and he turned to him again to learn how to market his knowledge of gamblers' schemes. Green and Tappan both knew that national markets made participants vulnerable to the venality and bad judgments of their associates. Tappan had a large silk business and he had firsthand experience with the problems of credit in an expanding economy. He was also an abolitionist, with experience in organized benevolence. He brought the two together and used a network of ministers, lawyers, and abolitionists to gather information on inland merchants requiring credit, and he sold the services of the Mercantile Agency by subscription to city merchants who needed credit information on distant customers.[94]

Green decided the A.S.G. could start its own version of a "Mercantile Agency" to gather information on clerks who would gamble. Through a combination of undercover work and moral blackmail, Green would find out who was gambling and note it all down for the careful merchants who had subscribed to "The Intelligence Office, J. H. Green, Chief Agent." Subscribers had the right to look in a "private book" that contained the names of persons who frequented gambling houses. The association's agent would first warn and admonish individuals who appeared to be commencing a career of gambling, but when warning and admonition failed, they would inform a subscribing employer that he had a gambler on his payroll. Subscriptions to the services of the Intelligence Office were offered at varying rates, depending on the number of employees and on the amount of trust the association calculated as necessary for a particular business. Banking associations, insurance companies, and railroad companies could subscribe for a fee of $100 a year. Bankers and "Banking Agencies" were to pay $50 for the same services, and manufacturing associations and "other Associations employing a number of clerks and officers" were asked to pay from $25 to $100 depending on the number of employees. "Merchants, Jobbers, etc." were offered rates pegged to the number of hands employed.[95]

When the A.S.G. held its first and only anniversary meeting in the spring of 1851, Havens spent most of his presidential address defending the Intelligence Office. Critics announced that the Intelligence Office had transformed the association into a nest of spies. It was an accusation that had been leveled against Tappan as well, although most of those who attacked the Mercantile Agency as "Jesuitical" abolitionist spies came from the South and may well have resented Tappan's abolitionism as much as his mercantile endeavors.[96] Attacks against the A.S.G., however, had gone beyond mere "comment" and turned into "abuse." The association's plans to lecture on gambling, to circulate tracts, and to work to pass laws against gambling had passed unnoticed. "But," Havens continued, "the moment that we place the finger on the sore spot of personal deportment, there is an extraordinary nervousness awakened or stimulated lest we tred on individual rights."[97] The anonymous critics worried that the association's spies would make mistakes and injure innocent parties with slanderous reports. Havens defended the office's "scrutiny and observation of character" because he believed the association was simply doing for hire what any man had a right to do for himself. Green's network of spies turned against the very people who relished the way his undercover band caught rich merchants. It was one thing to inform readers, another to inform on them.

Havens did not believe that charging a fee for services changed the nature of scrutiny and observation, and he argued that, in the long run, careful scrutiny promoted the good of the mercantile community. Socially distanced, but still financially interdependent, relations of employers and employees, of commercial creditors and commercial debtors, required "sentinels" like the association on the dangerous "shoals of commerce." Havens went on to make his points explicit, and the ministers who followed him on the podium, Rev. J. B. Grinnell and Rev. John Pierpont (both of whom had come down from Boston to address the American Temperance Union meeting in New York the same week) directly acknowledged the ways an antigambling association might serve the merchants' interests, and therefore the interests of society, as they saw it, as a whole.[98] Pierpont opened with the requisite tale of a ruined clerk who had committed suicide and asked, "Merchants of New York, is it not for your interest to sustain an institution like this to check the cause of such serious losses?" For Pierpont the association was *"insurance,"* to "aid in the protection of your interests as well as the morals of the community generally, from the piratical incursions of the gambler."[99] In Pierpont's address, although they were equated in his imagination, interests preceded morals. And so direct an acknowledgment of self-interest undercut exactly that benevolent vision which evangelical reform was designed to promote.

Havens never specified the origins of the attacks on the Intelligence Office, but the association ran into trouble by mixing finance and character and by promoting naked self-interest without its necessary drape of disinterest.[100] The A.S.G. lost the benevolent middle class as surely as it had lost the working class. Green's bad character did not help his crusade. It had been one thing for him to write dramatic fictions and to assert that trade was undermined by gamblers who wrote and spoke in secret codes. It was one thing for him to perform card tricks and tell the story of his life as a gambler, admitting that he had been jailed for cheating, even if he did not admit cheating. But it was another thing for him to presume to judge the character of young men and to offer to spy on those who read his revelations. Green was exposing a system of underground communication, a system of signs and signals, unintelligible, he said, to his reform-minded audiences but used with the complicity of their trusted sons and employees to empty their purses. It was not news anyone wanted to hear.

Green could not hide his association behind a simple practicality. The particular need he sought to fill involved a volatile combination of personal and financial worth. His reports, like Tappan's credit reports and like the secret letters of *The Secret Band of Brothers*, involved a mixture of physical and financial description. From them one could recognize an individual and recognize an individual's pattern of paying bills, in Tappan's case, or, in Green's case, of spending money or carrying out an employer's trust. Both of them assumed that character would determine credit and financial standing and both of them tried to find substitutes for the kind of knowledge which had been generated easily in a village of familiars. What made Tappan's agency significant was the way it combined older assumptions about character and older methods of personal observation with newer methods of communication and finance, and a growing faith in the power of information to solve the problems of credit in an expanding economy.[101]

Green the ex-gambler, writer of popular fiction for boys, was not Lewis Tappan, merchant, abolitionist, member of a respectable religious family. He shared some of Tappan's visions and some of his troubles, but he did not share his social position. Although Green and Tappan were both accused of spying, of trying to market surveillance, Green spied on people at their leisure and made it into a business. Nor was Green like the reformed drunks who even if they lapsed merely used their falls to illustrate the enormous power of alcohol. If Green returned to gambling he would have had to use the money given to finance a charitable crusade to defraud innocent victims. His weakness in the face of vice was tantamount to power over others. Gamblers who had to make their living where others worked harmed the innocent. Green's crusade ended in laughter, accusations of fraud, and resentment, but unlike P. T. Barnum he could not use a conjunction of laughter and fraud to turn a profit.

Neil Harris has explored how an "operational aesthetic" could be said to have characterized the Jacksonian middle-class imagination. P. T. Barnum's extraordinary success can be explained by his adept manipulation of popular sentiment. Barnum presented puzzling "humbugs" that provided audiences with a sort of shadow play of the perplexing ideological questions of the early nineteenth-century republic. Harris explained that naive audiences relished Barnum's deceptions and enjoyed his revelations. Barnum prospered by reducing complicated aesthetic experience to "simple evaluation," and Harris concluded that the "practice of humbugging solved some special problems of the mass sensibility, problems particularly acute in America, where cultural ambitions outstripped cultural achievements."[102] Barnum presented occasions for calculated assessments open to everyman, and his humbugs became expressions of a democratic epistemology. He made a world in which "one could decide for oneself," and he made a fortune.

Green, despite his technical skills with cards and his precise technical revelations about cheating, could not move into the realm of mass entertainment. He was too busy reforming leisure to envision its commercial possibilities. Money stayed too close to the surface of Green's works, and undisguised money was not a very entertaining topic. Barnum put something—mermaids, singers, midgets, buffalo hunts—between his customers and his profits and he offered them deceptions that were clever constructions. Green did not have clever constructions to hide, to expose, or to reveal. He exposed only the venality and greed that lurked in the heart of economic man and then turned and sold his services as a spy on those who might have accepted his revelations of greed. In effect Green misread the ideological project of middle-class audiences who were busy discovering the virtues of economic man.

He also misread a working class who might have seen him as someone who could expose hypocrisy and greed. Green painted a world governed by suspicion and distrust, but he ignored any remnants of mutuality and reciprocity that might still have characterized a working-class vision of leisure in northern cities. In books like *The Secret Band of Brothers,* he exposed a wildly exaggerated fictional greed, but when he came out into the real world he chose to supervise the small gambles of clerks and employees rather than the more galling depredations of their employers. By choosing to expose the sins of workers and middle-class boys, rather than the dangerous sins of the rich, he barred himself from the cultural support of the world of popular, sensational journalism where exposures helped create a world of "objective fact." Dan Schiller recently argued that working-class readers shared assumptions about property, justice, and natural rights and that these shared assumptions shaped reporting in such papers as the *National Police Gazette,* where "publicity and exposure" might be used to working-class ends "to redress the political corruption that led to permanent class divisions."[103]

Like the working-class readers of the penny press Green understood the class divisions of the marketplace. Owners of property depended on the propertyless to carry out their business, and this inequality could prove dangerous both to men of wealth and to those who worked for them. But instead of appealing to the poor by attacking permanent class divisions and describing men of wealth as selfish gamblers who lived off the toils of others, Green appealed to men of property who were looking for ways to protect their purses. His appeal lacked a vision of inspired benevolence and his portraits of gamblers had a faint whiff of sarcasm. The clerks and employees Green described gambling with their employers' money merely borrowed it, just as merchants borrowed from banks to speculate. They had every intention of repaying their loans—as soon as they began to win. It was just that they would never begin to win, and to cover their losses they were forced to continue the robberies that first financed their speculations.

Green's professional gamblers and their victims had turned the world of the merchants and their clerks upside down. Gamblers were men bent on a rational search for profits, but they rejected the social goal of accumulation. As Fowler had discovered, they lacked the acquisitive bump, the bump of capital. They reveled in the fruits of unearned wealth, but they offered no pious homilies to the steady wages that had made their wealth possible. By denying the irrationality and chance of gambling, Green had helped promote the rationality of a market economy, but the proper merchants and reformers he tried to woo needed to maintain an area outside the market. Green might have been a useful ally in the realm of fiction, but they did not rush to embrace him in the flesh. As a gambler he perverted the financial world that depended on credit and trust; as a reformer he upset the world of reform which depended on moral foundations outside the market and he fell victim to the contradictions at the heart of nineteenth-century market culture. As an author he promoted the universality of rational market relations, but when he became a reformer he entered a world whose rhetoric depended on distinctions between the calculating relations of the market and the sentimental relations outside it. When he became a reformer he also turned on his working-class readers.

In New York in 1851, the stories that had sometimes "thrilled" midwestern audiences provoked laughter. A reporter for the *New York Daily Tribune* described an audience more raucous than indignant, moved more to laughter than to moral outrage. He began his report by noting that "several ladies were present in the galleries and in the area of the Building, who seemed to take a lively interest in the proceedings." The audience then reappeared in the report in a series of parenthetical asides. Like other early nineteenth-century audiences, they applauded speakers and they shouted an occasional "Hear hear."[104] But they also gasped with "sensation" whenever statistics on gambling were announced, and they interrupted sermons and speeches by "laughter," by "roars of laughter," by "immoderate roars of laughter." One rendition of a gambling joke produced "(Immense laughter, in which the ladies heartily joined!)."[105]

When the New York audience began to laugh, Green's crusade was over. And so to a certain extent was the sentimental phase of antebellum moral reform. What Green had tried to take seriously as the moral dangers of moneymaking now looked like a mere parody of efforts to remake a moral world. He had so hopelessly muddled the cultural distinctions between humanitarian reform and self-interest, between the sympathetic heart and the self-interested purse, between recreation for self-improvement and simple entertainment that his reform association offered little more than jokes. He had voiced the unspeakable proposition that moral man was only economic man in a thin benevolent shell. To make matters worse, he went on to argue that character and rationality were but feeble safeguards for a society made up of self-interested individuals. Green had violated the cardinal sentimental precept that there were tender, empathetic relations outside the market. When audiences heard Green as speaking in parody, they deprived him of the hierarchical distance that might have created moral authority, but they also acknowledged that the market no longer needed the emotional support of sentiment.[106]

The middle class accepted parody, and Green became a parlor entertainer. He offered something like a postsentimental mockery of sentiment. He evoked the sentimental world of victimized boys and suffering parents, but by charging a fee and offering a service he painted a sentimental world no longer worthy of exalted thought or pious endeavor, and no longer worthy of the audience of mechanics and artisans who might have seen him as an ally. To the thousand or so white women and men in Green's audience, a society of self-interested individuals no longer appeared fragile, and they no longer took seriously the potential challenges of nonrational economic men. There were others, however—economic outsiders, like African-American city dwellers and poor immigrant women—who bought policy slips and continued to gamble on the possibility that the market economy was no more rational, no more just, than the random numbers of a lottery drawing.

Gambling on the Color Line

And what of everyday life? Everything here is calculated because everything is numbered: money, minutes, metres, kilogrammes, calories . . .;
and not only objects but also living thinking creatures, for there exists a
demography of animals and of people as well as of things. Yet people are
born, live and die. They live well or ill; but they live in everyday life,
where they make or fail to make a living either in the wider sense of
surviving or not surviving, or just surviving or living their lives to the
full. It is in everyday life that they rejoice and suffer; here and now.
— Henri Lefebvre, *Everyday Life in the Modern World*, 1968

The gambling propensity is another subsidiary trait of the barbarian
temperament. It is a concomitant variation of character of almost universal
prevalence among sporting men and among men given to warlike and
emulative activities generally. This trait also has a direct economic value.
It is recognized to be a hindrance to the highest industrial efficiency of the
aggregate in any community where it prevails in an appreciable degree.
— Thorstein Veblen, *The Theory of the Leisure Class*, 1899

W hen the Ex-Coloured Man, the eponymous narrator of
James Weldon Johnson's 1912 novel *The Autobiography
of an Ex-Coloured Man,* decided to start living as a white man in New
York (or rather to identify himself as neither black nor white and let
the world take him "for what it would"), his first concern was with
money. He passed a few days in self-indulgent pleasure spending what
little he had accumulated in his varied careers as a black man and then
turned his attention to "financial success." "I had made up my mind,"
he wrote, "that since I was not going to be a Negro, I would avail
myself of every possible opportunity to make a white man's success;
and that if it can be summed up in any one word means 'money.' "
For a time he let himself be consumed by the white man's love of gain

and delighted in his growing investments.[1] But he also suffered a growing sense that he had bargained away a portion of his soul in the relentless devotion to gain.

The Ex-Coloured Man had two financial experiences of New York, and they divide neatly along the lines of race. When the narrator had first arrived in New York as a black man, he had found a world of bohemian pleasure along Sixth Avenue. He patronized a Chinese restaurant whose walls were "literally covered with photographs or lithographs of every coloured man in America who had ever 'done anything.' " When musicians sometimes performed in a back room, tables were pushed against the wall and the floor was "given over to general dancing."[2] Here no gambling was allowed, but the Ex-Coloured Man was also ushered through New York's gambling world, where he wagered money on a variety of games. It was a closed world, and money lost one night might be won back the next. To describe its financial structure Johnson employed a series of circular images: money and dice passed around tables; men sat or stood in concentric circles playing or watching the play. Those who played bowed to fates beyond their control, and this acceptance of fate spread from the gaming table to much of the rest of life. As a gambler the Ex-Coloured Man saw his encounter with New York, as had pilgrims before him, as an encounter with "a great witch," a "fatally fascinating thing." New York was green and golden, a "place where there was lots of money and not much difficulty getting it," but success and failure were governed by the cruel goddess fate. "Some she at once crushes beneath her cruel feet; others she condemns to a fate like that of galley-slaves; a few she favours and fondles, riding them high on bubbles of fortune; then with a sudden breath she blows the bubbles out and laughs mockingly as she watches them fall."[3]

When he returned as a white man, his vision of New York changed. The narrator did the watching and the laughing. He took a new active role; he replaced caprice and passivity with rational action, exchanging gambling circles for rectilinear want ads and columns of figures, and a gambler's round tables for a real-estate investor's grid of streets and towering skyscrapers. He moved through New York finances on a path of "decided advancement," and now turned capitalist and real-estate magnate, he watched his money "grow from the first dollar." When "the fever was on him" as a black man, he descended through gambling circles, playing and losing first at pool and poker and finally at craps. When he "contract[ed] the money fever" as a white man, his "practical sense" took over and he turned his text into a balance sheet. But Johnson's bottom line was finally race, not capital, and the more capital the narrator's investments produced, the more his passing became, as he put it, a "capital joke." For the Ex-Coloured Man financial return was not just money, but wonderful, mocking laughter and final disproof of the " 'theory that one drop of Negro blood renders a man unfit.' "[4]

The Ex-Coloured Man's moves from gambling to investment followed the contours of parallel economic universes, universes divided by race. His calculations revealed cultural and racial barriers in the supposedly neutral marketplace. Why did he have to become white to save and to succeed? When he surrendered his marked black body for an unmarked white body, the Ex-Coloured Man acquired the purposive, economic rationality that a century of liberal economic theory had made the foundation of human nature and the base of political stability within the republic. He went to business college; he worked; he "economized"; he pursued his studies; and he set goals. He denied himself the aesthetic pleasures of art and music and the physical pleasures of alcohol and tobacco, but he "derived a great deal of pleasure" from calculating the increase on his principle.[5]

His two selves have a deeper message as well. He maintained a dual identity, a double consciousness if you will, that granted a strong measure of cultural independence to his economic identity as an African American. He had not simply loosed a bourgeois economic man that had been hidden within his black skin: when he began to calculate, he changed his race. As a white man, however, he learned that every careful gain was simultaneously a cultural loss. In blackness was creativity; it was the source of the Ex-Coloured Man's music, and his key to the creative economy of "gifts" where money, goods, and inspiration moved freely in ever larger circles. The white man with the balance sheet stopped the flow, leaving the Ex-Coloured Man standing alone on the bottom line as "an ordinarily successful white man who has made a little money." But the ordinary white man who looked back over his former self adopted an elegiac tone: "When I sometimes open a little box in which I still keep my fast yellowing manuscripts, the only tangible remnants of a vanished dream, a dead ambition, a sacrificed talent, I cannot repress the thought that, after all, I have chosen the lesser part, that I have sold my birthright for a mess of pottage."[6]

Johnson was not the only writer to imagine venturing over social borders of race and class, and by the end of the nineteenth century several professional sociologists had made careers exploring the class lines of their social world. Like Johnson's narrator, they donned disguises, adopting the speech and manner of their informants and in disguise penetrated an alien world, most often a working-class world, to write about it from the inside. Such professional adventurers learned that barriers between classes were far less permeable than those described in the optimistic fictions produced by Horatio Alger, Jr., and others, and that despite their own acts of espionage traffic between classes, like traffic between the races, did not generally move freely back and forth.[7]

The Ex-Coloured Man's foray across the color line suggests a slightly different lesson. It is only in rare instances that one chooses one's race or one's gender, and such rare instances provide lucid commentary on the arbitrary structures of a world divided by gender and race and on the arbitrary constrictions of the social categories that pass for categories of nature. When the Ex-Coloured Man moved race into the realm of choice, Johnson exposed the great fallacies in the economic universals of the white nineteenth-century. In choosing his race, the Ex-Coloured Man simultaneously chose the economic characteristics that the long intellectual project of a liberal capitalist middle class had made a natural part of white men. By exercising choice he also challenged the racists and white supremacists who, since the emancipation of the slaves, had complained openly that blacks who refused to work for them, whatever their reasons, were indolent, lazy, superstitious, and by nature ill suited to the careful calculations of a market society. Furthermore, by taking a stance outside the supposed rational markets of the nineteenth century and choosing certain aspects of rationality rather than simply having them or inheriting them, Johnson's Ex-Coloured Man pointed to possible economic alternatives—to an artist's world of creative gifts, to a world of small dissident pleasures to be found in the waste, risks, and chances of gambling, and to exchanges of work and leisure which might have been governed by the cultural or spiritual logic of an African-American world.[8] Johnson's chosen complicity with the business world of the early twentieth century suggested that human beings made, rather than inherited, their economic natures. More important, the experiences of the Ex-Coloured Man make it possible for us to look for submerged economic alternatives that never made it into the texts of formal political economy, to explore the power of the irrational in that most rationalized sphere of human action. In certain nineteenth-century situations gambling provided access to just such alternative economies.

By the end of the century most states had passed the laws against gambling; law-abiding citizens embraced the quest for accumulation and indulged in only the most rational leisure pursuits. Gambling, driven underground, fed the coffers of early organized crime. Yet even if the money wound up in the hands of criminals, many, like the Ex-Coloured Man on his first visit to New York, continued to find rare pleasures in gambling. To study these small pleasures suggests alternatives to the ways the history of gambling and the history of personal finance have been written. Historians have emphasized gambling's ties to early organized crime and followed money into criminal operations, but if we turn the exploration of gambling back to the pleasures of those who bet, we may learn more about bettors than about gangsters. Why did people bet on numbers in spite of the enormous odds against them? Why, in effect, did they waste their money? Why did they defy tremendous cultural pressure to save and to accumulate? It would be too much to attribute to gambling a utopia of desire fulfilled, yet I would like to suggest that remnants of an alternative culture of irrational economics lie hidden in the early numbers betting and in the dream books designed to guide the miniscule speculations of numbers bettors and policy players. Poor people who wasted their pennies in unlikely speculations represented an indulgence that challenged middle-class injunctions to save. And the dream books, cheaply printed pamphlets offering the means of turning sleep into capital, suggest that even the very poor discovered the means of transforming economic matters into the stuff of play.[9]

Policy or, in slightly different form, numbers, had existed alongside the lottery since the middle of the eighteenth century. Those who wished to venture but who did not have the full price of a lottery ticket would "insure" a number with a broker, agent, friend, or scoundrel. For a small premium and a small return they could wager that particular number, or the numbers drawn on a given day or in a given order. It is not hard to see why policy might have troubled those who promoted lotteries. Policy bets were side bets, and neither the promoters nor the designated beneficiaries touched the money that changed hands. It was not drawn into the rational channels that the lottery (whatever its origins in irrational economies governed by fate and superstition) was made to serve. If the lottery had an immoral, irrational, or corrupt component, that was surely all that remained when adventurers and profiteers reduced it to the inexact science of policy.[10] Policy also allowed those who had only the smallest sums to wager to venture and to play, and middle-class reformers complained that policy was a besetting vice of the urban poor, especially poor African Americans. For players, however, to wager in the lottery or to venture at policy was to entertain fleeting utopian visions of an economic world where dreams came true. Like all utopias, however, the visions of players were but imperfect allegories for economic worlds that did not yet exist. The reformers who wrote on policy probably exaggerated the extent of play, but a study of those who consulted dream books and bought policy slips does lead us back to significant decisions about small amounts of money. And it is, I think, decisions about these small sums which offer a way into the splendid irrationalities of the economics of everyday life.

Against the Lottery: Waste, Idleness, and Superstition

The lottery played a significant role in financing large projects in the American colonies and the early republic. In a frontier society hard pressed for the means to underwrite capital-intensive projects, the lottery provided a pool of capital as well as the means of spreading the risk of large-scale undertakings. Between 1744 and 1774, one study concluded, at least 158 lotteries were authorized in the American colonies. Before the invention of the ternary combination that allowed multiple winners to be determined in a matter of minutes, thousands of individual lottery tickets and thousands of prizes or blanks were drawn over periods of months and even years. Public lotteries were licensed to build levies, lighthouses, docks, canals, bridges, roads, schoolhouses, colleges, churches, and even jails, and individuals conducted private lotteries to dispose of the real estate and personal property whose value exceeded the wherewithal of any single individual. In his long study of American lotteries, John Samuel Ezell concluded that the lotteries which were part of daily life in the colonies provoked little moral opposition. Increase Mather had frowned on their impiety; Cotton Mather had concluded that they returned nothing useful to the community; and in Pennsylvania, Quakers had consistently opposed them as encouraging immoral gaming. But their long if controversial history in Europe as well as the need for funds and the widespread acceptance, especially on the part of such moral authorities as educators and clergymen, of the projects they supported curtailed any sustained opposition. They were licensed as a form of voluntary taxation, a less painful way to finance the development and defense of the colonies.[11]

Lotteries as enterprises and as ways to raise revenue did not die with the Revolution, and at least another three hundred officially licensed ventures financed internal improvements throughout the early republic. As enterprises, lotteries grew increasingly complex, and professional operators took over services that had been performed by unpaid volunteers and friends of beneficiaries. Managers paid commissions to ticket brokers, and lotteries crossed state lines as brokers, who bought tickets at a discount, searched for customers willing to pay full face value. Entrepreneurs opened ticket brokerage houses throughout the country, and Ezell estimated that by 1815 every town of a thousand inhabitants supported at least one person whose business was selling chances in a variety of lotteries. Brokers also often exchanged local currencies, sold books and stationery, and performed some of the services of modern-day investment bankers. Large-scale lotteries proved highly profitable for their managers, contractors, ticket agents, brokers, and for the newspapers who accepted their advertisements, if not for those who adventured. At the same time a few worried reformers saw that small-scale, unlicensed lotteries and raffles distracted the poor from a routine of careful earning and measured expenditure.[12]

By the early 1820s moralists, increasingly schooled in the rational assumptions of the enlightenment, made it clear that simple capital accumulation was not the state's sole interest. Capital formation had to be accompanied by the mental formations that would ensure personal stability and widespread involvement in the ongoing search for wealth. While lotteries funded laudable projects, they allegedly destroyed the individuals who ventured in them, and critics beseeched

Drawing of Lottery Tickets.

From J. H. Green, *Gambling Unmasked! or, The personal experiences of the reformed gambler* (Philadelphia, 1847). Courtesy Yale University Library.

the public to consider the means they used to raise revenue as well as the ends. Lotteries raised money for good causes, but they violated an equally important public interest in making people into good citizens mindful of small accumulations and small expenditures. Critics noticed that lotteries appealed most to those slowest to learn the lessons of the market—to the urban poor, especially poor African Americans and recent immigrants. Lotteries drew them from their places of employment, entertained them with drawings carried out over several days, and filled them with false hopes and mistaken expectations. They also encouraged precisely the delusions that led the poor to steal from the rich.

Like the opposition to recreational gambling, opposition to the lottery has to be set against the changing economic structures of the urban Northeast. Hostility of the poor to the evident prosperity of the rich made the purses of the rich vulnerable to the designs of the poor. Lottery promoters encouraged the poor to look to the easy gain that was kin to stealing, and they did nothing to promote the self-discipline and delayed gratification that were to police the boundaries between classes. Opposition thus drew on the discourses of moral reform and self-control which fueled crusades for dietary reform and temperance. But reformers also presented ample evidence of the corruption and dishonesty of individual managers. Lotteries, which had once seemed so benign a means of finance, had become dangerous, critics argued, because they fostered an unseemly interest in the quick gain that denied the sanctity of steady, incremental accumulation; because they promoted the waste that undercut injunctions to save; because they celebrated the idleness that challenged the precise division of human life into periods of work and periods of leisure; and because they encouraged a dangerous dependence on modes of thinking now labeled as superstition and deemed to undermine the education in rational calculation that was to assure the fair dealings of a commercial republic. Those who adventured had chosen quick gain over delayed savings, waste over accumulation, idleness over work or leisure, and superstitious interpretation over calculation.

Although revelations of financial fraud among lottery managers as well as careful presentations of the logical fallacy of hoping for profit from a lottery wager helped turn public opinion against lotteries in the Northeast, it was finally the cultural or ideological contradictions implicit in officially sanctioned lotteries that brought the practice to a close. The lottery was dangerous because of what it did to the mental world of bettors. Certain ways of thinking and acting once considered easily within the range of human possibility began to appear as outmoded, irrational, and therefore dangerous to a bourgeoisie busily creating a world in its own likeness.[13]

Organized opposition began to appear in the 1820s in New York, where the press accused managers of fixing drawings, and more generally among Pennsylvania Quakers. Job Tyson, a Quaker lawyer from Philadelphia, emerged in the 1830s as the most important antilottery spokesman. He collected tales of fraud and abuse and described individuals who had won money only to lose it again in an insane thirst for gain. He found fifty-five debtors who had come before the Pennsylvania courts as a direct result of lottery speculation. He published his findings in his much-quoted *Brief Survey . . . of the Lottery System,* which served as a guidebook for antilottery movements throughout New England and the Northeast. The campaign he inspired was very successful. A profitable lottery could never be as covert as other forms of gaming, and opponents succeeded in repealing the licensing laws that assured state support and regulation. While the Society for the Prevention of Pauperism had despaired of closing the gambling houses that operated in secret, they had far greater success against the lottery. By 1840 lotteries had been explicitly prohibited in twelve states, and they were on the wane in the other fourteen. Organized opposition, the victim of its own successes, diminished in the 1840s and 1850s, and lotteries reappeared following the Civil War. The speed and relative facility of the lottery's temporary demise, however, should tell us a great deal about the construction of morality and finance in the 1830s.[14]

In September 1818 the New York State legislature, prompted by an exposé of cheating on the part of managers of the Medical Science Lottery, passed a law prohibiting any new lottery licenses after 1820. Charles N. Baldwin, the publisher of the *Republican Chronicle,* had described the scheme used to rig the drawing. "It is a fact," he began, "that in this present Lottery . . . there is SWINDLING in the management. A certain gentleman in town received intimation last week that a number *named* would be drawn on Friday last! and it was *drawn that day!* The number was insured *high* in several different places. A similar thing had happened once before in *this same lottery:* on examining the manager's files, the number appeared *soiled* as if it had been in a pocket several days! If this be true, *and we vouch for it,* it may be previously known who shall have the 100,000 dollars in this lottery. It deserves immediate attention by our magistrates." The lottery managers sued Baldwin for libel. He won his case when an investigation conducted by John Pintard confirmed truth of his allegations and the legislature agreed to limit the operations of lottery dealers. An act passed on April 18, 1819, forbid new licenses, raised penalties for unauthorized lotteries and for the sale of insurance, and further stipulated that lotteries currently licensed could be drawn only with bare arms.[15]

Henrietta Larson argued that the demise of the lottery was financial rather than moral. Lottery offices became stock brokerage firms; financial innovations, especially corporations, made it possible to spread monetary risk among many investors. "There was a veritable crusade," Larson wrote, "but I am inclined to think that not the reformers but the development of machinery for the sale of shares in corporations was responsible for the decline of lotteries."[16] The development was deeply dependent on ideological transformations. Like the lottery, savings banks, insurance companies, and stock speculation communicated a moral message within financial schemes. Viviana Zelizer has argued recently that the success of life insurance between 1840 and 1860 can be explained only by the decline of a deterministic religious ethos that had condemned life insurance as sacrilegious speculation on divine plans. Both savings banks and insurance provided alternative sources of capital for public and private projects and, more important, helped to turn the small accumulations of the poor to the ends of the rich. They did seem to offer the poor something in return. The poor who bought lottery tickets, critics sensed, were the least likely to benefit from the public projects and the internal improvements lotteries financed. Life insurance and savings accounts seemed better suited to financial justice, for both offered a possible return on investments and both tempered gain with moral message: insurance companies with financial consolation for the bereaved, savings banks with lessons in compound interest and steady accumulation.[17]

Reformers described the dire consequences of lottery gaming, and as for all forms of gaming, consequences followed class lines. The well-to-do, like John Pintard and his family, whose lottery speculations began in rational assessments of risk or in considered support for the projects a lottery was designed to finance, stayed sane, rational, and honest, whether they won or lost. But patterns in the commercial relations in New York suggested to Pintard that the lottery was a risky business, and he began to remark on bank clerks whose lottery speculations had led to crime and deceit. Realizations of financial and social risk perhaps prompted the wealthy to direct speculations to ventures that offered better security or better returns, and once they had done so they could join campaigns against the lottery with little regret and with little reduction in their own opportunities for pleasure or profit.[18]

Writers compiled sad histories of loss, despair, and self-destruction, but there is little of the sentimental charge that frequently informed pamphlets on drink and slavery. Lottery adventurers fell not by tragic weakness but by selfish search for gain without work. Reformers turned their attention away from tragic figures and advanced practical arguments on the futility of adventuring in the lottery. Time and again they repeated the calculation that proved that even to buy all the chances in a lottery was to be a sure loser. Their logic depended on a direct application of the arithmetical skills that by the 1830s had become part of the common school curriculum. They used these burgeoning skills in calculation and statistical analysis to separate the educated, the rational, and the intelligent who worked to abolish lotteries from those who could be led to bet. They addressed those who would "submit to the force of reason," who had separated themselves from the "great mass of superstitious and illiterate persons." The lottery drew in the superstitious and the illiterate by encouraging them to exercise their skills in interpreting hunches, signs, and dreams. Lottery players chose interpretation over calculation. "In what other game," Tyson asked in his *Brief Survey,* "is the subversion of reason so necessary for the success of the players as in that of lottery?"[19]

In an antilottery pamphlet published in 1841, Thomas Doyle, a former ticket vender, addressed an "intelligent public" who had already given up on the lottery. He exhorted them to act on behalf of those incapable of understanding the larger ills of the lottery and who might be prevailed upon to wager. He employed various logical weapons in his assault, confessing that statistics, "however dull and uninteresting," were necessary to comprehend the details of the lottery and to see just how managers made their money and bettors lost theirs. As had Tyson before him he explained that a 66-number lottery run as a ternary combination produced 76,076 tickets and that if 30,136 of them drew prizes, 45,760 would draw blanks. Furthermore, a disproportionate thirteen-eighteenths of a lottery's revenue went to pay the expenses of the management, leaving a meager five-eighteenths for supposed beneficiaries. A lottery's profits were its adventurers' losses, and even one who bought all the tickets and was thereby assured of winning all the prizes would not recover his investment. For a bourgeoisie increasingly obsessed with a return on every investment such losses were anathema. As Thomas Man put it (after a careful disquisition on the structure of lottery profits): "There is no rational man but would come to this conclusion; that he would no longer suffer such gross imposition! such an outrage on common sense! such a Tax on his Pocket, without any return!!!"[20]

And it became increasingly bothersome to lottery reformers that some citizens of the republic did not share their rational horror of loss and waste. The poor who risked a meager surplus on a lottery ticket must surely suffer some profound deformation of character. Lotteries attracted laboring men willing, as one wrote with horrified emphasis, to *"throw away"* a portion of their wages. Like drunks they consumed for no good end, reveling in the simple dissipation of pure waste.[21]

As we have seen, both Robert Bailey and Jonathan Green experimented with the means of turning gambling into an aspect of commercialized leisure. In both their careers the controversy and scandal they encountered can often be understood as a direct result of their experiments. It was not possible in the early nineteenth century to market overt venality as amusement. Not only were those who gambled at their leisure corrupt, they also seemed to aspire to the possibility of doing nothing—to inhabit an ideal state in which nothing was made and nothing was exchanged. Bailey and Green worked at what had become a criminalized trade, but when they transformed gambling into a trade they worked where others played and denied the disruptive idleness that lay at the heart of gambling in an expanding capitalist economy. Entrepreneurs were never idle, but idleness was the lure held out to victims and lottery adventurers. Early nineteenth-century northern reformers painted the lottery as a problem because successful lottery bettors were not even gambling entrepreneurs and they threatened to disrupt the ideal construction of life divided into periods of work and periods of leisure with an audacious celebration of waste and idleness. *"Idleness,"* Tyson complained, was "a concomitant of gambling. What has a greater tendency to remit exertions than the expectation of independence without it?" Or, more clearly as the author of an 1827 pamphlet *Lotteries Exposed* explained, lotteries encouraged "idleness by holding forth prospects of gain without labor."[22]

The prospect of idleness attracted those not yet drawn into the expansive celebration of free labor. To entertain the possibility of idleness was to engage in a small revolt against the bourgeois division of all life into labor and leisure. Slaves might well have entertained idleness as a preserve of independence, but the one thing free labor did not mean, as Eric Foner has often argued, was freedom not to labor. Until gambling could be represented as a product to be consumed in a leisure tied to a constant toil of productive labor, the possibility of not working was exactly what the lottery offered and precisely why it offended those who had a stake in keeping people at work.[23]

By approving lotteries as a means to raise money, the state, although bent on putting people to work, encouraged not working. Tyson saw the perverse contradiction and concluded that while the government wanted to support "honourable sentiments and habitual industry" it instead promoted a system that fosters idleness and gives "nutriment to vice." It seemed to him that the system was directly at war with the "whole policy of the country whose every interest consists in making wealth the fruit of intelligent industry." Or, more sarcastically, "if it is the duty of the government to encourage idleness, that duty may be accomplished through the instrumentality of the *lottery*."[24]

The external appearance of idleness was a sure sign of specific mental capacity, or incapacity. Doyle's years in the lottery office had taught him that through the good offices of the lottery the multitude was not only impoverished but despite their losses went on expecting prizes and that such expectation produced a "dissipation of the mind which totally unfits individuals for any regular or legitimate trade; renders him disoriented with the slow gains derivable only from industry and attention to business." Recurrent complaints of the dissipation of lottery bettors linked them not only to wasters and wastrals, but to the drunks who increasingly preoccupied the imaginations of middle-class temperance reformers. Tyson, in a second pamphlet, complained that lottery venders were in cahoots with saloon keepers favoring profitable licensing laws rather than temperance and that saloon keepers returned the favor, supporting all manner of drawings. They profited from the lottery trade, not only by selling chances but by serving drinks both to the winners who were compelled to treat their friends in the celebration of victory and to the losers who sought consolation in alcohol.[25]

Tyson's studies of drunken, suicidal, and indebted winners taught him that even winners, flush with cash, could never be returned to the fold of rational accumulators. "It is," Tyson asserted, "a peculiar feature of lotteries, that success and miscarriage alike allure their votary to ruin." He compiled various anecdotal incidents in which a winning ticket had spelled its purchaser's doom. Lotteries had thus simultaneously enriched and destroyed a dentist, a mechanic, a laborer, a merchant clerk who "fatally came up with a prize," and even a lottery vender.[26] The victorious were victims of a compulsive disorder that forever barred their return to productive society. Moreover, they also refused to consume. Today we are familiar with lottery winners who produce detailed shopping lists (often sentimentalized as homes for aged parents), but their early nineteenth-century forebears were incapable of turning money into goods. Or at least that is what lottery reformers wanted to argue. Winners, isolated in a sort of madness, refused productive labor, sentimental consumption, and even the more common nineteenth-century idiom of advancement through social class. Rather than rising with newfound, if somewhat suspect, wealth, they wasted and wasted away, spreading infectious waste through family and friends.

Although critics saw that the rich and poor often shared the vice of idleness, some spending by the rich assured their return to the community of consumers. Even if goods purchased were useless, unrepublican, extravagant frippery, a single purchase was better than the boundless waste of lottery winners. Poor lottery winners used their winnings only to purchase more tickets and perhaps to finance an occasional alcoholic binge. The lesson behind Tyson's sad tales was that only slow and steady gain assured the sanity of its possessors and the safety of the republic. As George Brewster had written in 1828, "That man, who rises gradually into notice from obscurity, and who, by frugality, temperance, and perseverance in business becomes wealthy, is alone the happy man in the enjoyment of his possessions. He feels a complacency and a contentment, which that man knows nothing of, who starts up, at once, like the mushroom, from obscurity, into the ranks of the rich."[27]

Citizens who had shot up in a night like mushrooms could hardly assure a stable future for the republic, for in the discourse of lottery opponents political stability rested on the belief in the possibility of a gradual ascent from "poverty to mediocrity to affluence." This is "the very basis of our independence, the very foundation and building principles of republicanism—destroy it and we must fall." And the fall, "A Foe to Deception" was sure, rested in breeding, and here he drew lessons from the experience of slavery. "Let a man," he wrote, "who has been born and bred to nothing more than a common livelihood be suddenly put in possession of a fortune, will he know how to take care of it, more than the black would know how to take care of his liberty?" But Thomas Man, another reformer, used race to suggest that profiteers as well as bettors posed a threat to a worthy republican government. "At whose expense does the Broker obtain his wealth? At the expense, not of the Blood, Sinew, and Tear, of the poor African; but, equally shocking to the feelings of humanity, *at the expense of the Trial and Sweat* of the industrious, and most valuable inhabitants of every country; the hardy and virtuous Peasantry."[28]

The very presence of the lottery with its tempting lures to chance, fate, and idleness raised the troublesome possibility that economic rationality was neither universal, nor natural, nor instinctive. When Tyson and his allies listed likely victims they invariably focused on the poor and ignorant, defining them in opposition to the rich and intelligent and thereby giving a mental component to their otherwise economic construction of class. The ignorance of the poor and needy was defined precisely as their longing for the big prize in spite of the odds against it. Such wild hopes of winning could be based only on folly, on mistaken, irrational, or superstitious readings of reality. Furthermore, irrational longings distracted the poor from their labors, fostering a wild abandon that made vulnerable the purses of patron and employer. "These persons are mostly servants or poor people, who spend their time and means in this way, affording great temptation after they have policied away their own property to use that of others."[29]

Lottery players thought in curious and dangerous ways, for they had succumbed to the "long and brilliant advertisements" designed to "bewilder . . . minds and dazzle . . . eyes."[30] The fault, critics claimed, lay not with those who had created tempting advertisements but with those whose minds were too weak to resist their lures. This combination of the public commercialization of superstition and the kind of thinking it represented as existing in some large portion of the populous made lotteries anathema to those working to make the economy appear analogous to what they had deemed the highest forms of human rationality. It was unseemly to finance the public projects that stood as evidence of the rational progress of the republic with overt appeals to modes of thought now to be labeled superstitious, irrational, and retrograde. According to George Gordon, "the intelligent" never bet: "The more intelligent part of the community understand the quackery, and the falsity of the promises displayed on the many colored lures, which are posted about the lottery shops." The poor, caught in the "winding labyrinths of fallacy," had lost the "power of governing themselves" and were most easily deceived.

Gordon's formulations made it clear that anyone wishing to see himself as intelligent would foreswear the pleasure of taking chances in a lottery, and as in most reform movements he drew in those who had already abandoned vice.[31]

Public life, however, did not yet fully reflect economic rationality. Tyson found that lottery advertisements "literally disfigured" New York streets with the slogans and images that promised wondrous profits from small expense. He recognized that the iconography of the lottery was capitalism's promises without capitalism's processes. Promoters represented patrons' raw desires as gold coin raining like manna, and while just such a desire for wealth may have stood behind the growth of capitalism's markets, lottery promoters stripped it of the drapes of order, labor, and even consumption and celebrated money as anarchy and idleness. Streets so disfigured by raw desire (desire that could not be represented as goods to be bought) offered plenty to tempt or to please the eye. "Go along the streets," Tyson wrote, where lottery offices are stretched on either side, and watch the motions of rascally underlings; hear the persuasions that are made use of to entrap those who, perhaps for the sake of curiosity, stop at the door to see an interesting painting, or to listen to the notes of an artificial chorister." Brewster too complained of the lottery's visual lures. "There the 'Lucky Office,' or 'The Road to Wealth,' or 'Fortune's Home forever,' and such like epithets are to be seen, to all of which is added, some pictures of the goddess of golden favors, in the attitude of showering wealth among the scrambling rabble." The poor scrambling rabble, whatever their moments of expectation and pleasure, had been beguiled, deceived, and deluded. Exhausted by lottery speculations, they were left floundering on an ocean of chance, "minds . . . laid open to the ravages of superstition and immorality."[32]

By far the most important argument advanced by the lottery's opponents was that delusions and superstitions ran counter to public interest. "Why," the "Foe to Deception" wrote, "it is merely propagating superstition; and we may in vain endeavor to support science and literature, and spread universal knowledge when this powerful machine is brought to counteract us. But we well know that men of understanding scorn these things. What then? It is the credulous and illiterate that believe, and it is taking unjustifiable advantage of their ignorance. Now a man that will prey upon the weakness of his fellow mortals, and make use of their incapacities to aid his own personal prosperity, cannot be an honorable man or a republican." While the "Foe to Deception" may have entertained an exaggerated sense of republican honor, Tyson more clearly expressed the source of distress for those who watched bettors wager on a lottery. Like all forms of gambling, the lottery stood opposed to steady work: "Low dissipations, and idle phantasms of golden showers, from being long indulged, have so impaired his faculties and weakened his character as wholly to destroy his ability for any useful pursuit."[33]

Lotteries were also particularly loathsome as recreation. Tyson and the "Foe to Deception" both understood that lotteries were public entertainment. Lottery parlors offered more than a setting for the purchase of chances. They offered music, art, and conversation, and since drawings took place over weeks, months, and even years, they also offered an ongoing form of entertainment. Like those who frequented saloons and taverns and other "low dives," lottery patrons had declined to choose from the array of rational recreations—libraries, mechanics institutes, lectures—offered to city dwellers.

And their choice was construed as ample proof that lottery bettors were the irrational, the superstitious, and the poor, who could not calculate to their advantage. "Are they the wealthy, the intelligent, and the wary—those who can afford to adventure, are able to penetrate the subtleties of speculation—or the needy, the ignorant, the weak, and the desperate?"[34] J. A. Powers, a civil engineer who joined the crusade against lotteries in the early 1840s, determined that "domestic servants, day laborers and the poor and needy"—those in other words "most easily imposed upon"—were those most likely to buy lottery tickets. "Swarms of these persons daily visit these worse than gambling shops, where they risk their little all, and get nothing in return but the delightful anticipation of being rich when the 'drawing' takes place." Under the sweep of expansive utilitarianism, it is acceptable to see such anticipation as a purchasable commodity, but for Powers and his contemporaries such fleeting pleasures were less than nothing, and it was precisely these moments of waste that troubled a middle class bent on accumulation, compensation, and a commodity in return for every expense.[35] By wasting little bits of money, the swarming poor, organized neither as workers nor buyers nor sellers, reappropriated the rights to expressive extravagance that the rich had reserved for themselves.

Judging from the lottery's quick demise in the Northeast in the

1830s and 1840s, arguments that raised the spectre of waste and superstition were, in conjunction with other economic and social changes, effective. But in the 1850s lottery promoters in Maryland and Delaware discovered a means of marketing lotteries to would-be rational bettors and turned the complaints of Tyson and his allies on their heads. The agents did not appeal to the illiterate with glittering images of fortune; they wrote letters for the careful consideration of literate recipients. Emory & Co. bragged that their drawings, instead of spreading want and distress, had "rescued many a falling man from that grim monster poverty." And Colvin & Co. presented a Delaware lottery of 1853 as a business venture: "The wisest and best men are the buyers of Lottery Tickets, and why? Because they know the chances are more favorable at a small risk than in other speculations, and if they draw blanks they try again. The vicious, the drunkard, depend upon it, never spend their money in Lotteries; it is only the well-regulated mind that has the good sense to enter into a game of profit and loss. It is a singular, but well known fact, that gamblers never buy lottery tickets nor do those who patronize lotteries ever gamble."[36] So curious an assertion suggests that these promotions can be read as responses to the complaints of early critics. By the 1850s certain agents tried to innoculate themselves against the charges of antilottery reformers.[37] In the 1830s it would have been hard to persuade reformers that bettors had gone on to prosperous business careers. Poor people who speculated in lotteries whether they won or lost, shared the same fate: they wound up drunk, impoverished, in jail, or dead. Tyson found no exceptions. And his list of unhappy winners graced most antebellum pamphlets on the lottery.[38]

Among the lottery winners who came to unhappy ends Job Tyson might well have included Denmark Vesey, the man who tried to lead the slaves of Charleston, South Carolina, in an insurrection in 1822. Vesey, a literate seaman, purchased his freedom with $1,500 he won in a lottery that had been organized to support work on East Bay Street in Charleston. Once free, he set himself up in a carpenter's shop. Despite his prosperity Vesey stayed loyal to the African-American community of South Carolina, working and worshiping with slaves and free black men and women. In planning the revolt, he conspired with Gullah Jack Pritchard, a well-known conjurer, but also with leaders of the African Methodist Episcopal church. The judge who sentenced Vesey after his failed rebellion was puzzled that a man who was free and rich would have risked life, liberty, and personal prosperity in this way.

The historians Michael P. Johnson and James L. Roark suggest clues to the mysteries of Vesey's career. They contrasted his life with that of another free black man, William Ellison, who used his skills as a cotton-gin maker to save enough money to buy himself and then went on to buy land and slaves. Ellison, who earned in slow, methodical, and therefore acceptable fashion, fraternized with the wealthy planters who patronized his business and refused to risk his freedom for the community of bondsmen which had inspired Vesey.[39] Economic rationality, with its delayed gratification and purposive accumulation, was more than a set of principles to be taught by rote. It clearly had a large experiential component, a component slaves were by definition denied, and a component Vesey avoided by getting money and freedom in one blow. He became a rich man without abandoning the traditions of his community. And Vesey's life was ample illustration that money alone would not ensure loyalty to the principles of a white and bourgeois liberal political economy. As long as the lottery harbored the means of creating moneyed dissenters, revolutionaries, or idlers, it should not, its critics cried, be tolerated.

There were certainly those who might have turned William Ellison's experiences and skills to revolutionary ends, and antiabolitionist complaints about the dangers of literacy and calculation suggest slave owners knew full well that a little learning and a little ambition were dangerous to a human spirit in chains. It would also be a simplification to assert that Vesey's lottery winnings made him into a revolutionary; nevertheless his fate confirms the fears of northern reformers who worried that workers who speculated in the lottery and won would forget the lessons of free labor taught in the workplace. Their concerns suggest that despite assertions to the contrary, they were not entirely convinced of the economic foundations of human nature.[40]

If they had doubts about the instinctive rationality of immigrant white workers, some southern whites were convinced that the African Americans they judged idle, indolent, and thriftless would pose even greater problems. In a famous passage the unreconstructed but "genial" racist George Fitzhugh argued in 1866 that former slaves who worked too little made white free laborers work too much. "Political economy," he went on, "stands perplexed and baffled in presence of the negro. Capital can get no hold on him. Fashion cannot increase and multiply his wants, and make him again a slave, in the vain effort to supply artificial wants. How will the convention deal with a being that, being liberated, seems resolved to remain, really not merely, nominally free? How make him work ten hours a day, whose every present want can be supplied by laboring three hours a day?" Fitzhugh quickly buried his sense of the freed people's resolve to maintain a freedom of their own devising by denigrating it as a desire to revert to a "natural simple savage life." But in his own perverse way he suggested that those newly freed from slavery were dangerously free of the internal constraints and desires of a market society. They had a sense of work based on a construction of freedom which might allow them forever to resist the transformation of their labor into the means of production of surplus value.[41] They had put their own constructions on freedom and had neither the aspirations nor the desires that held free white labor within the order of a "free" market society. Concern for the economic character of former slaves is obviously the subtext of reconstruction drama, and conflicts between economics and culture were played out on a number of stages. Two enactments, I would like to suggest, can be discovered in the story of the Freedman's Savings and Trust Company in the South and the persistence of policy or numbers betting in the North.

The Freedman's Savings and Trust Company

Vesey's luck was an extraordinary thing. Most of the African Americans who missed out on the lessons of market rationality were not so fortunate. Lessons of accumulation (measured or not) were obviously denied to slaves, and the market was rigged against almost every free black man and woman who tried to enter it in northern and southern states. As Eugene Genovese has so often asserted, there was little in African cultural tradition to support an independent, purposive, and frugal black work ethic. Like the European peasants filling northern factories, slaves had neither the experiences nor the cultural traditions to make easy sense of the aggressive search for gain, of the individualism, industry, sobriety, and frugality so necessary to the construction of an industrial working class in the Northeast.[42]

Gerald Jaynes has recently argued that the inculcation of such a work ethic, with the ultimate aim of creating a black proletariat, stood behind the pact that sustained the Freedmen's Bureau. "Northern immigration," he wrote, "was to provide a class of free labor managers capable of inculcating the freedmen with discipline, thrift, intelligence, and that strong sense of self-righteousness that can only be purchased with the sober morality of the Protestant work ethic. For its part of the bargain, the bureau was to provide the minimal external force required to stabilize a preindustrial population so that their education might have enough continuity to succeed. In addition, the bureau was to protect the freedpeople from their own licentiousness, unscrupulous northern profiteers, and southern planters uncommitted to the gospel of free labor."[43] The work ethic drew barriers between certain forms of economic behavior, separating the praiseworthy from the censorable. But as Jaynes argues so well, even the best economic models and the finest economic plans are played out in historical circumstances that cannot be fully predicted.

The struggle over the economic loyalties of the freedpeople can be traced in the peculiar history of the Freedman's Savings and Trust Company, better known as the Freedman's Bank. The bank grew out of military savings banks begun during the war by Union generals in Norfolk, Virginia, and Beaufort, South Carolina. The military banks were designed specifically to shelter the bounty and pay of black soldiers. Because a soldier's pay was not integrated into the rationalized needs of daily life, it had always been perfect prey for ambitious purveyors of vice, gamblers and prostitutes in particular. Black soldiers were deemed particularly vulnerable. A reporter for the *Nation* remarked that recruits spent their pay "wastefully and improvidently." "For example after a regiment was paid off it was not unusual to see a soldier wearing two watches and two chains and some one of the little jewelry shops at Beaufort or Hilton Head would sell as many as seventy, more or less, worthless watches in one day."[44] Watches were one form of the pointless extravagances that savings banks might curtail.

The military savings banks seemed to have been, a congressional investigation concluded, "well-timed and suitable to the object in view." But at the close of the war savings banks held substantial sums in unclaimed deposits. John W. Alvord, a peripatetic Congregational minister and former abolitionist, picked up the crusade against waste and extravagance as well as the unclaimed capital still held in soldier's banks and began the Freedman's Savings and Trust Company. In

January 1865 he brought together in New York City an august, but very busy, collection of white philanthropists who agreed to serve as trustees for a savings bank designed for "persons heretofore held in slavery in the United States, or their descendants." On March 3, 1865, President Lincoln signed the law chartering the bank as a private, nonprofit, institution whose investments were to be confined to government securities. Alvord and his agents collected soldiers' pay and bounty money but, following demobilization in 1867, turned their efforts to the civilian population. Alvord asked no security of his trustees or of his officers and the bank never dropped its philanthropic trappings.[45] Half charity, half finance, the bank was a curious amphibious creation and full of anomalies from the start.

Alvord's agents presented the bank as a quasi-government organization, and they milked whatever sense of gratitude the freed people may have felt toward the victorious Union. They decorated passbooks with flags and images of Lincoln and filled them with pious adages and brief proverbs on savings. They also exploited the nonexistent connection between the bank and the Freedmen's Bureau. Yet there was a more sinister paradox in the bank's project. The bank was not designed for capital accumulation or for investment in the impoverished African-American communities: it was designed to build character, and it was presented with all the trappings of a missionary crusade, but a missionary crusade that drained assets from the communities most needing them. The bank's historian, Carl Osthaus, is inclined to accept the promoters' sincerity. They believed, he argued, that "training in thrift could transform ignorant freedmen, beset by temptation to idleness, intemperance, and gambling, into morally upright citizens."[46] But Frederick Douglass's brief stint in 1874 as president of the moribund bank ("I was married to a corpse," he said) led him to a more sarcastic assessment of the founders' intentions. "Their aim," Douglass wrote, "was now to instill into the minds of untutored Africans lessons of sobriety, wisdom, and economy, and to show them how to rise in the world. Like snowflakes in winter, the circulars, tracts and other papers were, by this benevolent institution, scattered among the sable millions, and they were told to 'look' to the Freedman's Bank and 'live.' "[47] Douglass noted the bank's presentation of salvation, but he acknowledged that it competed directly with the freedmen's compelling needs for homes and land, and with churches who turned to the community in desperate search for funds. By turning the freedmen's funds into capital for government securities, the Freedman's Savings Bank transformed freed people into creditors, assuring their interest in the prosperity and success of their debtor.[48]

Whether or not a coarse venality stood behind the bank is a matter of some debate, but whatever interpretation one grants the events, the Freedman's Savings Bank turned the small accumulations of former slaves to the ends of white investors and financiers. Those who deposited may well have had their own ideas about what savings meant, and it is important not to cast all savers into the mold of a white bourgeoisie. Like the laboring poor in northern cities who began to save in the 1820s, freed people may have placed hopes for independence or autonomy or even idleness in savings passbooks. They may have dreamed of projects dear to their communities or saved for their own versions of self-improvement. Osthaus also speculated that freed people may have found it convenient to deposit their money, that they may have calculated the gains of interest, felt compelled to support an institution that presented itself as a friend of the race, felt social pressure to save, or planned to buy a home or land or to protect their families against illness.[49] The story of the Freedman's Bank may well have caused them to alter their expectations.

In the late 1860s, the bank expanded rapidly, opening branches in any town with a significant black community. But the bank had neither funds nor staff nor the facilities for communication necessary to maintain a network of branch offices. It was, after all, as one historian put it, a "poor company seeking to establish itself in a poor land among poor people who had a wealth of needs." And as such it may well have been doomed from the beginning. Nevertheless, between 1865 and 1870 at least twenty thousand depositors opened and closed accounts, and before the bank closed its doors in 1874 over 100,000 people had deposited money in branches in thirty-seven cities. By 1872 some $3,684,739.97 had been deposited in the bank, more than enough to transform it from a missionary organization to a financial empire. The bank moved its headquarters from New York to Washington, D.C., in 1870, and changes in the charter allowed directors to invest in real estate. Bank officers joined the great barbecue in Grant's Washington. It was not until the bank was on the verge of collapse that directors amended the charter to grant the bank the right to offer loans and mortgages "in the vicinity of the agency or branch of said company from which deposits are received."[50] By then it was too late. The funds of the freed people had become a gold mine for a few speculators, and the directors had no way to cover their losses when the failure of Jay Cooke's banking house sped the country into the Panic of 1873. The profiteers who had pocketed gains from stock schemes and fraudulent investments left behind them a legacy of mistrust. Years later W. E. B. Du Bois wrote, "In one sad day came the crash,—all the hard-earned dollars of freedmen disappeared; but that was the least of the loss,—all the faith in saving went too, and much of the faith in men; and that was a loss that a Nation which to-day sneers at Negro shiftlessness has never yet made good."[51]

In 1910, J. H. Hayes testified before Congress in support of a bill to reimburse depositors who had lost money in the bank's collapse. He explained how the money had come into the bank. "The Negro forty-five years ago did not have much discretion and could not read signs. He was simply being led by the white men who had authority and whom they believed the Government had sent and so we turned loose every dollar we could rake and scrape and save in the hope of making something of ourselves."[52] Hayes may well have adopted a victim's tone to address himself to a Congress that had the power to right past wrongs, but the tactics of the Freedman's Savings Bank suggest that the freed people could read signs and that the bank was presented to them with an elaborate set of symbolic trappings. Not only were passbooks full of the iconography of emancipation, but savings were encouraged through presentation of careful calculations that in the long run entailed sweeping cultural changes in African-American communities.

After ample illustrations of pious workmen whose temperate habits had netted them fortunes late in life (brick carriers who had become great merchants) and homey proverbs of prosperity ("Tall oaks from little acorns grow." "DESPISE NOT THE DAY OF SMALL THINGS." "ECON-OMY THE ROAD TO WEALTH. SAVE YOUR MONEY! Save the pennies, and the dollars will take care of themselves.") the directors presented savers with tabular illustrations of increasing wealth. The bank offered ways to transform traditional patterns of saving and spending, or as the directors construed it, wasting, money. In the Freedman's Bank the intentions, experiences, expectations of northern reformers frequently met the intentions, experiences, and expectations of the freed people. And the bank's proponents set the bank in exact opposition to traditional patterns of expenditure. They labeled the lottery shop the "Bank of Idleness," the liquor store the "Bank of Misery," and the savings bank the "Bank of Happiness."[53] They advised savers to give up cigars and whisky, informing them that they would thereby save ten cents a day and after a year of 312 working days they would have saved $31.20.

> How nice to have that much cash to put by at Christmas!
> *Now, what will you do with it?* Will you put it away in an old stocking, or hide it in a crack in the floor, where bad folks may steal it, or mice eat it up? Or, suppose it isn't stolen or eaten up by mice; if safe hid away it would be making nothing for you. It would be like the unfaithful steward's talent, which the Bible tells of! You know his Lord, when he came condemned him for having his talent in a napkin. He called him a "wicked and slothful servant."
> Instead, then of hiding your savings in a napkin, put it in the bank, where it will be making money for you. You will get, we will say, six per cent interest for it.[54]

The bank marshaled celebrations at Christmas, biblical injunction, and precise calculation, all of which could have been read by freed people in distinctive ways, but mixed together for the bank's ends they led individual savers into the calculations and desires of a market society—a society, the bank reminded them, they were to furnish with a proletariat: "If you work hard you will earn money the same as other folks. Not one of you need remain poor if you are careful and do not spend money for candy, or whiskey, or costly clothes. As for food, cheap, hearty victuals—beef, fish, bread, coffee—will do for men and women better than pies, cakes, and such things which cost more money and give you less strength."[55] By urging the reduction of expenditure to necessity, the bank tried to eliminate the disruption of idleness, outlandish desire, and extravagance.

In 1867 the bank tempted savers with a description of a contented farmer surrounded by his proud wife and respectful children. Here was a man who by foreswearing tobacco and whisky had managed to accumulate five hundred dollars by saving ten cents a day for ten years. Household strife had been transformed into contests over who could save the most, and in his long labors even the farmer had been transformed: "He would not be content to work for hire all his life. He could buy his piece of land and become a thriving farmer! The earth would be working for him day and night. He would see his flocks and herds grazing on his pastures. He would drive his own horse and wagon to market. He would enlarge his fields by his gains. He would become a good citizen, giving freely to the school and church, and all things that make for peace and freedom and justice."[56]

Such didactic prosperity was very different from the prosperity proposed by the lottery. Lotteries presented gain with the wrong lessons; advertisers displayed money without chains, without social obligation, and without the obligation to work, to earn, or even to spend. The promises of the bank, on the other hand, were all bound up in work and purposive expenditure. Behind the freedman's fancied gain, contentment, and prosperity was hard labor. The savings bank might have offered him ownership and the right to work for himself, but it never offered him the right not to work and the right not to spend. The thriving farmer, admired by loving wife and loyal children, moving from his land to market in his own carriage was caught up in long, productive toil and fully integrated into the aspirations and loyalties of commerce.

Integration was never as painless as the promotion literature imagined it to be. The Freedman's Savings Bank, like the other large financial institutions that promised gain beyond the simple earnings of productive labor, kept stumbling into its troublesome likeness to the gambling behavior it condemned. When the Democratic Congress, still sitting in early January 1876, investigated the affairs of the bank, they accused the Washington directors of gross deception, mismanagement, and of staging a raid on the freedmen's money. The cabal of D. L. Eaton, H. D. Cooke, and William S. Huntington, they concluded, had "held high carnival over the freedmen's hard-earned and sweat-stained savings, which in an evil hour they had been cajoled into trusting them with for safe-keeping and profitable investment." And the bank's failure was inevitable once the trustees had been lured into a "fancy stock gamble."[57]

Certain Freedman's Savings Bank patrons had foreseen the confusion that burst the bubble in Washington. In the summer of 1869 mechanics in Mobile, Alabama, "fitted up a new office because the old one looked more 'like a policy shop than a bank.' "[58] They had learned that they needed a symbolic vocabulary of banking to mark saving as different from policy. Without furnishings what made the transactions different? Money changed hands, marks were made on a ledger, and exchange was reduced to ciphers. But the all-important moral difference between betting and saving, the invisible intentions of those who entered banks rather than policy shops, had to be made visible, had to be marked and celebrated in the structured appearance of the bank. Frederick Douglass clearly understood the code when he described his pleasures in the Washington office. The managers had

> erected on one of the most desirable and expensive sites in the national capital one of the most costly and splendid buildings of the time, finished on the inside with black walnut and furnished with marble counters and all the modern improvements. The magnificent dimensions of the building bore testimony to its flourishing condition. In passing it on the street I often peeped into its spacious windows, and looked down the row of its gentlemanly and elegantly dressed colored clerks, with their pens behind their ears and buttonhole bouquets in their coat-fronts, and felt my very eyes enriched. It was a sight I had never expected to see. I was amazed with the facility with which they counted the money. They threw it off by the thousands with the dexterity, if not the accuracy, of old and experienced clerks. The whole thing was beautiful.[59]

Douglass's gentle irony seems to suggest that, like Johnson, he registered the cultural losses his lightning calculators might have suffered. He came to understand the bank as polished facade: while the eyes may have been enriched, the purse was impoverished; while clerks counted with dexterity, they ignored the accuracy that is the very ground of calculation.

Not everyone shared Douglass's aesthetic economy. An article by a reporter for the *Savannah Morning News* was read into the House Report of the Select Committee on the Freedman's Bank. The reporter singled out William J. "Daddy" Wilson, the black cashier of the Washington branch, and Thomas Boston, his assistant, making them comic figures in the financial charade. He described the behavior of poor depositors as well:

> Indeed, the modern savings-bank is little more than a lottery, and has too many of the worst features of the lottery, as it was managed by northern men in Southern States. The colored man was a good patron of the lottery; it was his weakness and his sin. He would go without food or raiment if he could get money enough to buy a ticket. And he bought that ticket in the innocent belief that it would bring him a fortune.

135

> The same natural impulse finds him with his little savings and his rags
> at the counter of the Freedman's Savings-Bank and Trust Company to
> deposit his money in the happy belief that Daddy Wilson will make it
> grow him a fortune.[60]

The reporter had several intersecting intentions here: to accuse the
North of robbing the South, to accuse the bank's directors of using
philanthropy as a mask for greed and gain, and to mock the credulity
of the black community. But however racist his tone, his equation of
the "natural impulse" to bet with the "natural impulse" to save would
have made the bank's promoters wince. Their whole project depended
on drawing a distinction between the two, and on this front their
ideological failure is as significant as their financial failure. They did
not make people believe that it was in their interest to save and,
beyond saving, that life began and ended in the precise calculations of
accumulated interest. Policy players who used dreams to interpret the
economy and to produce the numbers on which they acted had another
economic agenda.

Policy Play

The northern press had long singled out African Americans of both
sexes as the particular patrons of the lottery, although patrons were
certainly numerous in many poor and immigrant communities. When
lotteries became too expensive or after they had been abolished in the
Northeast, poor adventurers gave their patronage to policy dealers,
who let them wager pennies or nickels on the numbers drawn in
official and unofficial lotteries. States established ternary systems to
determine winning numbers in a matter of minutes, hoping to cut
down on policy play. Policy, however, can be played on any random
production of numbers. Within the African-American community,
betting perhaps gave pleasure to bettors, and from time to time it
returned profits to the black community. This was more than one
could say for the Freedman's Saving Bank.

Abram L. Harris concluded his 1936 study *The Negro as Capitalist*
with the lament that "in spite of the fact that since the beginning of
the present century, individual Negroes have accumulated sizable
fortunes in the practice of medicine, from real estate promotions, from

the operation of Negro newspapers and of such recreational enterprises as pool rooms, from the manufacture of hair straightening and skin bleaching goods, and, in most recent years, from the lottery business known as playing the numbers, Negro life has never afforded the economic basis for the development of a real black middle class."[61] Although some would shudder at Harris's inclusion of the profits from numbers betting in a list of capitalist fortunes, as work it was, as many had suspected, little different from banking. Policy writers, like bankers, offered sage counsel. In a similar vein a reporter on the staff of the *Chicago Daily News* argued that at the turn of the century "gambling was one of the few lines of prosperous activity open to colored men." But he recognized that means and ends were significant in white judgments of propriety and prosperity. "Politically some would like to keep it so even at the expense of holding back the race as a whole from progress."[62]

Even earlier, Charles White, a man who billed himself "the popular Ethiopian Comedian," included a well-dressed policy writer in his 1847 "The Policy Players; an Ethiopian Sketch in One Scene." His writer served the community as interpreter of dreams and financial counselor. An old man concerned about an injured son described the funeral he had dreamed. "I had a curious dream," he confessed, "an' if dar is no one around, I'll tell you, case dat's what brought me down here, thinking dat the boy might die, and, if he should, I might hit you for enough to bury him." The price of lumber was high, and the old man worried that if his son should die, he would be unable to purchase a coffin. The revelation was played for farce rather than sentiment, and after careful consideration the operator told him which numbers his dream meant him to play. He then proceeded to rig the results in the old man's favor, posting exactly the numbers he had played. The brief drama was a simple shell for minstrel numbers, but it suggests why policy dealers might have been regarded with favor by those who played.[63]

The players who turned dreams into cash carried on a logical revolt against the rampant rationality of nineteenth-century business civilization. Policy preserved a place to exercise the powers of superstition and interpretation; it offered the lure of idleness. Policy players exercised forms of power that openly challenged the rational assumptions of a market economy. In the 1930s, the French surrealist librarian Georges Bataille proposed that one look for the origins of economics in the desire for loss, not for gain. Building on the work of Marcel Mauss, he constructed a vision of waste which challenged capitalism's myth of its own origins in barter for gain. Policy players enacted a similar challenge. They had none of the "natural instincts" of economic men. They were idle and superstitious; they interpreted, they did not calculate; and they insisted that waste, not accumulation, set life in motion. To bet on dreams and hunches against very long odds was not simply a rational response to a closed economy but was the means of opening the closed economy to the play of the imagination—play based on a distinct vision of human nature and its expression in the market.[64] Like all alternatives to the agenda of market capitalism, it was construed by some as dangerous.

In the 1840s the *National Police Gazette* found plenty of danger in the urban policy shops. The paper declared that "almost every negro servant and porter are daily customers of these dens" and included policy players in their figures of class conflict of the urban North because, reporters concluded, the opportunity to bet tiny amounts would prove irresistible temptation to impoverished players. Those who would have hesitated before grand larceny might feel free to pilfer the small change careless employers left lying about. They advised readers to question all servants and to fire those who played because since almost everyone was better off than policy players, every purse was sure temptation. They concluded that policy attracted the poor with "the luxury of a pinch of indulgence admeasured to the extent of their capital." Amounts appeared so insignificant (at least to those who had more to spare) that the poor who had once made it "a rule to save their earnings to accomplish the purchase of a ticket" in legal lotteries now abandoned even such minimal frugal discipline and ventured pennies at whim. Adventurers included not just porters and servants but "thousands of our poorer white population" and "almost every negro, whether male or female, in the city."[65]

The police payed little heed to the *National Police Gazette*'s cries, but the editors engineered their own coup and uncovered the anxious policy play of the black porter who had robbed Tiffany, Young, and Ellis. The paper counted his apprehension among the "first achievements" of its "professional career." After an investigation, one writer concluded that there was "no species of gambling so pernicious, so demoralizing, so ruinous in every sense, so provocative of crime as the policy business," and the paper repeated the warning it had published before.

We found that the alluring infection had spread from its negro victims to the poorer white classes of the city—that it was making pilferers of every servant who engaged in it—that it was plucking the crust from the infatuated laborer, and that it was sowing broadcast among bar-keepers and clerks, the seeds of an illusory hope, whose pernicious germ must ripen into fraud or downright theft; and pursuing our inquiries into the gloomiest chapter of results, we looked into prisons and have found the mischievous problem worked to an accurate deduction, by finding an average of two thirds of the convicts for petty thefts ascribing their recent pilferings to the ungovernable cravings of a morbid appetite for policy gambling.[66]

As the National Police Gazette pushed its campaign against policy and against the metropolitan police who seemed to ignore it, descriptions of vice grew more intense: "The evil of all other modes of gaming sink into insignificance in comparison with this, as it is the only one which extends its havoc to the poor, and its corrupting mania to the females of that class. Out of a colored population of more than ten thousand souls, nine-tenths are its victims, and the laboring women of the whites are daily won to its infatuation in a rapidly increasing proportion." Here were women and blacks, the least likely of nineteenth-century economic actors, drawn in by "swarms of wan-dering pickers-up" who had been sent by policy backers "to penetrate into their very dwellings, and to dog them to places of work, for the last few pennies which a latent sense of prudence had reserved for food."[67] That policy play might violate a "latent sense of prudence" made the pennies worth risking. Even writers in the National Police Gazette sensed that it was not desperation for gain that drove policy players to bet, but the right to make decisions about small sums of money. Like all poor people who gambled in the early nineteenth century, policy players appeared to lawmakers and reformers to violate the iron necessity that ought to have governed their expenditures.

Reformers tried to curtail expression of economic independence by explaining how the indulgences of the poor, whatever their origins and whatever their size, fed the coffers of criminals. They appealed to what they hoped was an embryonic rationality, but such appeals, just as they had in exposés of the irrationality of betting on the lottery, went unheeded. Even after five years in a lottery office, Thomas Doyle was unable to recognize the problems inherent in addressing thoughtful appeals to the thoughtless. "As very few, save the unthinking portion of the community are familiar with this form of evil, we would ask them to reflect but a single minute upon the chances against them." But how the unthinking portion of the community were going to reflect was something of a problem, and policy allowed them to play "by fancy, or as some pretend, by *calculation*."[68]

In 1856, eleven years later, a "man about town" writing for the *New York Times* echoed earlier cries and tried to move from descriptions of the exteriors of policy shops to the interiors of policy players. There were, he was sure, at least a thousand shops in the city where policies were sold for as little as a penny on numbers drawn in the Baltimore lottery. Interested readers might recognize shops by the following "signs": the word "exchange," "a white washed shop window," a white curtain, or a dingy-looking shop window with a "score of half dollars and one or two gold coins displayed in the inside." "If you stand in front," he continued, "and see a poor German, a negro whitewasher and a woman enter, you may depend upon it that in a room behind the store they do a lively business selling policies." Win or lose, the "colored players seemed to take it the easiest. One of them broke out with 'I plays my money on forty four / And if it comes I work no more.' "[69]

The woman, the whitewasher, the poor German, and even a rag-picker all came to the policy shop to play on their dreams. "Women who had come out with baskets on their arms, apparently to go to market, were congregated in knots relating their visions—little children came running in with play from their mothers who were possibly confined to their home for want of shoes or clothes to come out." Betting alongside those who had pawned their clothes "were some respectable looking men . . . but they seemed to place as much reliance on their dreams as the simplest. Superstition seemed to be the prime mover of it all. Some of the players requested me to interpret their dreams for them. Others wished to know whether my dreams were good . . . and what were my ideas for the morning drawing."[70] Like the worried father in the minstrel play, policy players made dreams public. The women discussing their visions exchanged dreams, transforming the most private of imaginative forms into communal property. They all became interpreters, but they did so in ways precisely designed to resist the rational calculations of middle-class life.

140

In his study of black Philadelphia in the 1890s, W.E.B. Du Bois grouped such interpreters with the "submerged tenth" (the criminals, prostitutes, loafers, gamblers, and sharpers given, in a remarkable phrase, to "shrewd laziness, shameless lewdness, cunning crime") of the African-American community. While the white press may have marked all black men and women as policy players, Du Bois was far more discriminating. "The gambling instinct is widespread, as in all low classes," he wrote, "and, together with sexual looseness, is their greatest vice; it is carried on in clubs, in private houses, in pool-rooms and on the street." Like Johnson, Du Bois found that gambling clubs welcomed newcomers to the city by offering them simple amusements. Policy was a rather different form of amusement, but as long as it offered conversation and entertainment to the very poor it would attract players. Du Bois quoted from a report on policy play published in the *Philadelphia Ledger* in 1897 which complained that women, men, and even children played openly in the slum sections of the city. The paper worried that policy diverted not only the minute savings of lottery bettors who waited to adventure until they had accumulated enough for a ticket, but even the minute savings of drinkers. "Persons who have not the price of a drink may gamble away the few pennies they possess in a policy shop."[71]

After the Civil War, the white press dropped descriptions of colorful bettors and made policy a part of their crusades against metropolitan corruption. Because policy or numbers betting was a commercial enterprise, parlors operated with police cooperation, and reform papers used columns to describe bribed officers and their place in the structure of the policy racket. It was hard to get evidence against individual policy writers, who needed only a pencil and a slip of paper to run a business, but criminal backers ensured their own profits with systematic bookkeeping and carefully bribed individual officers and local police captains. They also cultivated corruption at higher levels and maintained cordial relations with ranking city politicians.[72] Reporters and state politicians took on corruption.

In 1894, when the New York State legislature began to investigate police corruption in New York City, a committee chaired by Clarence Lexow of Rockland County listened to various figures from the world of organized crime and vice. Pushed by the Rev. Charles Parkhurst's escalating moral crusade against the alliance of lawbreakers, police, and politicians, upstate Republican legislators began what turned out to be a searching investigation of the New York City Police Department. The committee conducted hearings between February and December of 1894, listening to witnesses who after some initial reticence revealed, as one student of New York police put it, a "systematic and pervasive pattern of police corruption, brutality, election fraud, payoffs for appointment and promotions, political interference in transfers and assignments, police involvement in confidence frauds, and the police conception that they were above the law."[73]

Several men (called "writers") who ran numbers parlors testified about the workings of the racket in various neighborhoods of the city. Since the objects of investigation were bribed policemen and corrupted captains, and not numbers runners, backers, or writers, even criminal witnesses were unusually candid. They explained to Clarence Lexow and his colleagues just who bet in the illegal lottery and just how the small bets of poor people fed the coffers of criminal businessmen. They explained that policy writers, like policemen, grew richest where neighborhoods were poorest: "They do not play such big amounts, but the quantity more than covers that." Still, the commissioner doubted his witnesses. "The districts occupied by the poorer class of people are the best districts?" he asked again. "A. Yes, and have the most policy shops."[74]

By the 1890s policy in New York was a well-organized racket. A group of backers known as "policy kings" had divided the city into districts. They funded operations, employed runners, bribed precinct captains and individual policemen, provided protection, and supplied the winning numbers they purchased from a telegraph operator in Jersey City who supplied them with coded results from lotteries drawn in Covington and Frankfort, Kentucky. Individual writers kept one-quarter of their profits after they had returned money for protection and rent to backers. Players watched to see if they had hit a "day number" (a number drawn anywhere in any of the day's drawings); a "station number" (a number drawn at a particular point in the sequence); a "saddle" (a combination of two numbers); a "gig" (a combination of three numbers); or a "horse" (a combination of four numbers) and were paid off according to their wagers.[75]

Dream Books

Demography and big-time organization were only part of the story of policy gambling, and the commission asked questions that led policy writers back to the mental world of those who placed bets with them. The commission took a particular interest in the language of numbers bettors, asking witnesses for definitions of slang terms. What were "gigs, saddles, and station numbers?" How did bettors name and choose their combinations? Witnesses, somewhat hesitantly, described various gigs and saddles, but the committee was disappointed when policy writers would not verify a "Lexow gig" that would have confirmed the committee's existence in the eyes of those they were investigating. There were, however, policemen's gigs, beer gigs, washer women's gigs, dead gigs, Irish gigs, sick gigs, money gigs, working gigs, "Negro gigs," and gigs for various days of the week and for famous criminals. It had taken one writer three or four months to learn the numbers of his neighborhood gigs. Another witness explained that in certain neighborhoods a policeman's gig was 7–13–20. Anyone who dreamed of a policeman or who saw something unusual happen to a policeman or who encountered a drunken policeman would play the policeman's gig. Doubting that such random events led to financial decisions, the legislator asked, "You mean to say if a policeman ran up against the Broadway cable car and got the worst of the collision, you mean to say that people would run in and play the police gig?" The witness explained that they "would take the police gig, take the number of the car and run the combination." This manner of reordering random events continued to astonish the commissioners, but it suggests that the search for calculations of certainty and order so characteristic of the late nineteenth-century business community and its bureaucracy had equally able practitioners who operated in a different mode.[76] Like businessmen, policy players arrived at calculations, at figures that were to provide a base for action, but figures for numbers bettors were not keys to an ever more rationalized and plotted universe. They were just figures, random, irrational figures, and their equivalents were in the unquantifiable substance of dreams, not in the accumulation of profits.

A guide to the pattern hidden in such accidental happenings and their numerical equivalents could be found in dream books. "There is dream books," J. Lawrence Carny, the policy writer, explained to the investigators, " 'Common Sally,' and the 'Three Witches,' and 'Wheel of Fortune;' now these books have every word in the dictionary, I guess, and they will have the lucky number opposite; if a fellow dreams he has seen a horse, if he is riding horseback, he will pick up the book and if he finds it 49 first, he will take out that."[77] Although witnesses asserted that there was no system in the play of policy, the dream books provided a system for interpreting the random events of

OLD AUNT DINAH'S
POLICY
DREAM BOOK.

COMPRISING A BRIEF COLLECTION OF DREAMS,
WHICH HAVE BEEN INTERPRETED AND PLAY-
ED WITH WONDERFUL SUCCESS TO THE
DREAMER.

From *Old Aunt Dinah's Policy Dream Book* (New York, ca. 1851), title page. Collection of the author.

the world and, more important, the means of ordering and acting on the chaos. The actions impoverished dreaming policy bettors took were economic actions, even if they involved the expense of a single penny. It is appropriate that dreams—the least controlled and least predictable site of human imagining—led straight to the economy, a region that remained for the poor the least predictable site of human expression. Dream books quite literally contained the knowledge or information that made play possible. But what kind of knowledge was it?

American dream books were a continuation of a long tradition of popular knowledge, a sort of vernacular divination that offered keys to the unknown future. They were also part of the nineteenth-century proliferation of guides, keys, and manuals of interpretation which detailed such arcane and mysterious subjects as the language of flowers. The first American dream book, *The New Book of Knowledge,* was published in Boston in 1767, but what made it American was largely its place of publication. Chapbooks, with similar interpretations, had been circulating in Europe since the sixteenth century. Like the American almanacs that often included chapters on the interpretation of dreams, European dream books frequently followed interpretations advanced by the Greek physician Artemidorus in the second century A.D. Artemidorus worked by analogy, by the juxtaposition of public and private elements whose patterns revealed the divine message hidden in dreams. As S. R. F. Price put it, Artemidorus understood that a "web of metaphor connects dream imagery and the real world. The interpretation of dreams was based on normative assumptions widespread in Artemidorus's day, and dreams thus belonged not to a baffling private universe but to the public sphere." Dreams offered every man access to the plans of the gods, but like all divination, meaning rested on correct interpretation. A dream that failed to predict the future accurately had been interpreted incorrectly. The fault lay not in the system but in the interpreter, and the dreamer might search for alternative readings.[78]

By the late nineteenth century, American dream books offered a number of alternative interpretations. Dream books for policy players, often printed as cheap pamphlets by popular publishers in Chicago, New York, and Baltimore, contain a remnant of Artemidorus's popular divination, but American divination is written in the language of African-American popular culture. The "web of metaphor" which connected the baffling present of the dream to its realization in the future was spun by the conjurers and seers who had once interpreted plantation life for fellow slaves.[79] Obviously dream books were marketed to urban, literate (largely northern) audiences, among whom they may well have competed not only with rational explanation but with storefront fortunetellers. However, by naming "Old Aunt Dinah," "Old Aunt Madge," and "The Gypsy Witch" or the Arabs "Professor Abdullah" and in the 1920s "Professor Uriah Konje" as fictional authors, publishers based expertise on folk wisdom derived from slave communities or on exotic knowledge increasingly lost to city dwellers. They called upon the interpreters, the wise figures of Africa and the Orient, who were privy to knowledge invisible to modern men and women. While the interpretations they advanced may have been arbitrary, superficial, and invented quite recently, the authors themselves were figures who embodied traditional principles of interpretation.[80]

Their knowledge could be construed in a number of ways and, like all forms of power, brought to serve various ends. On the one hand dream books were trivial souvenirs printed to be given away by dealers in patent medicines, owners of invalid hotels, producers of popular dramas, and joke-and-song-book publishers. They also seem to have provided parlor entertainment for the urban middle class. Numbers, in these instances, are presented as curious asides, and dreams are read as keys to courtship for young girls, the means of finding lost objects, and assurances of wealth and well-being. On the cover of one dream book, whose contents include an ample supply of policy numbers, are two well-dressed white couples happily engaged in some blindfold parlor play. Inside we find that to dream of a "Negro is Despondency. 14, 69."[81]

To trivialize dream books as middle-class popular culture is to ignore the ways middle-class play here is filtered through African-American seers. The presence of these seers, however gestural, is evidence of the African-American hand in northern popular culture and of the survival of folk beliefs. As the historian Lawrence Levine put it: "By the end of the seventeenth century, urbanization, the growth of science, the development of attitudes of self-help and of more efficient agencies of control, such as insurance companies and fire-fighting brigades, helped to diminish the force of magical folk beliefs, especially among the urban educated and middle classes, but the old patterns of thought and the traditional faiths survived among large segments of the population, particularly in rural areas, and they survived well beyond the seventeenth century." Although others date the triumph of enlightenment rationality somewhat later, Levine's point about the persistence of superstition helps us understand the importance of the African figures who presided over the language of dreams.[82] Dream books were a preserve of irrational superstitions, but presented in cheap pamphlets to bettors in both African-American and poor white communities.[83]

Even in the meanest pamphlets, prefaces established the position of interpreters. *The Gypsy Witch Dream Book and Policy Player's Guide* of 1903 began: "The art of interpretation being crude and unreliable, at first, has made rapid strides in the last two centuries, until today we present the most reliable and authentic dream book ever published, the garnering of material for which has occupied several years of careful research."[84] Like many forms of "traditional" knowledge, interpretations were recycled without revision, but the system was elastic and books were expanded to include advances in technology. A revised version of the *Gypsy Witch Dream Book,* appearing in 1930 boasted that it now included such "modern subjects" as airplanes, automobiles, elevators, and the tango. "The modern is more apt to awaken with a mind saturated with a night's dreams of an automobile than with any lingering memory of a dream of a white ox—yet both are here duly described." With no alteration, a method of interpretation embraced new material. "Automobile—to dream of riding in one signifies threatened danger from an unexpected source, and possible loss of property. To operate one: temptation in love matters. 21, 39"[85]

In his *Report on Gambling in New York,* first published in 1851, J. H. Green quoted at length from *Old Aunt Dinah's Policy Dream Book.* Aunt Dinah was free with advice to bettors, and the dreams of policy players began to be reduced to exact quantification.

> To dream of seeing a person's corpse, lying on a bed, is a good dream for the dreamer. If the scene is viewed with surprise and awe, it is good to play fifty-sixth fourth, or your age and the person's age in a gig. If you interest yourself in describing the scene to some other person, it is a sure sign of its being drawn soon, which will be *safer to play heavy.* . . .
> To dream of seeing a negro man, or one of very dark complexion, is a favorable token for the dreamer for fourteen first. If the person be very dark, inclining to jet black, it is more favorable. If the viewing of the person is very exciting to you, the number may with safety be anticipated very soon, and would advise the player to play heavy, as it is a *sure thing.*

By the end of the century Dinah's readings had been reduced to mockery and to simple ciphers. Dream books listed numerical equivalents without so much as a nod to the narrative substitutions that had stood between dream content and number.[86] Rather than deciphering dreams, dream books offered a reciphering that brought dreams into line with the lottery's random production of numbers, and it is here that they seem to comment on and to subvert the spreading quantification of nineteenth-century life.[87]

By the middle of the nineteenth century, players read dream books to arrive at a number to bet, to arrive at the coordinates to plot themselves in the economic landscape, and not for the science of interpretation. Exactly how dreams came to signify certain numbers is one subject dream books never address. They describe in detail theories of dreams and dream interpretation, but calculations of numerical equivalents remained the product of ancient traditions and mysterious arts. Dream books thus promoted a popular exoticism that they pitted in logical revolt against the overarching rationality of late nineteenth-century culture. "A dream," asserted the *Policy Player's Lucky Number Dream Book,* "is a motion or fiction of the soul, signifying good or evil to come, and it dependeth on the character or class as to whether it may signify its true meaning or directly the contrary."[88]

Other popular (unscientific) dream interpretations similarly challenged the triumphant materialism of late nineteenth-century culture, but they approached dreaming audiences in different ways. In 1884 one eccentric writer from Peoria, Illinois, James Monroe, published twelve issues of a periodical devoted to interpreting dreams. He used *The Dream Investigator and Oneirocritica* to promote a guide to his symbolic language of dreams. Like policy players, he assumed dreams were spoken in a "common language of dreams," and he broke dream narratives into key words. Although dreams may have foreshadowed future events, Monroe made no mention of their efficacy for gamblers. He encouraged readers to send him unusual or puzzling dreams to decipher, dreams he then explained, not by personal inspiration or intuition, but "in accordance with rules" he had devised. Dreams were thus revealed, if after the fact, as commentary on Lincoln's assassination or as foreshadowing results of current political campaigns. Dreams had predicted the election of Grover Cleveland and the difficulties of the Republican party. Monroe's dream grammar was not flawless, and he frequently published corrections and qualifications. Some figures, however, did not change. Monroe's sign of Republican problems was a reader's dream of "Negroes breaking up a political meeting." "Negroes," he asserted, "represent scoundrels, error, ignorance, misfortune, disease, and death. A very favorable opinion of negroes entertained by the dreamer, undoubtedly have [sic] its effect in dreams and consequently would require modification of the foregoing definition."[89] Or in a similar vein, "Indians, Negros and Foreigners represent enemies, opponents and uncongenial persons, and sometimes diseases. Disease being most frequently represented by negros. But the peculiar ideas of the waking mind of some persons in regard to Indians and negros will cause some exceptions to the foregoing rules in their dreams."[90]

Monroe's dreaming subjects, like the well-dressed couples in the parlor, were white. "Foreigners, Indians, and negros" were objects dreamed, not dreamers themselves. Policy players' dream books, on the other hand, acknowledge African-American subjectivity. They often comment directly on race, frequently reversing the power relations of the waking world. For the Gypsy Witch, to dream of being abandoned "by influential people signifies happiness," to dream of a "NEGRO—Denotes happiness, many powerful friends. 6, 14, 19, 78"[91] "To dream of seeing a negro man . . . is a favorable token for the dreamer." "To see a Negro in your sleep denotes an honorable and successful career. 121. To quarrel with him denotes disaster. 321." "To dream of a white man means lawsuits, and that your liberty is in danger. 876."[92]

Dream books applied numbers to entities that could not be quantified and in so doing violated the very logic on which quantification and calculation were based. Bettors arrived at a number to play not by any computation, but by interpretation, association, and analogue. That the systems were of no rational use made the elaboration of systems all the more striking. Ciphered dreams, explained by the exotic representatives of unscientific thought like Aunt Sally, Professor Abdullah, and the Gypsy Witch, fitted well in the systemic vacuum and worked for those Doyle had labeled the "unthinking portion of the community." While those in power mediated economic structures through calculations of profit and loss, estimates of production and consumption, policy players (who, like all gamblers, neither produced nor consumed) operated economically with the unmeasurable material of dreams.[93]

When the symbolic language of dreams was refigured in the wholly symbolic language of number, figures brought dreams into line with economic calculation. They also suggested that the status of the sleeper to his dream might have been identical with the status of a poor person to the economy. In neither case were they in control. Varied dream interpretations were linked by the assumption that dreams were spoken in some common language and that language was open to interpretation. Interpretation was designed to provide a guide for action in the world. But the language of dreams has a curious linguistic status:

to understand the language of dreams is to interpret, to translate, but never to manipulate, its symbols. So it was not just numbers but also this enforced passivity of practitioners which made dreams the appropriate analogue of the economy. Poor people, especially poor African Americans, had the same position in their dreams as they did in the markets. In both systems they were interpreters, but they were not agents. When the Ex-Coloured Man switched to the active verbs of white men's finance, he became an agent, a calculator, but he had lost the artistry of interpretation.

Now if we return to the descriptions of exactly who was likely to play policy (the ignorant, the superstitious, and the stupid) we find ourselves in the midst of those defined outside the quantitative culture that dominated daily life at the end of the last century. Numbers bettors were outsiders using quantification for their own ends and violating precisely the disjunction (just as they had used idleness to challenge the perfect dyad of work and leisure) between the scientific calculation of the waking mind and the irrational associations of the sleeping. After studying the kinds of thinking encouraged by nineteenth-century education, Daniel Calhoun concluded, "When the good bureaucratic society took pride in the number within its audiences who could step into performer roles, it ignored the variety of ways in which it froze out people's thinking."[94] We are beginning to see the complex beauty of worlds on the outside, worlds where those frozen in patterns of superstitious thinking at least preserved the power of their dreams. With the counsel of dream books and the "services" of numbers writers, even if poor bettors were not the most active participants in the market culture in which they lived, they were among its most innovative interpreters.

The Gambling Instinct and the Instinct for Accumulation

In the 1820s the pedagogue George Brewster had called a gambler who ascribed success to chance a "practical *Atheist*," and in 1813 one A. O. Stansbury had accused those who gambled in lotteries of flirting with disbelief and violating the second commandment by calling upon God to witness profane and silly lots.[95] By the end of the century Thorstein Veblen found the connection between gambling and belief running in precisely the opposite direction. According to Veblen only under the rational constructions of liberal Protestantism did gambling defy devotion, for in every other instance he found gamblers among the devout adherents of the most animistic creeds. Gamblers and believers shared an animistic universe not quite accounted for in the matter-of-fact causation that now ruled a world dominated by practical industry. To follow Veblen would be to argue that gambling, and along with it a belief in luck (like belief in animistic creeds), was a vestige of an older world, in his phrase an "archaic trait" that characterized the "sporting temperament and the temperament of the delinquent classes."[96]

> As a general rule the classes that are low in economic efficiency, or in intelligence, or both, are peculiarly devout,—as for instance the Negro population of the South, much of the lower class foreign population, much of the rural population. . . . So also such fragments as we possess of a specialized or hereditary indigent class, or a segregated criminal or dissolute class; although among these latter the devout habit of mind is apt to take the form of a naive animistic belief in luck and in the efficacy of shamanistic practices perhaps more frequently than it takes the form of a formal adherence to any accredited creed.[97]

Gamblers inhabited an unhappy space between an agricultural and handicraft world explained by acts of God and an industrial world explained by a rational science. It was something of a battle zone, and numbers bettors, or policy players, made a curious little world in the no man's land beneath the salvos of the two sides.

The language of race, instinct, and evolution continued to creep through the debates on gambling. Gambling did seem an instance where the vices and habits of the very rich and very poor intersected, but behavior had to be constructed differently for different classes. What was for the poor a dangerous vice was for the prosperous the cultivation of the uncertainties (or of the "conspicuous waste") that assured humanity would continue to evolve in the future.

Writers also turned gambling into a metaphor for all uncertainty. The psychologist Clemens France, who conducted studies of gambling in the United States at the turn of the century, concluded finally that a healthy desire for certitude stood behind the impulse to gamble. Like Veblen, he identified gamblers with strong faith. "We are here dealing with that same great passion for certitude which is the cornerstone of science, philosophy and religion—the desire to put the element of chance out of the game." And the search for certainty or faith inspired the risk-taking that had made human history.[98]

France read an ethical caution into the end of his discussion and advised those who worried that gambling was destructive to rechannel risk-taking activities into harmless pursuits. Society might control instinctual impulses and redirect them to designated ends, but human evolution depended on its risk takers. He was willing to mark the gambling of the poor as aberrant, criminal, and dangerous, but he was not willing to forgo the necessity for risk in the evolution of humanity. If France had been more generous, he might have seen the same search for risk in the policy play of the very poor and, in that search for risk, the same belief in change and motion that propelled human history. Policy players avoided the static calculations of the bottom line and kept money moving. But their opening moves were in waste, not in accumulation, in spending, but not in consuming, and in idleness, not in productive labor. "Harlem Pete," the author of a mid-twentieth-century dream book, understood their dissent from measured gain and summarized the policy players' epistemological model. It began in the irrational moves of waste. "If you want to be rich, Give! If you want to be poor, Grasp! If you want abundance, Scatter! If you want to be needy, Hoard."[99]

4

Devils in Their Gambling Hells

From his brimstone bed, at break of day
A-walking the Devil is gone,
To look at his little snug farm of the World
And see how his stock went on.
—Robert Southey

The farmer is the man
The farmer is the man
Lives on credit till the fall
And his pants are wearing thin
His condition it's a sin
He's forgot that he's the man that feeds them all
—Populist song

In January 1892 a Minnesota wheat farmer or, as he described himself, "an old man with one arm," wrote to the chairman of the House Committee on Agriculture in support of a bill designed to prohibit options trading on agricultural commodities. As a former National Farmers Alliance lecturer he figured he knew the "minds and hearts of the farmers of the United States," and he spoke for them when he said that the "horrible curse of wheat gambling has been one of the chief causes of our misfortunes." "The gambling in food products," he continued, "utterly destroys anything that could be called a market. What business has a man (or a devil) selling or pretending to sell, a food product which he does not possess? . . . These men who 'operate' on the boards of trade (more appropriately called gambling hells) have no right to the consideration of honest men than the devil has to a seat in heaven."[1]

The one-armed farmer was not the only witness who saw the devil's hand in commodities speculation and confronted speculators and grain traders with accusations of evil. Another described the "ghouls" who depressed the price of farm products, and another was sure that speculators saved themselves from damnation only by feigning death-bed conversions. "It is satan rebuking sin; it is the old story: The devil got sick, the devil a saint would be: The devil got well, the devil a saint was he." If Congress would stop speculators selling grain "before it *is*," he went on, "the worst hole out of hell will dry up."[2]

The presence of metaphoric devils in the debate over futures trading in agricultural commodities is important because it suggests a moral and intellectual component to late nineteenth-century economic questions, a component often camouflaged in more monochromatic histories of speculation. Those who won money speculating had long been thought subject to manic instability, but they began to appear to farmers as diabolical in the 1870s, when the number of bushels and bales of wheat traded on the exchanges began to exceed the annual production.[3] It seemed to those who labored to produce wheat, cotton, corn, and hogs that such excess sales and the profits they generated violated the logical, moral, and economic laws that governed markets. Farmers pictured speculators operating in a world where supply was no longer determined by weather and labor and where prices no longer followed the laws of supply and demand. Such men profited from sales of wheat not only that they had never seen and did not own, but that did not exist. And since farmers believed that wealth originated with crops in the field, those who lived off exchanges appeared to be modern incarnations of the scheming gamblers who brought nothing to market but tricks and ruses and crept away with profits to which they had no right.

The farmers perhaps exaggerated the evil in speculators' ancestry, but they used metaphors of diabolical gambling to respond to transformations in their economic lives. Commodity speculation flourished in the last quarter of the century. A standard grading system made it possible to trade in elevator receipts. But trading in elevator receipts also made it possible to sell futures short (to contract to sell commodities one did not own for delivery at a later date) and to profit, therefore, in falling as well as in rising markets. For farmers, who calculated economic worth through virtuous production, short sellers were troubling figures. Short sellers had an interest in driving prices down, and

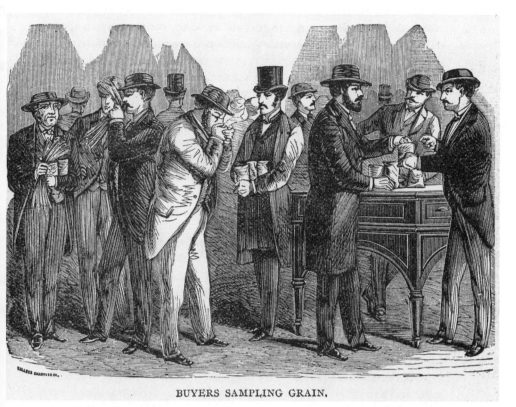

BUYERS SAMPLING GRAIN.

From John Philip Quinn, *19th Century Black Art: or, Gambling Exposed* (Chicago, 1891). Courtesy Yale University Library.

farmers were sure they created an artificial oversupply by selling crops that did not exist. The sale of fake produce, farmers argued, drove down the prices they got for the real. They saw a market perverted by short-selling speculators whose self-interest in reducing prices ran exactly counter to their own in rising prices, and they accused speculators of assuring their own gain by venal manipulation of markets whose neutrality they trumpeted but whose processes they in fact controlled.

Whether speculators actually manipulated prices was less important than the simple fact that prices could be manipulated. The farmers attacked a system that marketed agricultural produce less with the producer in mind than with the speculator. Throughout the 1890s, as the Chicago Board of Trade adopted regulations to curb abuses, they responded directly to agrarian allegations. They contended that speculative markets were as necessary to the producers as they were to the speculators. They encouraged farmers to turn to the sophisticated market transactions that would help them hedge against a bad harvest, but in the early 1890s the farmers expressed their doubts about speculative hedges.

Farmers also battled speculators on the Board of Trade over the origin and nature of prices for agricultural commodities. They did not simply haggle over price, they asked whether prices arose out of fair exchanges between buyers and sellers. Were prices public information? The questions were heated ones for those on both sides of the debate. The greediest of the new speculators appeared to profit from simple price changes and, worse, to support the fake exchanges, known as bucket shops, where they manipulated prices and called their gambling speculation.

Although such market innovations as trading in elevator receipts and settling contracts on the basis of price differences have often been described by economic historians as the simple and necessary development of complete markets, the Minnesota farmer, and others like him, offer a glimpse of a real dispute, not simply over the profits from the grain trade but over explanations of their origins as well. Speculators defended themselves by asserting that every buyer implied a seller and explained that they simply made money from one another by fair exchange. The farmers rejected justification by exchange alone and argued that only those who produced wealth had a right to share in profits. Farmers claimed that speculators lived off the labor of others and that they contributed nothing to the stable community of producers.

The members of the Board of Trade accepted many of the farmers' complaints, but they turned them against bucket shops, where they admitted gamblers operated. It was in fact in bucket shops, the board said, that evil proprietors traded with customers on simple price differences. Bucket shops were brokerage offices, often in small towns, that only appeared to be grain exchanges, for there customers could trade on simple price differences but could neither buy nor sell real bushels of wheat, bales of cotton, lots of pork bellies, or actual shares of stock. At their best bucket shops competed with "legitimate" exchanges for a portion of the futures market; at their worst they were confidence schemes based on gambling opportunities created by the rise and fall of stock or commodity prices. Bucket shops proved trouble-some adversaries for the Board of Trade for they were as much kin and double as villainous opposite. Each time the board tried to close the bucket shops, accusing operators of gambling and fraud, bucket-shop proprietors returned the accusations and raised anew moral questions about the origins of profits from sales on grain exchanges. In the last decades of the nineteenth century, the Board of Trade succeeded in es-tablishing itself as the legitimate market for commodities and the legiti-mate channel for the profits produced by the proliferation of exchange. But the victory involved a far-reaching cultural shift, an alteration in the ways people explained their behavior. Gambling again served as "negative analogue," as the form of behavior whose rejection helped legitimate innovations in the production of wealth.

The conflict over commodities speculation, it is true, must be set against decades of declining prices for agricultural commodities, a long period of currency contraction, and a growing popular political awareness, especially among the debt-ridden farmers of the South and West, of the economic inequalities of an industrial society. Why, they asked, were speculators entitled to wealth? What of value had they brought to market? Short-selling speculators personified the far-reach-ing market transformations that brought even agricultural produce into the age of mechanical reproduction, and farmers tried to under-stand just how markets now operated. It is wrong, I think, to assume that angry farmers simply made speculators scapegoats for their eco-nomic problems. What I would like to suggest is that although the evo-lution of markets often assumes a necessary, natural, or logical guise, the battle over commodities trading helps us see that the direction of market evolution was a matter of contention. To agrarian critics it seemed that speculators had stolen profits they did not deserve, but they appeared as particularly evil because they stole by logical machinations that reversed the proper order of things. Farmers complained that spec-ulators made markets in "wind wheat" which molded the market in real wheat, and furthermore that they usurped from actual producers and actual consumers the power of making prices for goods they made and used. Speculators appeared to be gambling fiends who violated the laws of the simple market and perverted its social relations.[4]

Agrarian protestors used a distinct vocabulary, but the attempt to use moral language to confront economic change resembles behavior the anthropologist Michael Taussig studied in South American peasants. The devil served Bolivian and Colombian peasants as a conceptual tool, he argued, and helped to explain or to mediate clashes between "two different systems of production and exchange."[5] Taussig found that on plantations in Colombia and in mines in Bolivia when peasant men were forced to work for wages, and when wage labor replaced traditional patterns of reciprocity and traditional forms of production, peasants turned to devil worship to explain the dialectic of destruction and production which characterized capitalist economic relations. Those men, newly molded into a proletariat, who made contracts with the devil appeared to acknowledge that production for gain was unnatural. The devil's wages destroyed all that was human, fertile, and reproductive: "The worker makes a lot of money by selling his soul to the devil, but this is reciprocated by nonrepetitive and final events: a premature and agonizing death and the barrenness of soil and wages. Rather than an exchange that reinforces and perpetuates a set of perennial reciprocal exchanges like the peasant's relation to the tree crops, the devil contract is exchange that ends all exchange—the contract with money which absolves the social contract and the soul of man." Taussig concluded that the superstitions he studied were not some vestige of a prior era of peasant life, but rather entailed "a systematic critique of the encroachments of the capitalist mode of production."[6]

In the United States at the end of the nineteenth century, farmers turned to metaphoric devils when the production of wealth was divorced from both productive labor and from the very existence of goods themselves.[7] The change within an already deeply capitalist and commercial economy to an economy based on speculative wealth was less shattering than the change from an economy based on reciprocity, kinship, and equal exchange to one that was modern and, as Taussig put it, "asymmetrical, nonreciprocal, exploitative, and destructive."[8] Nevertheless, debates surrounding speculation in the late nineteenth century suggest that capitalism had not fully flowered in the minds and hearts of all men and women and that changes even in an already asymmetrical economy can raise troubling questions.

One strain in the farmers' doubts led all the way back to skirmishes in the moral revolution at the origins of capitalism. For all the apparent secular rationality that seemed to distance nineteenth-century farmers and speculators from their ancestors, there is a medieval quality in the discourse over the Chicago markets. When the farmers called upon the devil we find traces, however faint, of a world where the economy was embedded in the spiritual and where undue gain condemned a man to hell. Speculators, like tenth-century usurers, were making money from nothing. Both were idlers who made profits even while they slept; both had money that reproduced itself without labor. And such magical reproduction was surely diabolical. Jacques Le Goff has suggested that the invention of purgatory permitted the gradual acceptance of usury and that the legitimation of profits made from lending money was intimately related to the rise of capitalism. Usurers were "the instigators of capitalism," but they instigated little so long as they were caught in the devil's grasp. The unrepentant usurer, the devil's friend on earth and his rightful prey at death, gradually escaped the eternal fires of hell for the temporal sufferings of purgatory. "The hope of escaping Hell, thanks to Purgatory, permitted the usurer to propel the economy and society of the thirteenth century ahead toward capitalism."[9]

The escape from hell was a cultural fact. Not only was the practice of usury moderated, but new values gave the usurer a new face. Profits from moneylending were no longer theft, but a "salary" earned in the labor of lending and a just compensation for risk.[10] Economic innovation and epistemological innovation went hand in hand. Grain traders and commodities speculators in the late nineteenth-century United States also renamed themselves, called themselves producers of markets and prices and rid themselves of the moral evil that clung to those who gambled, who pocketed profits that were not their due. In so doing they helped instigate a world of abstract finance and mass production, a world where producers and consumers no longer made the prices for the goods they exchanged, and where even the labor of farmers produced wealth for those who did not toil.[11]

The change was not simple, seamless, or free of conflict. Le Goff's medieval usurer in hell served as an obstacle to economic change, and the nineteenth-century farmers who evoked the devil called up just such diabolical powers of obstruction. They turned to the representative of absolute moral evil and used the symbolic power of the devil to question the ways wealth and power were distributed in the late nineteenth-century industrial economy. But they used the devil as well to challenge a world where economic discourse was increasingly restricted to rational problems of regulation and reform, and their moral pleas often fell on deaf ears.

Agrarians accused grain traders and speculators of gambling and, worse, of gambling in a game they had rigged. They returned to the rich cultural legacy of gambling. In the 1880s and 1890s a corporate economy of speculative finance and mass production could, with the help of gambling metaphors, be imagined as an economy run from hell. The devil's presence in letters to Congress suggests that the farmers' quarrel with the Board of Trade was moral, cultural, and epistemological as well as economic. "A change in the mode of production," Taussig reminds us, "is also a change in the mode of perception." And as Walter Benn Michaels has suggested, literary and philosophical representations of nineteenth-century markets involved an ontological quarrel over the status of money and a metaphysical quarrel over the nature of reality in a speculative economy, as well as a moral quarrel over the source of wealth. Writers, as well as workers, farmers, and social critics, asked whether value was to be a "function of production or of speculation?"[12] To farmers who worked in the soil, speculators made something from nothing. The angriest agrarians believed that speculators had embraced a search for wealth that approached the blasphemous: they had appropriated divine powers of creation and had begun to live off the spoils of an unnatural pact with the devil.[13] It could end only in barren silence and parched earth as people went on trading what they did not have and what did not exist.

Speculators on the Chicago commodities exchange finally used a debate about gambling, an activity scorned by a working class wary of unearned wealth and by a professional middle class still searching to validate only the most rational forms of money-making, to construct a cultural (but not a financial) solution to the problems of speculation. Farmers were not alone in seeing gambling devils in the markets. The Board of Trade, sharing the farmers' cultural discourse, also attacked gambling devils. But the gamblers they attacked were those who speculated outside what they defined as safe, rational, and organized markets. By identifying the devil as a gambler and by trying to eliminate gamblers from their midst, capitalists, in general, and the Chicago Board of Trade, in particular, engineered a transformation in the nature of markets and in the nature of the economic reality those markets produced. In their efforts at self-reform, especially in the campaigns against bucket shops, members of the Board of Trade exorcized evil from their midst, shifted the label gambler away from themselves, and attacked those they said gambled on the prices they produced. In their hands the devil became a sort of imp of the perverse, a maker of small market problems, no longer the redoubtable figure of moral evil. By purging a world of vice and corruption on the edges of their market, they purified the speculation practiced within it and thus transformed their agrarian critics into deluded victims in need of their professional protection and sage advice. They called prices things and called themselves their producers. "The movement of *prices*" substituted "for the flow of commodities themselves," and in the corporate economy the market resumed its natural camouflage.[14]

In the 1840s, as we have seen, merchants and moralists had used the danger of gambling to help define persons worthy of trust and credit. In the 1890s the Chicago Board of Trade and its various allies, associates, and enemies used gambling to try to understand just how and why markets had changed and to determine who had a right to the profits they generated.[15] Like the Old Maid in the card game, the accusation of gambling passed from hand to hand. The bucket shops and a few admitted gamblers were left holding it at the end. One Chicago character, John Philip Quinn, a reformed carny gambler who claimed also to have been a commodities broker, wrote a series of books reasserting the old gambler's plaints about the hypocrisy of those who made fortunes speculating while condemning the practices of smalltime gamblers. He gambled and attacked gamblers and played a small part as a moral fool in the battles over gambling and prices. He shared the stage with farmers, Populists, and various supporters of agrarian interests who voiced doubts about the source of speculative profits and accused speculators not only of gambling but of rigging the game as well. Bigtime speculators, especially in Chicago, challenged bucket-shop operators who mocked their labor and did indeed seem to be gambling on the rise and fall in prices for agricultural commodities. In the bucket shops, the directors of the Board of Trade discovered gamblers masquerading as speculators and taking bets from farmers and clerks who had been duped into gambling on the changes in commodities prices. The Board of Trade saw trading on prices alone as a counterfeit of their exchange. Farmers accused the speculators of counterfeiting their crops and profiting on sales of an imaginary crop they called "wind wheat." Quinn, meanwhile, defrauded farmers with fake gold bricks, dealt cards to midwestern fairgoers, and, changing his cap, ran a brokerage house in Chicago. He accused the farmers of greed and the speculators of gambling on the rise and fall of prices. Trying to pass the buck, they all exchanged accusations of gambling.

Speculation and Production

Accusations of gambling had powerful resonance for a society whose moral basis still lay, rhetorically at least, with producers, and they illustrate just how speculation (metaphysical and economic) remained a problem for a culture based on practical thought and useful production. To understand the way speculation figured in the agrarian protests, we need to return to long-running doubts about the validity and safety of speculative profits. The investigation will take us back not only to Adam Smith and artisans and republicans of the early nineteenth century but also to the historians of many persuasions who have grappled with the problems of speculative wealth. Gambling, as we have seen, was deemed wrong because gamblers who produced nothing necessarily lived off the labor of others. They also violated the basic laws of commerce and took, as Beecher said, "without rendering an equivalent."[16] Promoters of middle-class economic virtue singled out gamblers as men bent on the self-interested pursuit of gain but lacking the virtues that transformed greedy men into members of the capitalist community. Because gamblers cared little about accumulating wealth or holding on to it, they were bad owners, and as bad owners they could not be trusted to abide by the social covenant of property.

Speculators were tarred with the same brush. In the 1830s articulate artisans, virtuous yeomen, and outspoken mechanics had barred them, along with idle aristocrats, from the "phalanx of honest worth and independence" which supported the commercial and political life of the republic. They characterized speculators as unstable men who held the most ephemeral wealth and who turned their money into only the most useless of luxury goods. Along with lawyers and moneylenders, they were barred even from the most inclusive constructions of the "producing classes." But gradually through the nineteenth century, through a reconstruction of the ethical standards of capitalism, speculators managed to shed their aura of evil. They were like gamblers, yet they were neither so useless nor so heartless as gamblers. They stood somewhere between the two moral poles of the capitalist economy, between the most diabolical of gamblers and the most virtuous of investors. Like gamblers they seemed to produce nothing. However, until grading and standard contracts made short selling possible (and speculators were able to make "disloyal" side bets against what seemed the common communal interest in rising prices), they behaved like investors and held property hoping for a rise in value.[17]

By the fifteenth century, speculation had come to mean "contemplation of a profound far reaching or subtle character; abstract or hypothetical reasoning in subjects of a deep, abstruse, or conjectural nature." In the eighteenth century Adam Smith used it this way in *Wealth of Nations* describing "philosophers, or men of speculation whose trade is not to do anything, but to observe everything." Smith also associated trade and speculation in another way: it was not until the middle of the eighteenth century that speculation had taken on its financial connotations, and again in *Wealth of Nations* Smith referred to merchants who sometimes made "sudden fortunes, . . . by what is called the trade of speculation."[18] Although few recognized speculation as a legitimate trade before the end of the nineteenth century, Smith's "what is called" interests me here because it provides a tag on a word whose meanings are shifting and are, perhaps, subject to cultural and political debate. Speculation, in its financial sense, continued to carry its tag for the next few decades. Timothy Dwight, in his 1821 *Travels in New England,* saw people expecting fortunes from rising land values and described the evils stemming from "what has been proverbially called in this country speculation." And thirteen years later a writer in *Tait's Magazine* referred to the "evils produced by that species of gambling named speculation."[19]

Such attacks on speculation were part of the physiocratic critique of mercantilism and part of a lingering republican suspicion of commerce. Abolitionists, sentimental novelists, feminists, and all those who defended an area of heart and home free of the market also attacked speculation. Although the gravest sin had been the creation of a market in human beings (and, as Harriet Beecher Stowe reminded her readers, those who speculated in human souls had no hope of escaping the fires of hell), speculators continued to commit lesser sins against both man and nature. When Lydia Maria Child commented on life in New York in the 1840s, she found a landscape altered by speculators. She described Brooklyn land speculators desecrating a revolutionary burying ground by turning out the bones of dead soldiers. With the same cavalier indifference speculators turned out the living as well. A "band of speculators" carried away by "unwholesome excitement" approached a poor, ignorant farmer. They offered him $70,000 for his farm and put $10,000 in silver and gold coins on his table; "he looked at them, fingered them over, seemed bewildered, and agreed to give a decisive answer on the morrow. The next morning found him a raving maniac! And thus he now roams about, recklessly tearing up the flowers he once loved so dearly."[20]

For Child the evil behind commercial life, even in New York, and behind her deranged farmer, was speculation in human beings, and she read through all commerce to find slavery. She asked whether it was not possible that the "age of Commerce" was no better than the "age of War." Were merchant princes so great an "advance upon feudal chieftains"; had self-interest and "cunning" after all made for "human improvement"? Child had strong doubts about the celebrated fairness of market society. She was sure that things of the heart were far more valuable than the objects of the market, and she often presented her criticisms of commerce in brief parables of madness and corruption.[21] Elements of her sentimental celebration of the fruits of the earth and her warnings about the risk of insanity in speculative wealth reappeared in the late nineteenth-century criticisms of grain markets, but short-selling grain speculators were denounced as more distinctly evil than even the most greedy land speculators.

Child voiced a sentimental critique of speculation that often had great force. Like the one-armed Minnesota farmer, she witnessed damnation and destruction in the haste for gain. Those who tried to stop futures trading, along with those who tried to legitimate it by drawing distinctions between gambling and speculation, returned to the language of damnation, but damnation was constructed out of concerns about rampant commerce in a republic of free-laboring producers. Speculation raised anew questions politicians and moralists had been asking for a century. Was the United States a republic of honest producers? Were those who toiled free to reap the fruits of their labor? Was self-interest simply selfishness disguised? Were profits produced without productive labor the dangerous signs of corruption and decay?

Much of the recent work on the late eighteenth- and early nineteenth-century United States has centered around the commercial intentions of American farmers and the various popular incarnations of republicanism. We now know that American farmers were not just hardy yeoman pursuing lives of simple subsistence and that, as Richard Hofstadter wrote, despite the resonant power of the agrarian myth, American agriculture was commercial from the start and that American farmers were well integrated into world markets. In this commercial context even their ambition to provide a comfortable competence for their families bound them ever more tightly to the commercial relations of capitalism. But bondage to markets did not come with a ready-made interpretation, and even at the end of the nineteenth century farmers were still trying to figure what their bonds to speculative markets meant.[22]

In northern cities artisans who were caught up in the same process of expansion also worried about their own independence and about providing for their families. Commerce was tempered by a world view shaped by the values of what Sean Wilentz has called "artisan republicanism." Both Wilentz and Steven Watts have sought to qualify claims to a universal American celebration of self-interest and to sever republicanism from a necessary connection to a liberal celebration of the rational pursuit of gain and acquisitive individualism. For Wilentz the republicanism of early nineteenth-century New York artisans can be understood only against a backdrop of craft traditions. Key concepts of republicanism—"independence, virtue, equality, citizenship, and commonwealth (or community)"—are best explained by reference to ideals of trades that emphasized the virtues of community, political equality, and the right of all citizens to exercise natural political rights. The small shop, not the self-interested acquisitive individual, was the embodiment of republican values.[23]

Steven Watts also found evidence of anxiety over the ascendancy of commercial values in the first decades of the nineteenth century. Merchants and speculators embraced the commercial economy, but others "could not reconcile the private pursuit of profit with civic virtue and voiced fears that economic growth would lead the republic to 'luxury' and 'decline.' " For Watts it was the War of 1812 that bridged the republican past and the liberal future. The war served as a catalyst for the formulation of the politics of the marketplace and for the ideological shift into nineteenth-century liberalism. Watts argued that the shift took place around the intellectual and moral conviction "that pursuit of many self interests would result in the public good, that politics was the arena for sorting and settling the interests of self-controlled individuals, that energy in foreign affairs and productive home market in political economy best promoted the expansive young republic; and finally that progress and growth rather than decay and decline promised to color the future of the United States."[24] Watts's actors looked toward the liberal republicanism of individual opportunity, rational calculation, and self-discipline; Wilentz's toward a "moral order in which all craftsmen could eventually become self-governing, independent, competent masters," in other words toward an artisan republic in which one labored for the public good, not for personal gain.[25]

In an argument based far more on ideology than on actors, Joyce Appleby has asserted that understanding the changing interpretations of self-interest is essential to understanding the transformation of classical republicanism into economic liberalism and that a belief in economic rationality was intimately linked to the rise of republican politics. Hers was a world of ideas far less troubled by conflict and contradiction than the economic and political worlds described by Wilentz and Watts. "We find it a bit stale," she has written, "and . . . a little depressing to be told that people inevitably pursue personal advantage, but we are living at the end of this world view, not at the dawn when it contained exciting possibilities. Its social impact must be measured against the old conviction that human beings were impulsive, fickle, passionate, unruly, and likely to come to no good end regardless of what they did. Self-interest in market transactions presumed a rationality that was actually complimentary to human nature. Men and women made choices that served them well."[26]

These differing interpretations have enhanced our understanding of the political economy of the early nineteenth century. The recurrent attacks on speculation and recurrent expressions of doubt about the origins of speculative wealth suggest the enduring power of a republican criticism of commerce, and late in the century we can still hear echoes of the old dialogue. Attacks on gambling and speculation contain an artisan emphasis on the community of producers as well as a classical emphasis on the dangers of idleness and excess and a sentimental vision of worthy natural toil. The representation of selfish corruption necessary to republican definitions of good and evil gradually migrated from speculators to gamblers. Successful speculators were redeemed by visions of progress and growth, by testimony to their participation in the market economy. Greed, venality, and corruption shifted to gamblers. Failed speculators were gamblers; selfish speculators, who disregarded a common interest in the value of property, were gamblers. The very rich and the very poor whose risks and excesses fell outside the pale of what had emerged as rational self-interest were gamblers.

By the end of the nineteenth century, commercial speculation, incorporated into an optimistic vision of growth, no longer threatened the republic with corruption and decline. In the republican context of the 1840s, the indebted gambler, the man who would sell his vote for cash, whether citizen or representative, was far more dangerous than the speculator who bore the risks of economic development.[27] But doubts remained. Each of the century's "panics," "depressions," and "retrenchments" brought out grinning speculators who gambled on the misfortunes of their fellow citizens. Excess speculation was offered as a cause of panics and depressions, but any change in prices produced speculative profits and even in a falling market well-positioned speculators won money while others suffered. As Philip Hone watched brokerage houses collapse in the panic of 1837, he was sure those that fell first housed gamblers and not investors.[28] Although he was trying to reassure himself that his own ventures were safe and sane, he located the cultural problem of speculation. It was possible that speculators resembled gamblers and that their profits were private gain that was not being turned to public virtue. In their search for gain they harbored the personal corruption that threatened the social order. By the beginning of the twentieth century the writer of a popular economic tract could describe market speculation as "an inherent part of human nature."[29] The elevation of man the speculator required the destruction of man the gambler.

Once again, to turn to Appleby, the economists' model of human nature meant that "homo faber, man the doer, took precedence over man the believer, man the thinker, man the contemplator—even man the sinner."[30] It was man the speculator, however, who preserved something of man the thinker, man the contemplator, and, in an economic universe geared to actual production, something of man the sinner. The gambling evil that clung to speculation came, not only from flirtation with risk, a flirtation finally celebrated in the folklore of capitalism, but from a refusal to "launder" money by passing it through a productive economy. It was production, making something, exercising a trade, that made money, profits, and the self-interested pursuit of gain, moral and ethical.[31] In economic literature of the early nineteenth century, gamblers' money was illegitimate money that never passed through the market. Even in the most didactic and prescriptive literature, gamblers rarely won money that had been earned as wages, and even when they turned their winnings into commodities they kept their assets liquid. They won inherited money or money carried in trust, and they purchased portable wealth (clothing, jewelry) that might be wagered at the next turn.

It was this particularly irreverent attitude toward property that made gambling and speculation deeply troubling to people who saw independence, rooted in the ownership of property, as the preserve of the republic. In a gamblers' hands all property was liquid. Even if commercial speculation gradually lost its onus, land speculation, despite the tributes of developers and the revisions of frontier historians, continued to trouble many observers. As Child had insisted, neither the sacred rights of the dead nor the affectionate bonds of the living could stop the depredations of the speculative market in land. The confrontation between the land speculator and the settler offered an emblematic version of a confrontation between commerce and virtue, a starting point for politicians, reformers, and, in the twentieth century, historians. The British land reformer William Harbutt Dawson wrote in the 1890s, "Speculation in land may justly be regarded as one of the greatest evils associated with the institution of private property in the soil. Rightly described, it is nothing more or less than gambling over the probabilities and possibilities of social progress in one form or another."[32] Editors on the American frontier also found the gambler in the land speculator. Professional speculators "produce more poverty than potatoes and consume more midnight oil in playing poker than of God's sunshine in the game of raising wheat and corn."[33]

The polemic against speculation, common as it was in political rhetoric, also fed a current in the historiography of the American frontier. Paul Wallace Gates first turned his attention to speculators when he began writing about the history of public land policy in the 1930s. He argued that land speculators, though representing many levels of wealth and present throughout the history of the American frontier, were evil. In the past actions of absentee land speculators Gates found ample reason for the distress of early twentieth-century farmers. Speculation was the product of a mistaken land policy that had brought about monstrous inequalities in the distribution and ownership of government lands. Absentee speculators who were slow to pay local taxes had delayed the development of western communities, and if western towns had dispersed settlement, poor schools, few churches, bad roads, and peculiar locations, they had only to look to their speculative pasts.

Gates began writing during the Depression, and what troubled him most was the extent of tenancy in what was meant to have been a democratic land system. Gates acknowledged that land hunger had propelled white settlers across the continent and that even settlers often speculated in lands neighboring those they farmed. He did not indict settlers for the poverty of their descendants, however. Eastern speculators, land agents, and loan sharks were responsible for the heavy tax burdens that forced farmers into bad farming practices and into debt. Absentee speculators had corrupted western legislatures that "opposed land reform, fought other agrarian legislation, championed protective tariff duties, and condemned monetary heresies. They represented the creditor, the large property owners, the railroads and the rising industrialists."[34] Gates rejected arguments by agricultural economists who "said that tenancy was the inevitable result of the commercialization of farming and rising land values." Such impersonal forces may have played a part, but poverty was hardly inevitable and "tenancy got its start in the Middle West as a result of the activities of land speculators and moneylenders."[35]

Gates finally left speculators room to wiggle off the hook with a tribute to their dynamic presence on the American frontier, but he left their redemption to the next two generations of his students. Like gamblers, speculators may have treated property with cavalier irreverence, caring for wealth rather than the community of virtuous producers, but they shared with land-hungry settlers an interest in rising land values. Even if they lived at a distance, land speculators stood to gain only with rising prices and their greed benefited all. When a community's interest was defined as an interest in rising land values the speculator began to emerge as a local hero.

Historians lobbied for the redemption of land speculators by using arguments flush with the powerful magic of value-laden terms. The economist Richard Ely, although in other ways sympathetic to agrarian criticisms of capitalism, emphasized the skills of speculators and their service as colonizers. They brought land into "use." They "worked" as capitalists and provided a "social service" as taxpayers and moneylenders.[36] The speculator was transformed from a selfish gambler to a self-sacrificing pioneer and from an exceptional figure of evil to a benign aspect of every settler.[37]

And finally Ray Allen Billington even adopted some of Frederick Jackson Turner's poetic cadences and made the speculator a central figure in the parade of western development. Writing in 1945, he tried to correct Turner's omission of speculators, and he described speculators who had little in common with Child's defilers of graves and destroyers of flowers or with Gates's sinister companions of usurers and landlords. He represented the speculator as a soldier and as a pioneer. "Forging steadily ahead to mark out the best lands, pleading always with purchasers for long over-due payments, suffering risks that reduced their profits to a minimum, and enduring the hatred that frontiersmen reserved for tax collectors, absentee landlords, and others who tried to wring cash from flat western pocket books, [speculators] were as omnipresent along the cutting edge of civilization as the axe-swinging pioneers themselves."[38] Billington's series of participles—"forging," "pleading," "suffering," "enduring"—have rather more often described settlers than speculators. His heroic phrasing, however, offers an important instance of linguistic redemption of speculative activity.

With Billington, the opposition between settlers and speculators which had shaped so much of early nineteenth-century political rhetoric and had structured Gates's criticism of government land policies disappeared. All settlers who bought more land than they could farm and held it for a rise in value were speculators. By expanding the definition of speculation, most settlers became speculators or at least shared with absent speculators a common set of interests. According to Daniel Feller the opposition between settlers and speculators finally revealed more about the language of party politics than actual conflicts over settlement. Feller argued that even speculating politicians like Andrew Jackson clung to the language of an agrarian ideal. Feller wrote, "The settler ideal portrayed the American not as he was but as he wished to think of himself; the image of the speculator concentrated in an external figure the characteristics men did not want to acknowledge in themselves."[39]

We learn as much from arguments about speculation about the politics of historians and the rhetoric of politicians as we do about the labors of land speculators. Perhaps speculators did contribute to the advance of white settlement, but how those contributions have been conceived and described is as important as what speculators might have done. Speculation had offered Gates an explanation for the political and economic anomalies of the West. But legislatures who did not respond to local interests as well as the unequal distribution of land appeared anomalous only to a sensibility schooled in an agrarian critique of capitalism. If all the world was bent on capitalist growth then the speculator posed no problems, or rather he posed only those of the efficient or inefficient use of capital. In the 1970s Gates's language of condemnation and Billington's strident emotional verbs were replaced with the scientific language of economic efficiency. For economic model builders the speculator is a natural man, an efficient operator dealing with opportunity costs. Speculators created an effective land market.

One economic historian, Robert Swierenga, lauded the passing of the era of the progressive school of land historiography, of the "moralistic and unsystematic nature of much of the research," and cheered its replacement by dispassionate, econometric analysis. Like Edward Rastatter, he concluded that speculators were just doing their job; they were neither devils, nor misers, nor monopolists; they neither retarded nor "distorted the settlement of public lands."[40] Although die-hard agrarians would reject the salvation of the speculator, like the medieval usurers, land speculators were rescued from hell by semantic transformations and by a redefinition of the human project which put profits at the center of community activity. Good speculators were separated, not from bad speculators who promoted ruinous practices that sacrificed the long-term interests of communities of settlers to their own short-term gains, but from incompetent speculators who failed to realize an adequate profit on their risks. In the last analysis all of them were rational economic actors working out of self-interest to maximize profits.

The opposition between producers of agricultural commodities and speculators in agricultural commodities is based on a similar sense of an agrarian ideal, but speculation in real estate and in public lands and speculation in agricultural commodities raise different issues. By the end of the century, the economic circumstances of farmers made it difficult for them to imagine their common interest with speculators, especially with short-selling speculators who stood to profit from declining prices. The short-selling commodities trader who reveled in falling prices and appeared to undermine struggling farmers by driving prices down and by buying and selling things that did not exist could be redeemed only by extending the definition of common interest to include an interest in the production of markets and prices. In effect, by making markets and prices into products, commodities speculators altered that basic creed of economic liberalism which found markets and prices in the basic stuff of human nature.

By comparison the redemption of the real-estate speculator appears a simpler matter. Real estate has never been a fungible commodity and, because even in the most speculative real-estate markets one could not sell land or building lots short nor could one contract for houses to be "built or sold short," speculators and settlers have shared a common interest in rising land values. Once grading made agricultural commodities completely interchangeable and short selling possible, commodity trading lost its basis in physical reality. One could trade in the idea of wheat more easily than in wheat itself, and this shift altered the metaphysical structures that governed a logic of production and shaped exchanges based on real goods. The moral structures designed for communities of production and consumption fell apart.

So, in effect, did the psychological structures that wed speculators to the rational pursuit of gain. Real estate did not have the infinite powers of replication attributed to money and to wheat, and the vestige of reality still contained in real estate kept speculators sane. It would be difficult to imagine Child's farmer deranged by speculative profits in the 1880s. In Frank Norris's Chicago novel, *The Pit,* Curtis Jadwin stayed rational through his most successful real-estate dealings, but his ventures in wheat, as Norris put it, "all but unseated reason itself." Jadwin, "the Great Bull," could not maintain his corner in wheat against the combined forces of nature's bounty and bearish speculators. A huge harvest played into the bears' hands and drove prices down. But Norris hesitated before a world of abstract finance and based his fictional logic on a tangible reality of wheat.[41] Nature worked retribution with brute symbolic force, but nature was the source of value. Like "country speculators," Norris refused to believe that wheat possessed the magical qualities of money, that it could appear and disappear and that it could be counted more than once without actual physical appearance.

In 1902 he published "A Deal in Wheat," a condensed moral parable on the agricultural economy. A farmer, ruined by low prices created by the machination of bear speculators, moved to Chicago and became a workingman. The workingman was then denied his bread as wheat prices rose following the machinations of the bulls. But the tragedy on the streets was overshadowed by the comic confrontations between bulls and bears in the wheat pit. "Upon my soul," a character shouted, "it's as good as a Gilbert and Sullivan show." But even Norris's short-selling bears couldn't quite divorce themselves from the constraints of real wheat. When they set about to break the corner, they created warehouse receipts for grain, not by machinations of fictitious products but by repeatedly delivering to themselves a single railroad car of wheat. The bulls laughed at the bears' tricks and they all "went on through their appointed way, jovial, contented, enthroned, and unassailable."[42]

In staging his comic opera Norris perhaps ignored a history of assault on his enthroned speculators. The "salvation" of the land speculator has been a slow intellectual project of the twentieth century, but speculation in agricultural produce required a more rapid legitimation. The common interest of speculators was in fluctuating, rather than rising, prices, and to base a moral market on fluctuation entailed revisions in the delicate relations between profits, progress, and rising prices. At the end of the nineteenth century, the possibility of short selling agricultural produce raised serious questions about the social meanings of speculation. Construed one way, short selling was a convenient hedge against the natural risks of produce markets. But for politicized farmers, short selling revealed precisely the ways a speculator's self-interest ran against the interests of the agricultural community. Even if farmers sold wheat they had not yet harvested for future delivery at a price below the current market, they told themselves they were still selling real wheat, a product they made and controlled, seeking to protect themselves from the vagaries of the market and to gain a just recompense for their labor. The farmers tried to distinguish "forward delivery," legitimate hedging, from speculation on wheat futures by brokers and traders. Farmers contracted for "forward sales," brokers for "future sales." Farmers contended they could deliver the commodities they had contracted to sell and that speculators and brokers merely adopted delivery clauses as convenient fictions. Although the Board of Trade would later use this argument against the bucket shops, it seemed to farmers that speculators on the Board of Trade had made the opening move in the usurpation of the power of real wheat and forever altered the relations between nature and markets in nature's produce.

Short selling wheat futures, farmers argued, was the brain child of the city dwellers, of men who had perhaps never seen, but had certainly never grown, a bushel of wheat. Short selling was, as one commentator put it, "repugnant to the mind of the average country speculator." He knew it was socially, morally, and psychologically more dangerous than even the most greedy real-estate speculation. One master of the National Grange was certain that excess speculation was a "prolific cause of embezzlements, thefts, and the betrayal of fiduciary trusts." A St. Louis merchant was sure that no one would "steal money to buy actual wheat."[43] Behind the ethical problem of theft was the ontological problem posed by profits from goods that "practically" had "no existence." "It is difficult," one speculator admitted in 1906, "for the average man to understand how the dealer who sells can make deliveries of, or how the dealer who buys can receive, what does not exist."[44]

Short selling completed the speculative markets, but it raised metaphysical questions that revealed to farmers and other producers just how the self-interested pursuit of gain, so carefully rendered benign by the power of the invisible hand, might still turn savage and destructive. Agrarian critics found it difficult to turn short sellers' self-interest in gain into an interest in what they had learned to accept as the common good. But members of the Chicago Board of Trade did succeed in making speculative markets the necessary means of commodities exchange.[45] By the end of the nineteenth century speculators had learned how to launder their money by creating a trade for themselves, by passing their money through markets of their own making, and by appropriating the rhetoric of production and applying it, with all its historic moral weight, to the price quotations—the products—they said they made. They measured themselves against gamblers who made nothing and against farmers who certainly made something, but who in the age of telegraph sales and world markets depended, not just on merchants, but on speculators to market their crops.

John Philip Quinn, the Reformed Gambler

The Chicago Board of Trade had enough trouble with renegade members without having sheltered so dubious a character as John

Philip Quinn, reformed gambler, ex-convict, author, and evangelist. But Quinn said he sold commodities in the pits, and at the end of the nineteenth century he used his experience there to attack the hypocrisy of those who lionized successful speculators while preaching the virtues of production. He offers a peculiar insight on transactions on the Chicago markets. Quinn is typical of the nineteenth-century gamblers who reformed and turned their prior practice of vice into an occasion to preach virtue. Their unsavory economic backgrounds kept them suspect, however, and they never made it into the pantheon of true reformers. Once devils they were always devils.

Quinn was born in Missouri in 1846. By his own account his father, a prosperous, slave-owning farmer, trusted his mischievous son with small sums of money and sent him off on small errands. Like the northern clerks in sensational tales of the Mississippi Valley who gambled with someone else's money, Quinn gambled his father's money with dishonest strangers in midwestern cities. At fourteen he stole a horse and ran away from home. He lost the horse in a three-card monte game and returned home the penitent prodigal. Quinn's contrition was short-lived, and after the war he joined the midwestern gambling circuit. He worked (or rather played) his way across the Dakotas in the late 1860s and gambled with marked cards at the Centennial in Philadelphia in 1876. He worked fairs in Indiana, Illinois, and Missouri and played in gambling halls and poolrooms in Chicago and St. Louis. Like a good devil, he followed what he called "the highway to hell" to Hot Springs, Arkansas, practiced a few confidence schemes, and sold agricultural commodities in Chicago. He also worked as a barber, ran a saloon, operated a hardware store, and sold piano dulcimers and shoes. He was married at least three times, arrested at least twice, and convicted of defrauding a farmer of three thousand dollars. He was converted when he found a battered testament under his prison shoemaker's bench, and when he was pardoned he set off on his last career as a writer, evangelist, and financial reformer.[46]

Quinn recounted his escapades in prologues to a series of encyclopedic accounts of gambling schemes. He supported his assertion that all gambling schemes were crooked with precise technical descriptions and personal anecdotes. He supported his contention that a gambler's life was a life of loss by interspersing his adventures with accounts of the deaths of family members. Every time he went off gambling someone in his family died. He managed, in this way, to kill off two sisters, his mother, a wife, and a child. To make amends, he turned his life into a cautionary tale. He donned prison stripes and started off on an evangelical lecture circuit. Quinn had in him as much of the vaudevillian as the preacher and spent his evangelical days talking about the race track and social gambling to "more than ordinarily miscellaneous" audiences (read working-class) at such places as the Young Man's Institute on the Bowery.[47] Despite his reform, Quinn was not quite finished with controversy, and in the spring of 1894 he eloped with his preaching partner's seventeen-year-old daughter. Unlike his evangelical descendants, he married her, and evangelist E. N. Goff eventually forgave his "aged son-in-law." The two men took their publicity and continued their revivals in New York and New Jersey.[48]

Like most gambling reformers, Quinn attacked the hypocrisy of those in power whose earnings had the least taint of speculation and tried to explain that professional speculators, like professional gamblers, merely dangled pretenses of luck and risk before gullible victims. Both, in fact, lived by elaborate schemes, schemes that ensured their profits and their victim's losses. The gambler was something of a pariah, yet he was no different from the "heartless operator who deliberates long and earnestly how he may most speedily and surely accomplish the ruin of the man for whom he professes the sincerest friendship." Nor was he far removed from the selfish speculator, "the far-seeing scoundrel who concocts a cunningly devised scheme for wrecking a railroad in whose stock . . . are invested funds on which the widow and orphan depend for subsistence—for these men society has no condemnation, the law no terrors, and the pulpit no denunciations. They build churches and found colleges; they preside at public gatherings and occupy posts of honor upon public committees. It is a trite aphorism that 'nothing succeeds like success,' and no more apt illustration of its truth could be given than the adulation bestowed upon men whose fortunes have been cemented by the groans of the unfortunate and the tears of the widow."[49] Quinn combined his melodrama with a moral language of producerism. Although as a gambler he had wandered as far as possible from those who performed productive labor, it was to labor that he turned for an audience later in his life. He used his own career to equate the men who operated on the Chicago Board of Trade with the crooked carny gamblers who wandered through the Midwest. He evoked the moral logic of producerism, explaining that in gamblers' slang the "man who plays against

From John Philip Quinn, *19th Century Black Art: or, Gambling Exposed* (Chicago, 1891), frontispiece. Courtesy Yale University Library.

the gambler is called a 'producer,' and what can that mean but fool or victim."[50] Indeed Quinn knew it meant far more: the equation of producers with suckers signified a shattering change in the morals of the market.

"Fiat Wheat" and "Fiat Money"

In 1892 Representative William Hatch of Missouri, chairman of the House Committee on Agriculture, introduced a bill to levy a prohibitive tax on speculative profits from futures dealings in agricultural commodities. Hatch hoped his bill would eliminate the trading in options, privileges, "puts," and "calls" that allowed professional speculators to profit from simple changes in prices but would leave untouched the "forward sales" of actual products by farmers, millers, elevator operators, and dealers in real wheat. They used forward sales to minimize the risks of both nature and markets. The distinction between the two kinds of futures dealings posed subtle problems of definition, and in the hopes of resolving them the committee entertained a parade of witnesses who articulated their views on the nature and structure of markets in agricultural commodities.

When Dr. Charles Macune appeared before the House Committee on Agriculture in 1892 representing the National Farmers Alliance and Industrial Union in support of the Hatch bill, he made Quinn's dread connection between suckers and producers explicit. Although speculators claimed to make money only from one another, it was obvious to Macune that they had "to catch a sucker," for they produced no wealth. That farmers, the most "moral" producers, had become gamblers' suckers, in spite of themselves, seemed particularly irksome. For Macune, the economist, journalist, and author of the subtreasury plan for marketing agricultural commodities, and for many of the farmers and agrarian reformers he represented, it was a matter of basic political principle that producers should regulate prices and that the worth of goods should be determined by the labor required to produce them. In Macune's logic, overproduction in cotton or in basic foodstuffs was impossible. It was not a glutted market that had produced low prices. Short-selling speculators, he was sure, were to be blamed for falling prices. He argued that speculators had freed themselves from the natural constraints that still determined when farmers arrived at the market with their produce, and that speculators so freed, trading among themselves, could conspire to further depress prices just as farmers tried to market their harvests. The worst "evil" in options trading lay, he concluded, in its effects on "spot" price quotations for real products. Sales of "wind wheat" had produced a fictional overproduction and bear speculators had reaped profits from two decades of falling agricultural prices.[51]

When the miller Charles Pillsbury testified in support of the Hatch bill to limit options trading, he aligned himself with the farmers, not for political reasons but because he saw a shared metaphysical interest in the reality of wheat and in the reality of market transactions. Pillsbury said he had never sold a bushel of wheat when he "did not have it." The sale of "wind wheat," he was sure, depressed prices by creating an artificial oversupply. Such artificial oversupplies violated the law of supply and demand, which for both the agrarians and the miller had ensured the reality, normalcy, and legitimacy of market transactions.[52] The proponents of real wheat clung to an older cultural logic that had once helped make markets the basis for social reality. For the members of the National Farmers Alliance such market transactions were tempered by an ethical base in a producer ideology and by some remnant of a labor theory of value. Those who speculated in commodities markets had abandoned all ethical bearings and embarked on a long gamble that produced only the most ethereal and corrupted forms of wealth. What the agrarians were defending may perhaps once have had an arbitrary character, but it seemed far less arbitrary to them than profits that had nothing to do with either production or exchange. In the dispute over futures trading agrarians were not resisting commerce itself but rather the transformation of commercial markets into vast casinos and the transformation of their labor into the direct means of producing wealth for those who produced nothing. "Phantom cotton," "spectral hogs," and "wind wheat" had turned even farmers' labor into a means of producing surplus value for speculative capitalists.[53]

Hatch's first bill passed the House on June 6, 1892, but the bill was delayed in the Senate when members of the Judiciary Committee worried that it was "class legislation" designed to benefit only agricultural producers and raised doubts about its constitutionality. It was finally approved by the Senate, but it was returned to the House too late for passage by the 52nd Congress. Subsequent measures shared similar fate, and in their failures, as Jonathan Lurie has illustrated, one can trace the aborted attempts at public regulation of markets.[54] Even failure can be evidence of immense imaginative labor, and what Macune and his Populist allies proposed here and elsewhere were alternatives to the culture of laissez-faire capitalism and its speculative markets. Macune's greatest contribution was the subtreasury plan, which offered a more far-reaching solution to both currency shortages and to the injustices of agricultural markets, but in the late 1880s and early 1890s members of the National Farmers Alliance directly attacked urban speculators who sold agricultural produce they did not have.

Gambling served both sides as a way to represent a moral disorder at the center of the economy.

Short selling agricultural produce exacerbated the problems endemic to late nineteenth-century markets. Those who traded in price differences, who dealt in options to buy ("calls") or options to sell ("puts") were profiting from simple changes in prices for commodities they had not produced and which often did not exist. Once they had envisioned a market dominated by short-selling speculators, the agrarians followed impeccable logic. Even if they erred in assuming that bear speculators had perverted markets, they adopted the position that markets were rigged against their interests. Speculators defied the seasonal market in produce and, it seemed to farmers, manipulated prices to their own benefit. Loosed from constraints of nature and freed from the necessity of making or marketing an actual crop, speculators could fulfill contracts by dumping fake products on the market just when farmers arrived with the real. In the calculation of prices, fake products looked just like the real, and fictitious wheat, hogs, and cotton competed with the real and added to the already severe demands on a contracted currency. In glutted markets, prices declined and interest rates rose. Indebted farmers worried as they watched speculators supersede the law of supply and demand and bury real produce under an avalanche of fictitious products.[55]

Agrarian critics also charged that markets were open to manipulation because speculators could turn time and information to their advantage. Speculators made profits in minutes, hours, and days while farmers labored over months but were forced to market crops in weeks. The disparity worked for the speculators, as did disparities between urban and rural sources of information and powers of its dissemination. Speculators seemed to make predictions based on information and statistics, and they would use such predictions to draw farmers who were trying to cover their risks into the markets. They would then turn to lies and rumors about insects, weather, or war and move prices in another direction. "Fictitious news," as Quinn put it, was "as potent an agency in advancing or depressing prices as . . . the genuine article." Speculators, alienated from the laws of nature and above the law of supply and demand that ensured the honesty of markets, had opened prices to the free play of speculative imagination.[56] Farmers drew further support for their position as they witnessed immediate disparities between the world prices quoted on the exchanges and the local prices they were paid for produce. From the earliest days of the Texas Alliance in the 1880s, Macune recognized that only cooperative marketing would bring "the world market into direct competition with local cotton buyers."[57] But all this left the man with an actual crop to market the potential victim of the wiles of selfish gamblers.

Macune told the Agricultural Committee that the National Farmers Alliance stood opposed to futures trading. "I have," he said, "held national office in that way since it was organized in 1887, and we have never had a national meeting in which there was not a unanimous protest against the present system of dealing in options and futures." Indeed, in Cleburne, Texas, in 1886, in St. Louis in December 1889, and again in Ocala, Florida, in December 1890 the Farmers' Alliance issued platforms with a specific plank that read: "We demand that Congress shall pass such laws as will effectively prevent the dealing in futures of all agricultural and mechanical productions; providing a stringent system of procedure in trials that will secure the prompt conviction, and imposing such penalties as shall secure the most perfect compliance with the law."[58]

Witnesses tried to define agricultural interests in regulatory legislation. J. H. Brigham, a "practical farmer" and the head of the National Grange, thought both futures sales and the transfer of contracts for futures sales were fine so long as an initial sale originated with a tangible product. "If a man sells it who has the right, or has acquired the right from somebody, we would care not how often contracts are transferred. . . . We want to hamstring the man who sells what he has not got; we want to cripple him and stop him from interfering with the producer."[59] Macune was more specific about the negotiability of futures contracts: "I do not understand by the bill that it would prohibit me from selling a future or making a future contract against grain which I possess, or grain I was in the act of going to produce; and the same thing with cotton. A step further, I do not understand it would make a grain contract nonnegotiable. . . . I mean by that, if I owned grain and issued you a contract for the delivery of that grain next May, or cotton, my understanding of the bill is not that it would prohibit you from reselling that contract. You would have no right, as I understand it, to make a new contract, but you could transfer that contract by negotiation."[60]

According to critics of speculation, sales of artificial produce also let brokers charge commissions on transfers that had nothing to do with actual production. Brokers looking to their own profits encouraged the sale of "wind wheat," and they too, therefore, were implicated in depressing prices. Fictitious dealings had upset the delicate mechanism that had once turned selfishness into enlightened self-interest. The unenlightened selfishness of the rigged market, producers complained, could lead only to anarchy. They had a right to complain, for they were convinced that they produced the wealth that fed speculators and brokers and their gambling clients.[61]

Macune challenged the perversion of real markets by fictional products. But his appearance before Congress in support of government regulation of commodities markets represented only a small skirmish in the battle over the nature of the late nineteenth-century economy. Macune had more powerful proposals in mind, and he set about to curb the excesses of speculation. He knew that, especially in the South, farmers' only assets were their crops. He also argued that speculative profits were not simple products of greed, but grew naturally in markets that squeezed crops, as quickly as possible, out of producers' hands. The solution was not to regulate the speculators, but to take the control of year-round markets away from them and to make speculation both unnecessary and impossible. To this end he proposed his system of subtreasuries. Properly implemented the subtreasury plan would have solved problems of currency contraction and farm debt and eliminated the very possibility of speculative profits on agricultural commodities. As Goodwyn described it, Macune's subtreasury "plan called for federal warehouses to be erected in every county in the nation that annually yielded over $500,000 worth of agricultural produce." Farmers would store crops in these subtreasuries, and wait for higher prices. While waiting they might borrow up to 80 percent of the local market price of their produce. These loans appeared as government-issued subtreasury certificates of deposit and they became the basis of exchange.[62] The farmers would be charged small fees for interest and storage but would have the right to sell their warehouse certificates whenever they pleased. Those who finally consumed agricultural produce would redeem certificates to the full amount of money advanced, plus interest and insurance.[63] When the Farmers Alliance embraced the subtreasury plan in 1889 the specific plank on futures speculation disappeared from party platforms.

As the populist writer Harry Tracy understood it, Macune's plan would allow the farmer to provide the basis for a flexible currency and thereby eliminate bankers. The farmers would control markets and the supply of currency and thereby eliminate both speculators and usurers. "Under this plan," he wrote in 1894, "the farmer stores his own product, delivers it to the manufacturer or consumer himself through his elected agent, instead of the speculator doing it." The subtreasury would also eliminate the wide fluctuations in cotton and grain prices that now produced a speculator's profits. It would do away with unnecessary costs paid by producers, "useless shipping, extravagant handling, useless and demoralizing speculation, and useless demoralizing usury."[64] It would also solve seasonal problems of currency contraction by expanding the volume of money available in the fall when it was needed, thus restoring to the people, control over the markets for the commodities they had produced.

The farmers were demanding democratic control over the monetary system, and the roots of their demand lay in the old arguments of the Greenback party and in the producer critique of speculation in an industrial economy. When agrarian reformers mounted their attack on agricultural speculation they drew on a variety of ideological resources in the American past. As Richard Hofstadter, Lawrence Goodwyn, Steven Hahn, Bruce Palmer, and others have pointed out, they turned to a republican politics that was itself based on a vision of a simple market still controlled by the law of supply and demand and inhabited by interdependent producers and consumers. They drew on the antimonopolism of the Grangers and maintained the Greenback vision of a flexible currency designed to meet the needs of the people and not those of bankers and gambling speculators.[65]

The preface to the Omaha platform written by Ignatius Donnelly in 1892 for the People's Party presented a vision of the American republic gone over to corruption and decay: "We meet in the midst of a nation brought to the verge of moral, political, and material ruin." Moral, political, and material ruin were inseparable, and the People's Party called for nothing less than the restoration of political and economic equality: "We seek to restore the government of the Republic to the hands of 'the plain people,' with whose class it originated."[66]

The plain people, the proper heirs of democracy, included both producers and consumers, but not bankers, gamblers, and speculators. The exclusion was important, and it reappeared with particular clarity in the debate over commodity prices. Witnesses who appeared in support of regulation argued that speculators and not consumers were the farmers' opposition. Witnesses opposed to regulation described urban consumers harmed by rising agricultural prices. The agrarians countered with a vision of the economy buttressed by prosperous farmers. The abolition of commodity speculation would benefit the consumer as well as producer, they said. It would relieve the indebted farmer who now spends all his money on interest and mere necessities. One sympathetic witness was sure that "increasing the purchasing power of the farmer will quicken all the movements of the commercial world, and transporter, manufacturer, artisan, and operative will find that constant employment so essential to prosperity, and all these blessings are likely to come to our people when we can assure that great host who inhabit the farms a fair compensation for the services they render society."[67]

The Chicago Board of Trade, on the other hand, presented a world divided between producers and consumers. H. H. Aldrich, a board member, testified that the board was heartily in favor of attempts to limit privileges or options trading and that they even now refused to enforce contracts without a clause requiring the delivery of commodities. He acknowledged that the production of continuous price quotations made "gambling transactions" possible, but these were the accidental outgrowth of the board's legitimate business. Such trades were not allowed in the pits, and the board did what it could to discipline members who traded in options on the "curb," where they were not subject to board regulation.

But the Hatch bill presented problems that went far beyond the exchange floor. Its opponents described it as class legislation designed to support the interests of a group who had become a distinct minority in American society. Farmers now made up only about 45 percent of the population, and they were wrong to see themselves arrayed against selfish speculators. The modern opposition was between farmers who produced and consumers who bought their production. Any rise in prices designed to benefit 45 percent of the people would harm the other 55 percent. Aldrich admitted that "the labor organizations of this country have been in favor of legislation of this kind, and why, because they say the existence of these produce exchanges . . . increases the price of their food." But like farmers, he contended, laborers were misinformed and tended to misplace blame. The board created neutral markets, which made the goods of the producer available to the consumer. Excess sales were a factor of the velocity of transfer and were a necessary part of the world markets designed to spread risk as far as possible. If excess sales did influence prices, the influence was fleeting. Whether products were fake or real, every completed transaction implied the existence of both a buyer and a seller, and profits and losses were calculated between them. In the midst of complex world markets, the individual farmer simply did not have the capital to bring his crops to market. Aldrich emphasized the board's services and called his critics misinformed. His tone served to enhance the professional reputation of the board, but his testimony also added to the division between farmers and urban workers. He described the opposition between them in ways that would best serve the interests of capitalists and speculators.[68]

Aldrich and Macune may have been using the same vocabulary, but they were talking about two very different worlds of production and exchange. Macune and the members of the Farmers Alliance had a far more inclusive vision of producers. Urban consumers who were also productive laborers were part of a community of producers. Farmers who purchased the products they made were both consumers and producers. This was the base of an economic order, and a law to benefit society's producers was not class legislation but a law for the good of all society. Aldrich envisioned producers and consumers as men of antithetical interests locked in market combat. The different visions of producers and their interests were part of two very different definitions of the social and economic world.

Farmers and speculators also evoked the law of supply and demand, but like production it meant two very different things. Throughout the hearings it served as a talisman for the natural legitimacy of market transactions. For farmers who had followed changing markets and increased production when prices rose, declining prices seemed a natural consequence of increased supply. Profits and losses came out of a market of real products and came back to producers, for good or ill. They even admitted they speculated but only when forced to avoid the vagaries of international markets and to protect themselves from the whims of nature. Those who sold "wind wheat" short had interrupted the natural process of changing prices. Farmers objected to commodities speculation because they believed artificial products created changes in actual prices. Speculators not only took profits that should have gone back to farmers, they profited from falling prices while farmers, who didn't sell short themselves, suffered. Speculators responded to farmers' charges by insisting that, whether products were real or not, exchanges between buyers and sellers ensured the natural legitimacy of market transactions. "Supply and demand should be allowed to regulate the price," Aldrich announced. We should "allow business to take its natural course." Even trades in artificial products followed the laws of supply and demand, he insisted. What could be the harm in sellers' selling to willing buyers that which did not exist?

Farmers, however, found a market operating by a different set of rules. One agrarian witness described a farmer's complaint: "Believing that the present system of marketing farm products is wholly artificial and destructive of values, the farmer desires a return to the normal conditions of supply and demand which he feels assured will give him a fair return for the service rendered and yet work no injury to the consumer, and he looks to Congress to restore to him the market of which he has been despoiled by the short seller." An embittered St. Louis hog merchant saw the so-called law as just another fiction of speculative traders. "They talk about supply and demand. Nonsense! It is nonsense! It is gambling that controls the values." Speculation, wrote another farmer, "ignores the law of nature in its efforts to get a fortune without work, sets at naught the laws of supply and demand, and under the guise of business assists and gives countenance to gambling which should be stopped."[69]

As Pillsbury understood it there were now two very different systems of markets: in Minneapolis and New Orleans, for example, real exchanges took place (and here powerful millers like Pillsbury might in fact control markets in real grain), but in Chicago and New York deals in fictitious products appeared to make prices for the real. Thanks to this perverse market structure, Pillsbury complained, the "law of supply and demand has been practically abrogated in the wheat business." He invoked the gambling analogy: "I do not know of a better illustration of the question—of course we do not play poker in the Northwest, but down South I understand they do; I have been there and I understand they do—I do not know of any better illustration than some gentlemen playing a game of poker and each start into a game of freeze-out with an equal amount of chips, but one fellow had a basket full under the table, bringing them up as they are needed. That is the position, in my opinion, of the meaning of short selling."[70]

Pillsbury's apologetic return to a crooked gambling metaphor was suggestive, and it is not far from Macune's perhaps more realistic assessment of what was wrong with the market. The law of supply and demand could never function fairly in markets dominated by well-heeled speculators and supplied with an inelastic, contracted, gold-based currency. The game was rigged. If there was not sufficient money to move what was offered and what was asked for, the law of supply and demand would cease to operate. The return to a fair and equitable market, according to Macune, required first a redefinition of money and a reestablishment of value based on the productive wealth of the country and not on the artificial commodity value of gold. Money, as the Populists understood it, was "a creation of law . . . a simple representation of value, an instrument of exchange and not in any true sense a commodity."[71] Macune and the economists of the National Farmers Alliance returned to the Greenback notion of a democratic currency whose value was based on the productive labor of American workers. Greenbacks, according to the *Workingman's Advocate* in 1866, were the "people's currency, elastic, cheap and inexportable, based on the entire wealth of the country."[72] The subtreasuries made it possible, as one North Carolina paper put it in 1891, to extend "to the land and crops of the land the same power as is given to gold money."[73]

But if we return to the devil for a minute we can see that Macune sensed that something more was at stake in his attempt to preserve the reality of wheat. The subtreasuries were a way of preventing the infinite reduplication of wheat for the benefit of those who did not work. If subtreasury warehouses filled with agricultural produce were to become the basis of natural wealth, counterfeit commodities would be very dangerous. "Bad" wheat, "bad" agricultural produce, would drive out the "good," and farmers would find themselves holding undervalued certificates, just as they now held undervalued crops. The value of currency based on agricultural produce had to be protected from artificial overproduction. Fiat currency, especially as Macune understood it in the early 1890s, precluded the very possibility of "fiat" wheat.[74]

And here he and his followers returned to the moral revolution at the beginnings of capitalism. Value, as he saw it, was to be based on the natural reproduction of wheat, cotton, and other products used to fulfill basic human needs, and not on the unnatural gain of money held at interest. Money now reproduced itself for bankers, speculators, moneylenders, and capitalists who were trying to extend its unnatural properties to natural products. Such an extension would end only in destruction and hell. Macune's vision of nature's fertility was free of such diabolical perversion. And he tried as best he could to turn the monetary structures of the nineteenth century toward an economy based on human labor and human need. He tried to preserve agricultural labor, and by extension all productive labor, as the basis of value and in so doing to resist the fetishization of agricultural commodities.[75] It was a small set-to in a battle over money, morality, and reality. But this time the market speculators and commodity gamblers practiced their sleight-of-hand on a series of definitions. Though farmers prospered in the early years of the twentieth century, in the bigger battle over the nature of prices and the origin of profits, speculators won and farmers lost.

The War against the Bucket Shops

In the four decades following the Civil War, the members of the Chicago Board of Trade negotiated a series of transformations that both dealt with the agrarian complaints and rendered the complainers mute. By agreeing to do battle against the bucket shops, they recast the conflict over options trading. They adopted a series of self-regulations that they hoped would assure the honesty and legitimacy of market transactions. But in the very act of providing markets for agricultural commodities, they transformed the historic opposition between republican producers and corrupt speculators into an endless market battle between producers and consumers. The Board of Trade set the rules for speculation on natural products in markets, and simultaneously set the rules for speculation on the nature of those markets. By waging war on the bucket shops, the members of the Board of Trade made the devil the gambler who counterfeited speculation and not the speculator who counterfeited crops. This displacement turned cries for reform from a criticism of the evil of speculation itself into an effort to eliminate the evils *from* speculation. Speculation and gambling were alike, the board admitted, but the evil was incidental to the one and essential to the other.[76] Gambling took place on the fringes of the market, and if it had to be eliminated to make speculation appear rational and natural so be it.

"There is no more dramatic story in all economic history," James E. Boyle wrote in 1920, "than that of the rise and fall of the bucket shops."[77] Boyle perhaps exaggerates, but seen in the light of the battle to legitimate speculative trading on agricultural commodities he may have been onto something. Just what were the bucket shops? The term "bucket shop" was first used in the United States in the 1870s to describe brokerage houses that had no real connection either to stock markets or commodities exchanges. Customers "bought" shares from proprietors or "sold" produce to them and calculated their profits or their losses simply on the basis of changing prices. Exchanges in bucket shops, like all gambling exchanges, were confined to the margins of markets. Customers neither intended to deliver nor to receive the grain they pretended to buy. The term "bucket shop," the justices of the Arkansas Supreme Court wrote in the early 1880s, "seems, from the explanations of witnesses, to denote a place where wagers are made upon the fluctuation in price of grain and other commodities. Any person who was able to put up the necessary margin could buy or sell an unlimited quantity of grain or cotton without regard to his financial ability to meet such obligations."[78]

According to John Hill, Jr., a crusading speculator writing in 1904, the idea of the bucket shop originated in London at mid-century. These English bucket shops were "rough dens" where the urban poor gathered to drink dregs of beer which had been collected in buckets from larger saloons. Hill's derivation from drink fitted with his reforming impulse. The *Oxford English Dictionary* offers a less romantic etymology, describing bucket shops as the resorts of smalltime grain traders who operated in alleys around the Board of Trade and dealt in lots as small as a thousand bushels. Deals on the board began in five-thousand bushel lots, but when trading was slack, dealers would send to the small traders for a "bucketful of orders." Whatever the exact etymology, the implications are similar. Bucket shops entertained a clientele that might have been barred from more "respectable" establishments and marked out the class lines of speculation. Proprietors and their customers bought and sold in small amounts, and their unlicensed transactions had only adverse bearing on exchanges taking place in "real" markets.[79]

For twenty years at the end of the nineteenth century, American bucket shops were the subject of passionate debates. They seemed to foster the worst distortions of a speculative market and to feed exactly the cunning and greed that had long threatened the republic of producers. Problems began, Jonathan Lurie noticed, when people mistook bucket shops for the Board of Trade, or worse, the Board of Trade for a bucket shop.[80] In order to legitimate speculative grain trading the Chicago Board of Trade had to eliminate trading that appeared to be no more than idle gambling on price differences. Elimination proved very difficult because all bucket-shop transactions were based on prices produced on legitimate exchanges. Establishing prices thus implicated the Board of Trade in every bucket-shop transaction, but it also finally provided legitimate grain traders with the occasion to assert themselves as productive members of a professional community who made something and performed a service. Speculators who traded on legitimate exchanges claimed they were the men who established the prices that made all trades possible.

But this cultural act of assertion did not go uncontested. American agrarians who were trying to envision a more democratic economy challenged the Board of Trade's claim to the right to set prices for all, and in so doing they sometimes found themselves in the curious position of defending bucket shops. Even if bucket-shop transactions were gambling transactions pure and simple, the Board of Trade's attack on the public produce exchanges was, they argued, a hypocritical assertion of morality masking a selfish desire to eliminate competition. "To put it in plain English," said a member of the Minneapolis Exchange, "the exchange enmity to bucket shops is that of a rival in business and not based on commercial ethics." By his reasoning bucket shops protected the farmers from a monopoly on price quotations and democratized speculation. Bucket-shop proprietors were, as C. C. Christie, the "bucket-shop king," liked to say at the end of the century, "independent operators."[81] Moreover, their very presence supported agrarian contentions that prices were public property produced by all who grew grain and all who consumed it, not by diabolical traders who tried to monopolize and to market something that rightfully belonged in the public domain. The Board of Trade and its allies answered agrarian critics by trying to persuade "country speculators" that every bucket-shop transaction went against a farmer's interest in rising prices and that trades in bucket shops made farmers easy victims of fraud and dishonesty.[82]

Although the Board of Trade had considerable difficulty with members who continued openly to trade on puts, calls, options, and prices, in the popular press the name bucket shop became associated with fake brokerage offices in small cities and market towns, especially in the Midwest. In bucket shops "the clerk, the day laborer, the barber, the newsboy, and the bootblack," along with farmers, "bored women," and "those of small estate," speculated with small amounts of money on small amounts of wheat. Concerned critics estimated that there were between eight hundred and a thousand bucket shops operating in small towns throughout the country. One Illinois circuit judge even concluded that the bucket shop evil had become so prevalent "that the betting upon the price of grain without intention of delivery may be said to have become the national mode of gambling."[83]

Bucket shops diverted money that might have gone to the legitimate exchanges, and at the same time they gave those exchanges a bad name. The worst of the bucket shops were confidence scams with fake wires and fake prices, but most of them just looked like branch offices of brokerage houses and advertised themselves as "produce exchanges." To the rural public, the exchanges and their illegitimate offspring were often more alike than different. The bucket shops maintained convenient locations, permitted dealing in fractional lots on small margins, and they charged smaller commissions than the legitimate grain and produce exchanges. It was also easier to do deals in bucket shops and the action was quicker. They were open longer hours, took fewer holidays, and welcomed those with little money. They played off the assumed class lines of speculation, and observers noted that they catered to speculators whose purchases were too small for the legitimate stock and commodity exchanges. They also attracted those who mistook the labor of speculation and were looking for entertainment and excitement.[84]

Price quotations were the lifeblood of the bucket shops. Customers (or suckers) would speculate (or bet) that the price would go one way and the proprietor would take the other side. To run such a business all one really needed was prices, but bucket shoppers added the latest technological innovations to encourage customers to part with money. They equipped themselves with ticker tapes and telegraph wires (supposedly running directly to the floor of the exchange), and they set up blackboards for posting prices and a few chairs for customers. There were honest establishments where people played with a pretense of speculation and mocked the pretensions of big-city speculators. But in some cases the wire ran only as far as the end of the rug, and, in a popular variation, prices, which had been written by clerks the night before, were unwound from a box. Some bucket shoppers simply manipulated the prices they posted and robbed their customers.[85] They also counterfeited the masculine world of the broker's office. According to one observer, bucket shops offered patrons free lunch, free cigars, free subscriptions to market letters, and private rooms with pictures of naked women. Even with these pictures, they still seemed semirespectable, and witnesses found they attracted those who would not "dream of entering a room where faro or roulette is played" or of being caught in a "poker room."[86]

Bucket shops accepted orders from customers for small lots of "May wheat" or "September wheat," but all sales were margin sales for which purchasers put up but a small percentage of a posted sale price, and when a margin was wiped out, a deal was closed. No orders to buy or to sell were ever exercised for customers on the exchanges. There was no neutral market; a bucket shop's profits were its customers' losses. And a bucket shop's one intention, as a contemporary put it, was to "freeze you out."[87] "Purchases" had no bearing on prices. Customers could never claim a right to have property delivered. And customers' losses were predictable because bucket-shop customers all bet that the price of grain would rise. The general public was, most observers pointed out, optimistic. The speculating public bought wheat it did not have; it did not sell wheat that did not exist. "Country speculators," as one critic put it, "are bulls."[88] They had a hard time selling short for, unlike the disinterested professionals who speculated in Chicago, those who bought wheat futures in the bucket shops had a stake in rising prices. If they followed Macune they did not believe in an agricultural surplus, and they could not bet against themselves.

Their faith in their labor as farmers, the Board of Trade argued, was their folly as speculators. Because their bets, however small, were predictable, added together they had the effect of driving prices down. Bucket-shop proprietors could use the small investments of country speculators to exercise orders on the exchanges which would influence prices. Farmers who thought they were backing themselves and their interest in rising prices were thus encouraging short sellers, whose interests ran precisely counter to their own. Not only were they gambling, they were influencing the odds in favor of their opponents. One journalist went so far as to blame country speculators and their follies in bucket shops for the declining agricultural prices of the 1880s. Overproduction was a myth promoted by "European consumers and their allies the American short-sellers." The real explanation for declining prices lay with country speculators who by trading in bucket shops deprived the market of support and left it at the mercy of the bears.[89]

Since bucket-shop transactions offered no fixed delivery dates, a bet on rising prices was not a hedge against a bad harvest. It was simply a reaffirmation, in a peculiar context, of a faith in productive labor. The problem was that such faith was becoming inappropriate, illogical, irrational, and perhaps dangerous in the late nineteenth-century economy. The dangers of overproduction, as Daniel Rodgers put it, upset "the certainty that hard work would bring economic success."[90] Bearish speculators turned the alliance between hard-working farmers and beneficent nature into a dangerous combination that produced devastating losses instead of just and moderate profits. But since the farmers argued that overproduction was the result of an artificial surplus created by short sellers who dumped "wind wheat" on the market in order to drive the prices down, the country speculators' held on to their belief in an alliance with nature, and their faith in a bull market was faith in their own labor and an affirmation of the reality of wheat. By insisting on the evils of artificial or "wind wheat," country speculators refused to recognize what the critic Walter Benn Michaels has described as the collaboration between "nature at her most productive and the unproductive speculator."[91] The farmers' faith in nature also made them easy victims of dishonest speculators. An honest bucket shop might lose money in an extended bull market but continue in operation to recoup losses when markets fell. A dishonest bucket shop simply would close up and disappear.[92]

The Board of Trade used these contradictions in the country speculator's position to legitimate speculation on a grander scale. They got out most of the tools in the late nineteenth-century cultural and legal workshop. They turned away from the moral language of the Populists, although with some irony they held onto the rhetoric of production. They evoked rationality, efficiency, and regulation. They used publicity, legislation, and litigation. In the long shadow of Haymarket they asked if their enemies were not "CRIMINALS, ANARCHISTS, OR

GAMBLERS?" They required delivery clauses in their contracts and lobbied for anti-bucket-shop statutes that would prohibit trades where delivery was impossible. They pushed for injunctions to prohibit bucket shops from using their price quotations. They drew on the "scientific knowledge" of professional economics and used it to create professional speculation. They argued that they possessed rare skills and that they used them to provide services to clients. They portrayed themselves as disinterested businessmen who belonged to "regular trade organizations" and had high ethical "standards of business integrity." They shunned the seductions of advertising which might make "reckless risks" attractive to amateur speculators. They announced publicly that they had made the efficient modern market for farm products. They labeled those who speculated off the exchanges incompetent "amateurs" who were deluded by greed, misled by gamblers, and in need of the advice and protection of professionals.[93] This external logic of professional service was supported by a series of internal reforms. The Board of Trade banned options trading during business hours, required enforceable delivery clauses in all contracts, and banished dealings in puts and calls from the exchange floor.

In the early 1890s William Taylor Baker, his son remembered, "applied the lash to big and little alike" and tried to rout the bucket-shop evil. During his five terms as president of the Board of Trade he suspended members who continued to trade in puts and calls and to trade after markets had closed. Convinced that he could kill off bucket shops by starving them out, he tried to keep price quotations from leaving the exchange floor for unauthorized dealers. But even he had trouble. In his fifth inaugural address he again asserted that the "extermination of bucket shops should continue to be the aim of this board." "They furnish the most attractive gambling hells in every city and village where they can effect a lodgement, and are more dangerous to public morals than other forms of gambling because of their quasi-respectability and immunity from police raids." Western Union Telegraph Company still wired the news on which bets were laid, and Baker chastised the telegraph company for selling price quotations to any who wished to purchase them. He exhorted members to maintain an "unimpeachable standard of business honor." He did manage to get the Post Office to mark letters to bucket shops "fraudulent" and, if his son is to be believed, to close 110 shops.[94]

The crusade was more than a one-man show. In good progressive fashion, the board also garnered the support of muckraking journalists to attack the bucket shops and of academic experts to endorse the legitimate exchanges, for, as Jonathan Lurie argued, the moral battle against the bucket shops was won as much by the progressive creation of a self-regulated "professional speculator" who provided a public service necessary for befuddled investors in complicated markets as by any description of the scandalous behavior of bucket shops.[95] Journalists attacked bucket shops with the full force of publicity. They illustrated the dangers of an unregulated market by exposing the worst of the bucket-shop frauds, and they compiled statistics to persuade the uninitiated that bucket-shop speculation was a form of irrational gambling that drove prices down.[96] They silenced the "naive and innocent" agrarian claim that responsibility, regulation, and rationality came from a direct and intimate relation with real work and real products with descriptions of modern markets.

Academics located the precise place of speculation in an evolving economy and illuminated speculators' contributions to the social world of the market. In his Columbia dissertation of 1896, the progressive economist Henry Crosby Emery argued that the speculator was merely the latest professional innovation in the long, slow development of the market. Steam transportation and the telegraph had so transformed markets that a new class of speculators had arisen to meet new needs. The producer assumed natural risks and handed market risks to traders who in turn handed the risks of "conjuncture" to speculators. And, Emery reminded his readers, these necessary market risks were not to be confused with the artificial and frivolous risks of gambling. The intent of speculation was public benefit, and the speculator was linked to the economic community because he had incurred the "duties" and acquired the "rights" of a holder of property.[97] Speculation was a "rational" solution to economic development; gambling was irrational flirtation with economic disaster.

Emery's argument had the effect, among other things, of labeling criticism of speculation foolish, "unreasonable," and misinformed. He added an aura of scientific necessity to his arguments by adopting evolutionary metaphors and arguing that those who failed to understand the importance of speculation had failed to comprehend the historic development of markets. It was not that the speculators had perverted the reality of farm labor but that agrarian critics of speculation had failed to grasp the reality of modern, efficient markets. They misunderstood them, they misused them, and they were responsible for the ills they decried. Small holders bound by the force of custom were "slow to take quick advantage of market conditions," and their ignorance was the root of the evil in speculation. "Here appears," he wrote, "the greatest evil of speculation, the moral evil of a reckless participation in the market by a wide outside public." There was no little irony in Emery's effort to blame the victim. After the Board of Trade had successfully expanded their definition of things they produced to include prices and markets (as well as professional knowledge and expertise) and claimed a legal property right to the prices they had made, they situated themselves under the sign of "production" and, with the help of Emery and other academic economists, took over the moral center of the early twentieth-century market.[98]

Chicago speculators pretended to share a cultural world of production with farmers. When they called upon the devil as a common figure of evil they gestured at an older world of more fluid class alliances. The farmers used the devil as an offensive weapon. The Board of Trade used the devil in defense. By fighting evil in the bucket shops they cleansed their own labor in a heroic crusade. They also moved the moral discourse of good and evil away from the market. Speculators were not capable of evil; they were guilty of "professional transgressions" and "technical errors," but not evil. Perhaps this is the drama Boyle saw in the battle over the bucket shops. The Board of Trade had done more than create a professional trade organization, it transferred the moral power of production to intangible things like prices and information. They knew that speculators were not gamblers, for in a fundamental sense gambling, in its purest form, always resisted organization by the market. Gamblers were neither producers nor consumers. All property in their hands was money at its most liquid; desire at its most antisocial. Gamblers stood in opposition to the market because they flaunted the laws of supply and demand. They entered the market to gratify a love of excitement. And when they did so, one economist contended, they "perverted" exchanges "from their true commercial purpose" and used them to "pander to one of the most depraving of human instincts."[99] Depraved, they mocked what had become the human community of the nineteenth century. They destroyed the sentimental world of the family, sucked life from the community of producers, and snubbed the community of consumers. But they also served as the necessary outsiders who helped consolidate a human project that encompassed all "rational" economic activity.

Professional speculators, on the other hand, were pure men of the market. They saw themselves, as one defender put it, as sane, levelheaded, and farseeing, as the men who possessed a "most uncommon form of common sense" and who "had the faculty of looking through all the conditions which affect the determining price factor in a particular case." They were neither optimists nor pessimists, and they were "capable of broad synthesis" and "unsparing analysis."[100] They may have lived off what appeared to be the labor of others, and they sometimes profited from vagaries of nature and imperfections in the laws of the market. It was markets that made their lives possible; it was markets that left open their return to the capitalist community of the late nineteenth and early twentieth centuries. Quinn, the aging gambler, sensed this when he chastised his audiences for joining speculators in prayers addressed to the "Mighty Dollar!" Like Thorstein Veblen, he knew that wealth presented as conspicuous display closed off inquiry into its origins. The great economic reformer Henry Demarest Lloyd also tried to explain that industry ruled by self-interest was anarchy and that selfishness unrestrained had created an evil and unbalanced society: "Our system, so fair in its theory and so fertile in its happiness and prosperity in its first century, is now, following the fate of systems, becoming artificial, technical, corrupt; and, as always happens in human institutions, after noon, power is stealing from the many to the few. Believing wealth to be good, the people believed the wealthy to be good. But, again in history, power has intoxicated and hardened its possessors, and Pharaohs are bred in counting-rooms as they were in palaces."[101]

Lloyd marshaled his great eloquence to end the masquerade of selfishness as self-interest. But the battle over the bucket shops proved the speculators on the Board of Trade as adept at the arts of disguise as their gambling forebears. They accepted clauses requiring delivery in all their standard contracts, but acknowledged among themselves that such clauses were little more than necessary fictions. And much in this complicated battle was left unresolved. In the 1890s state legislatures passed antibucket shop statutes, but statutes never fully succeeded in eliminating trading on price differences either on the exchange floor or off it. Nor was it ever quite clear how the simple elimination of options trading would help farmers. It was never possible to devise a law to distinguish between what the farmers saw as legitimate hedging and what they considered suspect futures dealing. Nor was it ever clear whether futures sales actually affected spot prices for real grain, whether buyers and sellers of futures contracts did anything to exacerbate falling prices in already cycling markets. Farmers and speculators seemed to be living in contradictory economic universes. Money passed between the two, but meaning did not. Either production meant what the agrarians said it did and it was based on tangible reality and all wealth began with those who brought real products to market, or it meant what the Board of Trade said that it did and its meaning expanded into the invisible, the intangible, and the miraculous, and the economy was let loose into the sprawling modern world of infinite abstraction. Board members used the courts and the press to assert their own version of production, and they used the battle against the bucket shops to give their version of production moral and ethical stature.

For twenty years the Board of Trade tried to close the bucket shops, but the directors and their lawyers kept stumbling into their own troublesome similarity to bucket shops. How could the board rid itself of its diabolical double without crippling itself and limiting the very practices that made modern speculative markets possible? They held to one of Baker's tactics and tried to keep Western Union from distributing price quotations to unauthorized dealers. They eventually obliged the telegraph company to sign contracts pledging not to furnish price quotations "to any bucket shop or place where they are used as a basis for bets or illegal contracts."

Western Union, and a few bucket-shop proprietors, asserted that prices were news and therefore public property and that the Board of Trade had no right to injunctions limiting their distribution and use. They charged the board with monopolistic restraint of trade and challenged its claim to a proprietary interest in quotations. They argued that since 95 percent of transactions in the pits involved no delivery, the boards' contracts were every bit as much gambling contracts as those written in bucket shops. Illegal origin made prices fair game.

The two sides also held two differing views of property, a conflict suggesting the extent to which the battle over commodities speculation involved a subtle alteration in the status of "reality." The board argued that the quotations were reflections of their "expertise" and real products of their "work." The bucket shops countered with an assertion that the Board of Trade had exercised no "creative faculty" in the creation of prices; they merely recorded transactions and therefore had no rights to quotations as mental property. And then they turned to a more agrarian vision of the world and argued that "nothing can be the object of property which has not corporeal substance."[102] Here, surely, was a devil quoting scripture from the floor of a bucket shop.

Lower courts decided cases both ways, and throughout the battle the Board of Trade tried to exercise an embargo on price quotations. The board soaped its windows and limited telephone and telegraph access. Bucket-shop proprietors rented offices with better views of the exchange floor and hired spies to "steal" prices. The complicated legal battle (but not the cultural battle) over price quotations ended with a Supreme Court decision in 1905. Writing for the majority in *Board of Trade of the City of Chicago* v. *Christie Grain and Stock Company*, Justice Oliver Wendell Holmes found that the Board of Trade's collection of price quotations was "like a trade secret." Prices were the "fruits" of their "work," and they were entitled to exercise "property rights" over them and to limit their distribution and use. That three-quarters of the transactions in the grain pits involved no transfer of grain did not change the nature of the markets. Nor did the fact that contracts far exceeded the "total receipts of grain in Chicago." Holmes made explicit the connection between wheat and money, and he argued that the excesses of the contracts were "no more wonderful than the enormous disproportion between the currency of the country and contracts for the payment of money." They encouraged rapid circulation and exchange. "Speculation of this kind by competent men," Holmes concluded, "is the self-adjustment of society to the probable. Its value is well known as a means of avoiding or mitigating catastrophes, equalizing prices and providing for periods of want. It is true that the success of the strong induces imitation by the weak, and that incompetent persons bring themselves to ruin by undertaking to speculate in their turn."[103]

Armed with Holmes's decision, the board sent a "special detective" off to close the remaining bucket shops. The poor man found the menace intractable. He would no sooner close a shop than it would open again in the next town under another name. In 1919 Boyle reported the detective still on the road but now, aided by a powerful ally, "informed public sentiment," Boyle was sure the tide was turning in the long battle against the bucket shops.[104]

Virtue and Commerce

Quinn's metamorphoses, from card player to commodities broker, from gambler to author, from ex-gambler on a vaudeville turn to evangelist on tour, are no more surprising than the transformations of commodities speculators into moral producers performing a social service. Although a larger cultural trend toward mass leisure allowed commercial gambling (in the twentieth century, at least) the legitimacy of the entertainment industry, commodities speculators, who had nothing to do with entertainment, called upon the whole legitimating rhetoric of nineteenth-century producerism. While to agrarians they appeared to reap profits where they had not sown, the Chicago Board of Trade adopted the agrarians' own logic and announced that they had made something after all—they had produced a market and they had produced prices. The transfer of real grain could not go on without the service they provided. Speculative markets offered the means of spreading risk, the means of hedging against the insecurities of agricultural production. Protection came at a price, and farmers refused to accept its costs without contest. To accept the board's services was to accept an alteration in the position and nature of markets. Trading on price differences, the board finally asserted, was every bit as real as commercial transactions in actual wheat. No matter that markets and prices were once thought to have arisen out of man's natural tendency to truck and barter, they were now the products of a modern industry, commodities produced in factories like everything else, and like all commodities, hiding the social relations behind them.

Henry Demarest Lloyd saw through the subtle but sweeping changes that lay behind the triumph of the Board of Trade. "Markets, like political parties," he complained, "are run by the Machine. The people are losing the power of making prices as well as nominations." The Board of Trade had eliminated "mock" speculation, "counterfeit trading" and illegitimate, irrational gambling and asserted the right to define the real, the genuine, the legitimate and the rational. The farmers who had come to Washington to support legislation to limit options trading asserted a vision of the factual world based on their productive labor. The moral market in real work had been invaded by a fiction. By the time the century ended, it was the fiction that defined the real. The hearings *Fictitious Dealing in Agricultural Products* had, in effect, served to legitimate real trading on fictitious products. The structures of the social world had shifted, and shifted dangerously, Lloyd knew, when the "man who works in the ground must take the price fixed for him by the man who works in the air."[105]

If we keep the market in agricultural products in the foreground, this transformation of fictitious crops into real profits was the actual Turnerian moment of the late nineteenth century. The virtuous yeomen who, in Jefferson's vision, were to protect the American republic from the corruptions of commerce had finally been overrun. Turner's great demographic insight of 1893—that there was no longer a line of white settlement advancing across the West into an area of open land—had been foreshadowed in the 1870s when trade began to exceed production and short sellers began to profit from a falling market. The delicate compromise between agrarian virtue and commercial industry which was the American vision of salvation in the nineteenth century shattered just as significantly in the Chicago wheat pits as on the frontier. Although we are used to thinking of land or space as our central national metaphor, if we think in terms of the market, the raw contradictions so carefully masked in the rhetoric of free land—in the vision of what Henry Nash Smith called the "fee simple empire"— stand exposed in another light. Here was commerce unredeemed. Here was the end of the dialectic between virtue and commerce.[106]

The Populists witnessed the demise of virtue, and in the early 1890s they warned the nation of the dangers of a soulless dependence on commerce alone. Although there were ample signs of decay, demagoguery, and political corruption, the end of the dialectic had not brought the country to a political and economic standstill. The activities of the Board of Trade helped move the standards for virtue into an abstracted realm of ethereal production, and they garnered cultural support for their markets in fictitious products. They scrambled to produce a new set of terms to justify their power. They adopted remnants of an ideology of virtuous producers, but they used the remnants to advance modern efficient markets where producers had no say. The producers called upon the devil in the shape of a gambler to signify what was left of the historic conviction that corruption and decay were to mark the final triumph of commerce.

And the devil has kept haunting the "price factories." In 1905 J. A. Everitt could still conjure with the remnant of evil in the market and called "speculators and gamblers in farm products . . . unholy, Godless things."[107] More recently in the crash of October 1987 the Faustian nature of the market reappeared, and the Securities and Exchange Commission, falling into the nineteenth-century logic of reform, set off to eliminate the gamblers who had perverted and distorted the stock market and scared off the timid investors and country speculators. Wall Street sacrificed its irrational gamblers (its computer traders, its index arbitragers) to reestablish the appearance of rationality and morality in the markets. Behind the curtain of rationality the markets continue to make extraordinary fortunes for those who control the forces of production set free from all basis in reality and for those who manipulate the prices of the commodities they sell to so-called customers. But as long as we maintain even a rhetorical faith in the ideology of production we can hope the devil will reappear to haunt his markets, real and unreal, in fictitious products. He will remind us just how immoral our profits once seemed.

Notes

Introduction

1. Robert Bailey, *The Life and Adventures of Robert Bailey from his Infancy up to December, 1821, Interspersed with Anecdotes and Religious and Moral Admonitions* (Richmond, Va., 1822), 119; John Philip Quinn, *19th Century Black Art; or, Gambling Exposed* (Chicago, 1891), 80. For yet another version of the same trick, see Jonathan Harrington Green, *An Exposure of the Arts and Miseries of Gambling; designed especially as a warning to the youthful and inexperienced against the evils of that odious and destructive vice* (Philadelphia, 1843), 217–219.

2. On the "construction" of the self in the eighteenth century see J. E. Crowley, *This Sheba, Self: The Conceptualization of Economic Life in Eighteenth-Century America* (Baltimore, Md., 1974); or, more generally, Max Weber, *The Protestant Ethic and the Spirit of Capitalism,* trans. Talcott Parsons (New York, 1958).

3. The original study of gambling as symbolic behavior is Clifford Geertz's well-known "Deep Play: Notes on the Balinese Cockfight," in his *The Interpretation of Cultures* (New York, 1973), 412–453. I have followed Geertz far enough to allow that gambling, in certain circumstances, was as much an attempt to make meaning as an attempt to make money. On the complex workings of reciprocal economies see Marshall Sahlins, *Stone Age Economics* (Chicago, 1972), and Karl Polanyi, *The Great Transformation: The Political and Economic Origins of Our Time* (Boston, 1957), 47–55, 272.

4. The phrase "negative analogue" is from Stephen Marcus's study of Victorian pornography, *The Other Victorians* (New York, 1966), 283. Karen Halttunen's discussion of the relations between gambling and speculation appears in *Confidence Men and Painted Women: A Study of Middle-Class Culture in America, 1830–1870* (New Haven, Conn., 1982), 16–20.

5. On northern entrepreneurs and their celebrations of risk and innovation see Anthony F. C. Wallace, *The Social Context of Innovation* (Princeton, N.J., 1982), 141–142.

6. See, for example, Herbert Asbury, *Sucker's Progress: An Informal History of Gambling in America from the Colonies to Canfield* (New York, 1938); Henry

Notes

Chafetz, *Play the Devil: A History of Gambling in the United States from 1492–1955* (New York, 1960); and Philip D. Jordan, *Frontier Law and Order* (Lincoln, Neb., 1970).

7. For dramatic, sentimental figures of Gold Rush gamblers, see Bret Harte's stories "The Luck of Roaring Camp" and "An Ingenue of the Sierras," in *The Outcasts of Poker Flat and Other Tales* (New York, 1961); Louise A. K. S. Clappe, *The Shirley Letters, Being Letters Written in 1851–1852 from the California Mines by "Dame Shirley"* (Chapel Hill, N.C., 1973), 20, 44, 123, contains precise descriptions of parallels between mining profits and gambling. See also E. L. Cleaveland, "Hasting to Be Rich: A Sermon Occasioned by the Present Excitement Respecting the Gold of California" (New Haven, Conn., 1849); and John M. Findlay, *People of Chance: Gambling in American Society from Jamestown to Las Vegas* (New York, 1986), 79–109.

8. On cowboys, see Andy Adams, *The Log of a Cowboy* (Garden City, N.Y., [1902]), 119–132; Robert R. Dykstra, *The Cattle Towns: A Social History of the Kansas Cattle Trading Centers, Abilene, Ellsworth, Wichita, Dodge City and Caldwell, 1867 to 1885* (New York, 1976), 122–134; Gary Cunningham, "Chance, Culture, and Compulsion: The Gambling Games of the Kansas Cattle Towns," *Nevada Historical Society Quarterly*, 26 (Winter 1983), 255–271.

9. George Devol, *Forty years a Gambler on the Mississippi* (Cincinnati, 1887); Joseph Baldwin, *Flush Times of Alabama and Mississippi* (New York, 1853); George William Featherstonhaugh, *Excursion through the Slave States, from Washington on the Potomac to the frontier of Mexico; with sketches of popular manners and geological notices* (London, 1844), 2:241–245; J. R. Talbot, *Turf, Cards and Temperance; or, Reminiscences in a Checkered Life* (Bristol, R.I., 1882); Edward Willet, *Flush Fred, the Mississippi Sport; or, Tough Times in Tennessee* (New York, 1884); Daniel B. Dumont, *The Old River Sport; or, A Man of Honor* (New York, 1886); John Morris [John O'Connor], *Wanderings of a Vagabond. An Autobiography* (New York, 1873); and Green, *Arts and Miseries of Gambling*.

10. On the construction of morality and economics in the nineteenth century and on the uneasy relations between religious and economic discourse see Louis Dumont, *From Mandeville to Marx: The Genesis and Triumph of Economic Ideology* (Chicago, 1977), 24–36; Viviana Zelizer, *Morals and Markets: The Development of Life Insurance in the United States* (New York, 1979), 73–78; Henry May, *Protestant Churches and Industrial America* (New York, 1949), 12–35. Much of May's analysis of clerical economics is based on material from Joseph Dorfman, *The Economic Mind in American Civilization, 1606–1865* (New York, 1946), 2:512–835. For a discussion of the construction of rationality in economic theory and the rationality of economic theory, see Maurice Godelier, *Rationality and Irrationality in Economics*, trans. Brian Pierce (New York, 1972), 10–13, 303–319.

11. See, for example, Daniel Horowitz, *The Morality of Spending: Attitudes toward the Consumer Society in America, 1875–1940* (Baltimore, 1985); and the introduction and essays in Richard W. Fox and T. J. Jackson Lears, eds., *The Culture of Consumption: Critical Essays in American History, 1880–1980* (New York, 1983).

12. See, for example, James Barron, "Has the Growth of Legal Gambling Made Society the Loser in the Long Run?" *New York Times*, May 31, 1989, A 18.

Chapter 1. *Rich Men, Poor Men*

1. See Bruce Laurie, *Working People of Philadelphia, 1800–1850* (Philadelphia, 1980), 55–56; Sean Wilentz, *Chants Democratic: New York City and the Rise of the American Working Class, 1788–1850* (New York, 1984), 257–271; Alan Dawley, *Class and Community: The Industrial Revolution in Lynn* (Cambridge, Mass., 1976); Paul G. Faler, *Mechanics and Manufacturers in the Early Industrial Revolution: Lynn, Massachusetts, 1780–1860* (Albany, N.Y., 1981).

2. National Institute of Law Enforcement and Criminal Justice, *The Development of the Law of Gambling, 1776–1976* (Washington, D.C., 1977), 237–238.

3. Timothy H. Breen, "Horses and Gentlemen: The Cultural Significance of Gambling among the Gentry of Virginia," *William and Mary Quarterly*, 3d ser., 34 (April 1977), 239–257.

4. Robert Bailey, *The Life and Adventures of Robert Bailey from his Infancy up to December, 1821* (Richmond, Va., 1822), 15, 28, 61–64, 340–343. Bailey perhaps perfected his dancing skills as one means of luring the wealthy into games. On the social meanings of dance in colonial Virginia see Rhys Isaac, *The Transformation of Virginia, 1740–1790* (Chapel Hill, N.C., 1982), 80–87.

5. Bailey, *Life and Adventures*, 39, 64, 81, 103. Bailey was not the only candidate of dubious background. On the lowered tone of legislative politics in postrevolutionary Virginia see Isaac, *The Transformation of Virginia*, 319.

6. Bailey, *Life and Adventures*, 119; for later versions of the same trick see Jonathan Harrington Green, *An Exposure of the Arts and Miseries of Gambling: Designed especially as a warning to the youthful and inexperienced against the evils of that odious and destructive vice* (Philadelphia, 1847 [1843]), 217–219; John Philip Quinn, *19th Century Black Art: or, Gambling Exposed* (Chicago, 1891), 80. Like slave traders, professional gamblers had commerce with insiders yet they were outside proper society. Andrew Steinmetz made this point explicit in his description of American gambling; see *The Gaming Table: Its Votaries and Victims in all Times and Countries, especially in England and in France,* (London, 1870), 1:234. Harriet Beecher Stowe had a fine sense of the social hypocrisy in dealings between slaveholders and slave traders; see her introduction of the "Man of Humanity" into Shelby's Kentucky parlor in *Uncle Tom's Cabin; or, Life among the Lowly* (New York, 1987 [1852]), 41–53.

7. Bailey, *Life and Adventures*, 103, 82, 123, 127, 340–343. On the "tavern ethos" see Isaac, *The Transformation of Virginia*, 94, 122.

8. Breen, "Horses and Gentlemen," 243; Geertz's famous essay is based on his fieldwork in Bali in 1958. Breen followed Geertz far enough to assert the symbolic significance of staged wagers, but rather than replace Bentham's concern about the irrationality of "deep play" with a Weberian sense of the importance of

meaning, Breen turned seeming irrationality into an instrumental assertion of power. Where Geertz had found in cockfights an open-ended or undetermined commentary on Balinese life, Breen found in horse races a far more limited or immediate assertion of class power. Clifford Geertz, "Deep Play: Notes on the Balinese Cockfight," in *The Interpretation of Cultures* (New York, 1973), 412–453; Isaac, *The Transformation of Virginia*, 104.

9. Bailey, *Life and Adventures*, 162, 180, 198, 219. Once again Isaac helps us locate Bailey along a cultural divide. Bailey made the generous hospitality that had once been the pride of wealthy Virginians into a business. See Isaac, *The Transformation of Virginia*, 302–303.

10. Isaac, *The Transformation of Virginia*, 303; see also Norbert Elias, *The Civilizing Process: The History of Manners*, trans. Edmund Jephcott (New York, 1978), 51–217.

11. Bailey, *Life and Adventures*, 41–42.

12. Bailey, *Life and Adventures*, 45–47.

13. Herbert Asbury, *Sucker's Progress: An Informal History of Gambling in America from the Colonies to Canfield* (New York, 1938), 5–6; *The Standard Hoyle: A complete guide and reliable authority upon all games of chance or skill now played in the United States whether of native or foreign introduction* (New York, 1887), 183; John Morris [John O'Connor], *Wanderings of a Vagabond* (New York, 1873), 63; J. R. Talbot, *Turf, Cards and Temperance; or, Reminiscences in a checkered life: containing the most important events in the life of J. R. Talbot, together with sketches of all leading men with whom, personally, this sporting man, politician and lecturer has come in contact* (Bristol, R.I., 1882), 22.

14. Hoyle's description of the game of faro was reprinted in Green, 110–117. The warning comes from Green, who added his own description of deceptions used by professionals. *Arts and Miseries*, 117, 118–146.

15. The tiger was the mark of a faro game and images of tigers graced establishments where faro was dealt. David W. Maurer, "The Argot of the Faro Bank," *American Speech*, 18 (February 1943), 3, 6–11.

16. *The American Hoyle; or, Gentleman's handbook of games, containing all the games played in the United States, with rules, descriptions and technicalities, adapted to the American methods of playing. By "Trumps"* (New York, 1864), 209; Green, *Arts and Miseries*, 121–122; Morris, *Wanderings of a Vagabond*, 56–65. One reformed gambler included elaborate schematic drawings of rigged faro boxes in his discussion of the game. See John Philip Quinn, *19th Century Black Art; or, Gambling Exposed* (Chicago, 1891), 56–76; and Quinn, *Fools of Fortune; or, Gambling and Gamblers comprehending a history of vice in ancient and modern times* (Chicago, 1890), 200–211.

17. Bailey, *Life and Adventures*, 207–208, 347.

18. Jane Carson, *Colonial Virginians at Play* (Williamsburg, Va., 1965), 53.

19. National Institute of Law Enforcement, *The Development of the Law of Gambling*, 238–239, 15–21.

20. Act of May 6, 1744, c.5, 5 Va. Stat. 229 (Hening, 1819), in National Institute of Law Enforcement, *The Development of the Law of Gambling,* 239–240.

21. Isaac, *The Transformation of Virginia,* 243–295.

22. William Stith, "The Sinful and Pernicious Nature of Gaming: A Sermon Preached before the General Assembly of Virginia at Williamsburg March 1, 1752" (Williamsburg, 1752), 14–15.

23. Stith, "The Sinful and Pernicious Nature of Gaming," 13, 16, 19, 21–22.

24. Samuel Davies, "Virginia's Danger and Remedy: Two Discourses Occasioned by the Severe Drought in Sundry Parts of the Country; and the Defeat of General Braddock" (Williamsburg, Va., 1756), 21, 26.

25. Davies, "Virginia's Danger and Remedy," 27.

26. Continental Congress, October 20, 1774, quoted in Isaac, *The Transformation of Virginia,* 247, from Peter Force, comp., *American Archives . . . ,* 4th ser. (Washington, D.C., 1837–1853), 1:915, col. 1.

27. Robert Peter, *The History of the Medical Department of Transylvania University* (Louisville, Ky., 1905), 49–63; John D. Wright, Jr., *Transylvania: Tutor to the West* (Lexington, Ky., 1975), 65–66, 83–84, 97; Charles Caldwell, *An Address on the Vice of Gambling Delivered to the Medical Pupils of Transylvania University, November 4, 1834* (Lexington, Ky., 1834), 23–24, 3; Charles Caldwell, *A Discourse on the Vice of Gambling, Delivered by appointment to the Anti-Gambling Society of Transylvania University, November 2d and 3d* (Lexington, Ky., 1835). For his many opinions on many subjects and his quarrels with various prominent figures see Charles Caldwell, *Autobiography of Charles Caldwell, M.D.* (Philadelphia, 1855).

28. Caldwell, *An Address on the Vice of Gambling,* 6, 10, 22, 21.

29. Caldwell, *An Address on the Vice of Gambling,* 17–18, 20, 26; Charles Caldwell, *A Discourse on the Vice of Gambling,* 32.

30. Caldwell, *An Address on the Vice of Gambling,* 23, 21, 16; Caldwell, *A Discourse on the Vice of Gambling,* 8.

31. Caldwell, *A Discourse on the Vice of Gambling,* 4–6.

32. Caldwell, *A Discourse on the Vice of Gambling,* 8, 11.

33. It has never been clear that Murrell had anything to do with the professional gamblers at Vicksburg. The publication of a sensational pamphlet and the forced confessions of some slaves and some itinerant healers in Madison County set the white people in western Mississippi on edge. Early in the summer of 1835 northern abolitionists had also stepped up their propaganda campaigns in the South. With abolitionist attacks ringing in their ears, with rumors and hangings fresh in their minds, "prominent" citizens (read slaveholders) of Vicksburg set about to celebrate Independence Day. They had also recently heard the outcry over the publication of a pamphlet detailing Murrell's plots, a pamphlet that by extension suggested that northern abolitionists who distributed tracts and pamphlets created the disorder they then condemned. Augustus Q. Walton [Virgil A. Stewart], *A History of the Detection, Conviction, Life and Designs of John A. Murel, the Great Western Land Pirate, together with his System of Villainy, and Plan*

Notes

of Exciting a Negro rebellion. Also a Catalogue of the Names of Four Hundred and Fifty-five of his Mystic Clan Fellows and Followers and a Statement of their efforts of Virgil A. Stewart, the young man who detected him (Cincinnati, Ohio, 1835); H. R. Howard, ed., The History of Virgil A. Stewart, and his Adventure Capturing and Exposing the Great "Western Land Pirate" and His Gang in Connexion with the Evidence: also of the Trials, Confessions, and Execution of a Number of Murel's Associates in the State of Mississippi during the summer of 1835, and the Execution of Five Professional Gamblers by the Citizens of Vicksburg, on the 6th of July 1835 (New York, 1836). On the spread of mob violence throughout the United States and on the connection of antiabolitionist violence with other forms of mob violence see Leonard L. Richards, "Gentlemen of Property and Standings": Anti-Abolition Mobs in Jacksonian America (New York, 1970), 3–19.

34. Caldwell, A Discourse on the Vice of Gambling, 18–29.
35. Caldwell, A Discourse on the Vice of Gambling, 33–34.
36. Caldwell, A Discourse on the Vice of Gambling, 41–42.
37. Caldwell, A Discourse on the Vice of Gambling, 11–13.
38. Caldwell, A Discourse on the Vice of Gambling, 11–12, 53–59. Reports on the Vicksburg hangings from the Natchez Courier, the Columbia [Miss.] Argus, the Lexington [Ky.] Intelligencer, the Lynchburg Virginian, and the Clinton Virginian and Evening Star were reprinted in Duff Green's United States Telegraph on July 28, 1835; August 3, 1835; August 4, 1835; August 8, 1835; and October 6, 1835; in his Niles' Weekly Register, Hezekiah Niles used reports from the New Orleans American and the Vicksburg Daily Register. See Niles' Weekly Registrar, July 25, 1835; August 1, 1835; and August 8, 1835. See also Thomas Brothers, The United States of North America as They Are; Not as They Are Generally Described: Being a Cure for Radicalism (London, 1840), 13–15, and Howard, ed., The History of Virgil A. Stewart, 250–265; George Featherstonhaugh, Excursion through the Slave States from Washington on the Potomac to the Frontier of Mexico; with Sketches of Popular Manners and Geological Notes, (London, 1844), 1:250–254n; H. S. Fulkerson, Random Recollections of Early Days in Mississippi (Vicksburg, Miss., 1885), 95–97. A defense of the Vicksburg citizens appeared in "Uses and Abuses of Lynch Law," American Whig Review, 13 (March 1851), 218–219; a journalist claimed that the verb "to lynch" had come into common use with the hangings at Vicksburg: see 'Cohee,' "Lynch Law," Harper's New Monthly Magazine, May 1859, 794. See also James E. Cutler, Lynch-Law: An Investigation into the History of Lynching in the United States (New York, 1905). John Morris argued that the whole incident had nothing to do with gambling, at least not as he defined it as high-minded sport, and that the Vicksburg mob, in a fit of ugly passion, had turned on some "low thieves" and "reckless desperadoes." Wanderings of a Vagabond, 338–345. For an interesting reading of the conjunction of southern and frontier aspects of the Vicksburg violence see John M. Findlay, People of Chance: Gambling in American Society from Jamestown to Las Vegas (New York, 1986), 64–71.

39. "The Vicksburg Tragedy," Niles' Weekly Register, August 1, 1835, 331.

40. "The Vicksburg Tragedy," 331; see also *Natchez Courier*, July 10, 1835, reprinted in the *United States Telegraph*, July 28, 1835, 814.

41. Caldwell, *A Discourse on the Vice of Gambling*, 12, 56. The English geologist George Featherstonhaugh had sympathy for seduced youths, but little for those who engineered the hangings. *Excursion through the Slave States*, 1:250.

42. Brothers, *The United States of North America as They Are*, 14–15, 261, 274–276, 297.

43. Brothers, *The United States of North America as They Are*, 13–15.

44. Featherstonhaugh, *Excursion through the Slave States*, 1:254n.

45. *Niles' Weekly Register*, September 5, 1835.

46. Joseph Baldwin, *The Flush Times of Alabama and Mississippi* (New York, 1854), 84, 89; Margaret L. Brown, ed., "John Peters' Diary of 1838–1841," *Mississippi Valley Historical Review*, 21 (March 1935), 536, see also 532, 533, 539; Peter Temin, *The Jacksonian Economy* (New York, 1969), 113–171; Douglass C. North, *The Economic Growth of the United States, 1790–1860* (New York, 1966), 73, 194–195; Findlay, *People of Chance*, 70–71; Leonard Bacon, "Duties Connected with the Present Commercial Distress: A Sermon Preached in the Center Church, New Haven, May 21, 1837, and repeated May 23" (New Haven, Conn., 1837), 15.

47. James Silk Buckingham, *The Slave States of America* (London, 1852), 456; George Devol, *Forty Years a Gambler on the Mississippi* (Cincinnati, Ohio, 1887), 295–296; see also Featherstonhaugh, *Excursion through the Slave States*, 1:242–243; Talbot, *Turf, Cards and Temperance*, 82; Philo Tower, *Slavery Unmasked, Being a Truthful Narrative of a Three Years' Residence and Journeying in Eleven Southern States: to which is added the invasion of Kansas including the last chapter of her wrongs* (Rochester, N.Y., 1856), 87; Louis C. Hunter, *Steamboats on Western Rivers: An Economic and Technological History* (Cambridge, Mass., 1949), 408–410; Morris, *Wanderings of a Vagabond*, 432–433.

48. Steven M. Stowe has explored the drama and display of southern authority in *Intimacy and Power in the Old South: Ritual in the Lives of the Planters* (Baltimore, Md., 1987), 5–49.

49. Findlay, *People of Chance*, 69. Findlay argues, correctly I think, that Vicksburg moved beyond a frontier economy in the mid 1830s and turned against the vices that had characterized commercial leisure in an earlier stage of development. He sees development, however, in terms of the opposition between East and West. It might be more fruitful for an understanding of the 1830s to see opposition between North and South. Robert Dykstra (*The Cattle Towns: A Social History of the Kansas Cattle Trading Centers Abilene, Ellsworth, Wichita, Dodge City and Caldwell, 1867 to 1885* [New York, 1976], 239–292) makes a similar argument (albeit with considerable detail on local politics) about moral reform and economic development in the Kansas cattle towns.

50. *Vicksburg Daily Register*, July 10, 1835, reprinted in *Niles' Weekly Register*, August 1, 1835, 380.

51. Richards, "*Gentlemen of Property and Standing*," 168–169, 16–17.

Notes

52. Clement Eaton, "Mob Violence in the Old South," *Mississippi Valley Historical Review,* 29 (December 1942), 351–370. See also Edwin A. Miles, "The Mississippi Slave Insurrection Scare of 1835," *Journal of Negro History,* 42 (January 1957), 48–61; and Clement Eaton, "Censorship of the Southern Mails," *American Historical Review,* 48 (January 1943), 266–280.

53. Dickson D. Bruce, Jr., *Violence and Culture in the Antebellum South* (Austin, Tex., 1979), 41–43.

54. *Niles' Weekly Register,* August 1, 1835, 331; *Natchez Courier,* July 10, 1835, reprinted in the *United States Telegraph,* July 28, 1835, 814.

55. Reprinted in Featherstonhaugh, *Excursion through the Slave States,* 1:253n; see also W. J. Cash, *The Mind of the South* (New York, 1941), 70–81.

56. The phrase "bullying insolence" is from Baldwin, *Flush Times,* 89. On steamboats and the economic development of the Mississippi Valley, see Hunter, *Steamboats on Western Rivers,* 30, and George Rogers Taylor, *The Transportation Revolution, 1815–1860* (New York, 1951), 66–67.

57. Paul Johnson, *A Shopkeepers' Millennium: Society and Revivals in Rochester, New York, 1815–1837* (New York, 1978), 6–8.

58. Brian Harrison, *Drink and the Victorians: The Temperance Question in England, 1815–1872* (Pittsburgh, Pa., 1971), 26.

59. Howard Rock, *Artisans of the New Republic: The Tradesmen of New York City in the Age of Jefferson* (New York, 1979), 298–300; Sidney Pomerantz, *New York: An American City* (New York, 1938), 485–488; Laurie, *The Working People of Philadelphia,* 53–66; Wilentz, *Chants Democratic,* 257–271.

60. Paul Faler found gamblers (along with drunks and pickpockets) in the rowdy crowds who turned out to watch militia musters around Lynn, Massachusetts, in the 1820s. *Mechanics and Manufacturers,* 129.

61. Wilentz, *Chants Democratic,* 263; for discussions of working-class "traditionalism" see Alan Dawley and Paul G. Faler, "Working-Class Culture and Politics in the Industrial Revolution: Sources of Loyalism and Rebellion," *Journal of Social History,* 9 (Summer 1976), 466–480; and Laurie, *Working People of Philadelphia,* 54; see also Faler, *Mechanics and Manufacturers,* and Dawley, *Class and Community;* and David Montgomery, "The Working Classes of the Pre-Industrial American City, 1780–1830," *Labor History,* 9 (Winter 1968), 3–22.

62. For descriptions of fancy New York gamblers see Jonathan Harrington Green, *Green's Report number 1 on Gambling and Gambling houses in New York* (New York, 1851), 58; Harrison Gray Buchanan, Esq., *Asmodeus; or, Legends of New York* (New York, 1848), 75–79. For a description of French gambling houses (which seemed to influence taste, decor, and style in northern houses the way England had influenced the South) see Olivier Grussi, *La vie quotidien des jouers sous l'anciene régime à Paris et à la cour* (Paris, 1985). See also J. Frank Kernan, *Reminiscences of the Old Fire Laddies* (New York, 1885), 101–105; *The Tricks and Traps of New York City* (New York, 1857), 52–59; for a reportage on New York's "very splendid hells," see *New York Herald,* July 30, 1835; George C. Foster, *New York in Slices by an Experienced Carver, being the original slices published in the*

New York Tribune (New York, 1849), 26–27. After the Civil War reporters and reformed gamblers turned to formulaic descriptions of New York gambling; see James D. McCabe, *Lights and Shadows of New York Life* (Philadelphia, 1872), 716, 721; Matthew Hale Smith, *Sunshine and Shadow in New York* (Hartford, Conn., 1868), 397; John Philip Quinn, *Fools of Fortune*, 186–187; Thomas Dewitt Talmadge, *Social Dynamite; or, The Wickedness of Modern Society* (Chicago, 1887), 147; T. Narcisse Doutney, *His Life Struggle* (Boston, 1887), 135; Robert G. Williams, *Thrilling Experience of the Welsh Evangelist, R. G. Williams, reformed drunkard and gambler; or, Forty-eight years in darkness and sin and eleven years in the light and love of Christ Jesus* (Chicago, 1896), 58; Talbot, *Turf, Cards and Temperance*, 24. The quotation on temptation to rustics is from James Alexander, *The Merchant's Clerk Cheered and Counseled* (New York, 1856), 34.

63. Kernan, *The Old Fire Laddies*, 104; Asbury, *Sucker's Progress*, 185–191.

64. *The Tricks and Traps of New York City*, 52–61; Foster, *New York in Slices*, 26–28; McCabe, *Lights and Shadows*, 716, 721.

65. John Pintard, *Letters from John Pintard to His Daughter Eliza Noel Pintard Davidson, 1816–1833* (New York, 1940), 1:153–154, 173–174; 3:1; on racing, 2:306, 3:249–250; on winning the lottery, 1:88–89.

66. Act of April 6, 1801, chap. 164, 5 [1801] *Laws of N.Y.*, 439 cited in *The Development of the Law of Gambling*, 144.

67. *Minutes of the Common Council of the City of New York, 1784–1831* (New York, 1917), March 4, 1807, 4:369; April 8, 1811, 6:546–547.

68. *Minutes of the Common Council*, March 18, 1812, 7:71–75; March 23, 1812, 7:83. James F. Richardson argues that gambling was so extensive in the 1840s that it enjoyed a practical legal immunity. He also cites an instance of a grand jury that claimed it could not get enough evidence to prosecute lottery and policy-shop operators. Most jurors admitted that they held lottery tickets themselves. *The New York Police: Colonial Times to 1901* (New York, 1970), 27, 57.

69. New York City Common Council, *The Report of the Police Watch Committee on the Conduct of the Police Magistrates and the Watch in entering the house of Joseph Collett, No. 42 Broad-Street, on the evening of 26th March, 1826* (New York, 1827), 3–19.

70. M. J. Heale, "The New York Society for the Prevention of Pauperism, 1817–1823," *New-York Historical Society Quarterly*, 55 (April 1971), 157, 162; Christine Stansell, *City of Women: Sex and Class in New York, 1789–1860* (Urbana, Ill., 1987), 33; Raymond A. Mohl, *Poverty in New York, 1783–1825* (New York, 1971), 241–258; Carroll Smith-Rosenberg, *Religion and the Rise of the American City: The New York City Mission Movement, 1812–1870* (Ithaca, N.Y., 1971), 4–5.

71. Engs's memories are reprinted in Emerson W. Keyes, *A History of Savings Banks in the United States From Their Inception in 1816 Down to 1877: With Discussions of Their Theory, Practical Workings and Incidents, Present Condition and Prospective Development* (New York, 1878), 318–319.

72. Society for the Prevention of Pauperism in New York City, *Report of a Committee on the Subject of Pauperism* (New York, 1818), 5–11; *The Second Annual*

Report of the Managers of the Society for the Prevention of Pauperism in New York City (New York, 1819), 17–61; *The Fourth Annual Report of the Managers of the Society for the Prevention of Pauperism in New York City* (New York, 1821), 6–21; Stansell, *City of Women*, 33–35; S.P.P., *Documents Relative to Savings Banks, Intemperance and Lotteries* (New York, 1819), 21.

73. S.P.P., *Report of a Committee*, 6–7.

74. S.P.P., *First Annual Report to the Managers of the Society for the Prevention of Pauperism,* (New York, 1818), 5.

75. S.P.P., *Second Annual Report*, 36; *Fourth Annual Report*, 11; Heale, "The New York Society for the Prevention of Pauperism," 165.

76. S.P.P., *Fourth Annual Report*, 23–24.

77. S.P.P., *Documents Relative to Savings Banks*, 8; on the stepping mill see S.P.P., *The Sixth Annual Report of the Managers of the Society for the Prevention of Pauperism,* (New York, 1823).

78. Keyes, *A History of Savings Banks in the United States*, 1:307–310, 519–522; on Eddy's correspondence with Colquhoun see Samuel L. Knapp, *The Life of Thomas Eddy* (New York, 1834), 248, 265–266.

79. *Minutes of the Common Council*, May 5, 1819, 10:367–368; Heale found as well that many of them were trustees of the Free School Society, governors or physicians for the New York Hospital, members of the New-York Historical Society, members of the New-York Athenæum, members of the Literary and Philosophical Society of New York, and managers of the American Bible Society. "The New York Society for the Prevention of Pauperism," 158–159. See also M. J. Heale, "From City Fathers to Social Critics: Humanitarianism and Government in New York, 1790–1860," *Journal of American History*, 63 (June 1976), 24–25. Mohl also described the tangled mercantile and philanthropic careers of Eddy, Pintard, and Griscom. Their interests, he found, included the Humane Society and the Magdalen Society, as well as various religious, financial, and literary enterprises. *Poverty in New York*, 241–243.

80. Keyes, *A History of Savings Banks in the United States*, 2:34, 566.

81. S.P.P., *Documents Relative to Savings Banks*, 4, 8; Emerson W. Keyes, *Special Report on Savings Banks* (Albany, N.Y., 1868), 12.

82. Stuart Bruchey, *The Roots of American Economic Growth, 1607–1861; An Essay in Social Causation* (New York, 1968), 143.

83. S.P.P., *Documents Relative to Savings Banks*, 4, 6, 14. Writing forty years after the inception of savings banks, Keyes acknowledged the efficacy of cultural change. "While a man has nothing, he is reckless, improvident; but the moment he has consecrated a portion of his earnings, however small, to a fixed and worthy purpose, invested them in a permanent and remunerative form, the desire to increase the amount takes full possession of him. To this end he practices self-denial, diligently employs otherwise unoccupied hours, and abandons habits of prodigality and self-indulgence." And, Keyes was happy to report, even when savers indulged in "an occasional unbending of the energies of mind and body," they opted for rational forms of recreation. Indeed the project begun by far-seeing

philanthropists to redraw the class loyalties established by loans had been so successful that by 1868 "thirty-one millions in the earnings of the poor are loaned to the rich on bond and mortgage in this State." Loans gave depositors an interest in public order, and Keyes was certain no depositors were among the draft rioters of 1863. Keyes, *Special Report*, 15, 16–17, 19. Keyes further asserted that the "humblest depositor" at the savings bank had more in common with an "Astor, a Stewart, or a Vanderbilt" than with "the poor patron of the soup-house." Keyes, *A History of Savings Banks*, 2:39, 566. The trustees' first report to the legislature is reprinted in Keyes, *A History of Savings Banks*, 1:342–345. Viviana Zelizer's study of life insurance suggests that its acceptance by the middle class likewise entailed a cultural shift that replaced the mutual financial obligation of family and kin with bureaucratic financial institutions. *Morals and Markets: The Development of Life Insurance in the United States* (New York, 1979), 44–65, 73–94. See also Stephen Thernstrom, *Poverty and Progress: Social Mobility in a Nineteenth Century City* (Cambridge, Mass., 1964), 124–126.

84. Bailey reduced his finances to a simple formula. "When money is low the furniture must go / And when that won't do the negroes too." *Life and Adventures*, 198. Nineteenth-century gamblers' autobiographies abound in similar experiences. See Williams, *Thrilling Experiences of the Welsh Evangelist*, 80; Mason Long, *The Life of Mason Long, the Converted Gambler* (Chicago, 1878), 129; John Horatio Shannon, *Live Life: Biographical Incidents with an Exposition of Gambling* (Philadelphia, 1885), 196; Talbot, *Turf, Cards and Temperance*, 17; Green, *Arts and Miseries*, 315.

85. E. H. Chapin, *Moral Aspects of City Life* (New York, 1854), 100–101; Alexander, *The Merchant's Clerk*, 37.

86. A. O. Hirschman, *The Passions and the Interests: Political Arguments for Capitalism before Its Triumph* (Princeton, N.J., 1977), 41–42, 55, 59–63.

87. Eliphalet Nott, "Address to the Candidates for the Degree of A. B. in Union College, delivered at the Annual Commencement, July 27th, 1814," *Columbia Magazine*, 1 (December 1814), 103.

88. Caldwell, "An Address on the Vice of Gambling," 17–24.

89. Karen Halttunen, *Confidence Men and Painted Women: A Study of Middle-Class Culture in America, 1830–1870* (New Haven, Conn., 1982), 14–16; Henry Ward Beecher, *Seven Lectures to Young Men on Various Important Subjects* (Indianapolis, Ind., 1844); Stuart M. Blumin has warned historians about too facile a use of the term "middle class" in this period. Even if one bears in mind Blumin's caution that the "middle class" became a class around the denial of the existence of class, it does seem that recreational gambling, like drink, would be antithetical to those who harbored even unacknowledged longings for advancement in the rational markets of the North. "The Hypothesis of Middle-Class Formation in Nineteenth-Century America: A Critique and Some Proposals," *American Historical Review*, 90 (April 1985), 299–338. See also Stuart M. Blumin, *The Emergence of the Middle Class: Social Experience in the American City, 1760–1900* (Cambridge, Mass., 1989), 108–229.

Notes

90. Mason Locke Weems, *God's Revenge Against gambling Exemplified in the Miserable Lives and Untimely Deaths of a Number of Persons of Both Sexes who had Sacrificed their Health, Wealth and Honor at Gaming Tables* (Philadelphia, 1816 [1811]), 34; on Weems eccentricities as a reformer see David S. Reynolds, *Beneath the American Renaissance: The Subversive Imagination in the Age of Emerson and Melville* (New York, 1988), 59–61.

91. William Alcott, *The Young Man's Guide* (Boston, 1834), 146, 160.

92. E. H. Chapin, "A Discourse on the Evils of Gaming," reprinted in Green, *Arts and Miseries*, 303.

93. Walter Benjamin, "Some Motifs in Baudelaire," *Illuminations*, trans. H. Zohn (New York, 1969), 177, 176–180. See also Green, *Arts and Miseries*, 238–240; Long, *The Life of Mason Long*, 125, 142–143.

94. Nott, "Address . . . Union College," 101–102; on Nott's troubles with Yates & McIntyre see John Samuel Ezell, *Fortune's Merry Wheel: The Lottery in America* (Cambridge, Mass., 1960), 214–215.

Chapter 2. The Mind of Economic Man

1. "Gambling and Its Consequences, Communicated by J. H. Green, the Reformed Gambler; with an Account of his Phrenological Developments," *American Phrenological Journal*, 8 (1846), 49; John D. Davies, *Phrenology Fad and Science: A 19th-Century American Crusade* (New Haven, Conn., 1955), 46–64; Madeleine B. Stern, *Heads and Headlines: The Phrenological Fowlers* (Norman, Okla., 1971); Ronald G. Walters, *American Reformers* (New York, 1978), 156–163. According to Roger Cooter it was in the Fowlers' hands that phrenology "acquired that nonintellectualist, healthean, watered, fruity, and farinaceaus—almost fundamentalist tone—that was chiefly to characterize its popular presentation." *The Cultural Meaning of Popular Science* (Cambridge, 1984), 156.

2. Thorstein Veblen, "The Preconceptions of the Classical Economists," from *The Place of Science in Modern Civilization*, in *The Portable Veblen*, ed. Max Lerner (New York, 1976), 266. On the construction of economic rationality see Jean-Christophe Agnew, *Worlds Apart: The Theater and the Market in Anglo-American Thought, 1550–1750* (Cambridge, 1986), 5–9; and Michael Taussig, *The Devil and Commodity Fetishism in South America* (Chapel Hill, N.C., 1980), 3–12. The historian J. E. Crowley studied the internalization of rational gain and the construction of restraint among American colonists in the eighteenth century. "Unrestrained, the individual was a source of social disorder; economically isolate, his human qualities were neglected. The moral evaluation of work was a way for colonists to maintain social wholeness." Crowley found that the role of work in maintaining social cohesion was gradually replaced by a celebration of individual economic rationality. *This Sheba, Self: The Conceptualization of Economic Life in Eighteenth-Century America* (Baltimore, Md., 1974), 13, 154.

3. On the appearance of "capitalist ideology, mediated and mystified . . . in

the phrenological head" and on phrenology's role in the triumph of bourgeois hegemony in industrializing England see Cooter, *The Cultural Meaning of Popular Science,* 71–85, 134–185, esp. 165–168. See also Burton Bledstein, *Culture of Professionalism: The Middle Class and the Development of Higher Education in America* (New York, 1976), 23–24.

4. Karen Halttunen, *Confidence Men and Painted Women: A Study of Middle-Class Culture in America, 1830–1870* (New Haven, Conn., 1982), 16–20.

5. I am using the term middle class here to suggest a broad social group who shared assumptions about domesticity, economic and civic virtue, and about the value of the rational pursuit of wealth. As Mary Ryan has argued, such values can be traced in dialogue about work, family, education, religion, and the construction of public and private life. Mary P. Ryan, *Cradle of the Middle Class: The Family in Oneida County, New York, 1790–1865* (Cambridge, Mass., 1981).

6. Georg Simmel, *The Phenomenon of Money,* trans. Tom Bottomer and David Frisby (London, 1978), 59–60, 73; Max Weber, *The Protestant Ethic and the Spirit of Capitalism,* trans. Talcott Parsons (New York, 1958), 167, 170–171; Joyce Appleby, *Capitalism and a New Social Order: The Republican Vision of the 1790s* (New York, 1984), 22; Carolyn Porter, *Seeing and Being: The Plight of the Participant Observer in Emerson, James, Adams, and Faulkner* (Middletown, Conn., 1981), 20.

7. Halttunen, *Confidence Men and Painted Women,* 11, 20; on gambling in cities see, for example, Harrison Gray Buchanan, *Asmodeus; or, Legends of New York* (New York, 1848); George Foster, *New York in Slices by an Experienced Carver* (New York, 1849); *The Tricks and Traps of New York;* Charles Burdett, *The Gambler; or, the Policeman's Story* (New York, 1848).

8. William Alcott, *The Young Man's Guide* (Boston, 1834), 136–160; Henry Ward Beecher, *Seven Lectures to Young Men* (Indianapolis, Ind., 1844) 103–130; E. L. Cleaveland, *Hasting to Be Rich: A Sermon Occasioned by the Present Excitement Respecting the Gold of California* (New Haven, Conn., 1849); Halttunen, *Confidence Men and Painted Women,* 16–20.

9. Thimbles was nothing more than the old shell game. Jonathan Harrington Green, *An Exposure of the Arts and Miseries of Gambling; designed especially as a warning to the youthful and inexperienced against the evils of that odious and destructive vice* (Philadelphia, 1843), 17–19.

10. Green, *Arts and Miseries,* 14. Green's warnings to victims were nothing new. Historians have found numerous pamphlets from the sixteenth century warning of the wiles of rogues and swindlers. See Agnew, *Worlds Apart,* 68–69, 73.

11. Stephen Marcus, *The Other Victorians* (New York, 1966), 283; see also Halttunen, *Confidence Men and Painted Women,* 16–20.

12. David Francis Bacon, *The Mystery of Iniquity: A Passage in the Secret History of American Politics, Illustrated by a View of Metropolitan Society* (New York, 1845), 5. On production see Beecher, *Seven Lectures,* 104; Alcott, *Young Man's Guide,* 145. On the abolition of gambling and the legitimation of speculative profits by

the northern middle class see Halttunen, *Confidence Men and Painted Women*, 16–20.

13. J. A. Dacus and James W. Buel, *A Tour of St. Louis; or, The Inside Life of a Great City* (St. Louis, Mo., 1878), 465–471; Green, *Arts and Miseries*, 171–172; Robert Bailey, *The Life and Adventures of Robert Bailey from his Infancy up to December 1821* (Richmond, 1822), 198–200; R. G. Williams, *Thrilling Experience of the Welsh Evangelist, R. G. Williams, reformed drunkard and gambler; or, Forty-eight years in darkness and sin and eleven years in the light and love of Christ Jesus* (Chicago, 1896), 80.

14. Weber, *The Protestant Ethic*, 170, 181; J.G.A. Pocock, *The Machiavellian Moment: Florentine Political Thought and the Atlantic Republican Tradition* (Princeton, N.J., 1975), 389–391; Appleby, *Capitalism and a New Social Order*, 9; Simmel, *The Phenomenon of Money*, 304–305; Marshall Sahlins, *Stone Age Economics* (Chicago, 1972), 12–13.

15. George Combe, *Notes on the United States of North America during a Phrenological Visit in 1838-9-40* (Philadelphia, 1841), 1:185; Jonathan Harrington Green, *Gambling Unmasked! or, The personal experiences of the reformed gambler, J. H. Green; designed as a warning to the young men of this country* (New York, 1844), 297; Halttunen, *Confidence Men and Painted Women*, 9. For an elaborate gamblers' plot to defeat Polk by using money wagered for him to fund a campaign against him see Bacon, *Mystery of Iniquity*.

16. Green, *Arts and Miseries*, 19.

17. David S. Reynolds, *Beneath the American Renaissance: The Subversive Imagination in the Age of Emerson and Melville* (New York, 1988), 55.

18. On separations in cultural discourse between masculine goals of the market and feminine goals of the heart see Ann Douglas, *The Feminization of American Culture* (New York, 1978), 11–12; for a brief discussion of an Anglo-American line between the language of morals and the language of the market see Sahlins, *Stone Age Economics*, 181–183.

19. Green, *Gambling Unmasked*, 7–8. On runaway apprentices see W. J. Rorabaugh, *The Craft Apprentice from Franklin to the Machine Age in America* (New York, 1986), 89–92.

20. Green, *Gambling Unmasked*, 9–21; Rev. John Richards told the story of Green's life in his "Discourse on Gambling delivered in the Congregational Meeting-House at Dartmouth College November 7, 1852" (Hanover, N.H., 1852), 12.

21. Green, *Gambling Unmasked*, 24–25, 76–77, 83; Jonathan Harrington Green, *Twelve Days in the Tombs; or, A Sketch of the Last Eight Years of the Reformed Gambler's Life* (New York, 1850), 121; Otto A. Rothert, *The Outlaws of Cave-in-Rock: Historical Accounts of the Famous Highwaymen and River Pirates Who Operated in Pioneer Days upon the Ohio and Mississippi Rivers and over the Old Natchez Trace* (Cleveland, Ohio, 1924), 37.

22. Green, *Gambling Unmasked*, 41, 105.

23. Green, *Twelve Days in the Tombs,* 11–13.

24. On the Mississippi see Robert Wiebe, *The Opening of American Society* (New York, 1984), 258; George Rogers Taylor, *The Transportation Revolution, 1815–1860* (New York, 1951), 63–70; on easy wealth and speculation see Joseph Baldwin, *The Flush Times of Alabama and Mississippi* (New York, 1853), 84. Green argued that "gamblers were abundant on the Mississippi and its tributaries." *Arts and Miseries,* 67. Green quotes one supporter as describing his books as "highly useful to young men, especially to those who design to travel South or West." *Gambling Unmasked,* 323.

25. Sean Wilentz, *Chants Democratic: New York City and the Rise of the American Working Class, 1788–1850* (New York, 1984), 182–190; Ryan, *Cradle of the Middle Class,* 208–209.

26. On the dangers of "worker-intellectuals" to bourgeois definitions of class and the importance of the literary aspirations of failed or failing artisans see Jacques Rancière, *La nuit des proletaires: Archives du rêve ouvrier* (Paris, 1981), 7–8; Rancière, "Le bon temps; ou, La barrière des plaisirs," *Les revoltes logiques,* 7 (Spring 1978), 30; Donald Reid, "The Night of the Proletarians: Deconstruction and Social History," *Radical History Review,* 28–30 (1984), 451, 453.

27. Green, *Twelve Days in the Tombs,* 26–46.

28. Ryan, *Cradle of the Middle Class,* 110–111; see also Walters, *American Reformers,* 92.

29. Green, *Arts and Miseries,* 317. Paul Johnson, *A Shopkeeper's Millennium: Society and Revivals in Rochester, New York, 1815–1837* (New York, 1978), 6–8, 139; see also David Brion Davis, *The Problem of Slavery in the Age of Revolution, 1770–1823* (Ithaca, N.Y., 1975), 251.

30. John Ashworth, "The Relationship between Capitalism and Humanitarianism," *American Historical Review,* 92 (October 1987), 823, 824. See also Thomas L. Haskell, "Capitalism and the Origins of the Humanitarian Sensibility, Part 1," *American Historical Review,* 90 (April 1985) 339–361; Part 2, *American Historical Review,* 90 (June 1985), 547–66; Haskell, "Convention and Hegemonic Interest in the Debate over Antislavery: A Reply to Davis and Ashworth," *American Historical Review,* 92 (October 1987), 829–878; and David Brion Davis, "Reflections on Abolitionism and Ideological Hegemony," *American Historical Review,* 92 (October 1987), 797–812.

31. Leonore Davidoff and Catherine Hall, *Family Fortunes: Men and Women of the English Middle Class, 1780–1850* (London, 1987), 20.

32. Green, *Gambling Unmasked,* 310; Green, *Twelve Days in the Tombs,* 41, 35, 26–27, 156–169.

33. Carroll Smith Rosenberg, "Beauty, the Beast, and the Militant Woman," in *Disorderly Conduct: Visions of Gender in Victorian America* (New York, 1978), 113–114, 117; see also Barbara J. Berg, *The Remembered Gate: Origins of American Feminism: The Woman and the City, 1800–1860* (New York, 1978), 178, 186.

34. Green, *Twelve Days in the Tombs,* 190, 182, 208, 210, 178–179.

Notes

35. New Haven *Palladium*, reprinted in Green, *Twelve Days in the Tombs*, 78.
36. Green, *Twelve Days in the Tombs*, 10. On professional reformers see Walters, *American Reformers*, 13–15.
37. Green, *Twelve Days in the Tombs*, 182, 198–200; Walters, *American Reformers*, 22, 35, 130–134; Brian Harrison, *Drink and the Victorians: The Temperance Question in England, 1815–1872* (Pittsburgh, Pa., 1971), 32, 49–50, 129–132. On the Washingtonians see Ruth M. Alexander, "We are Engaged as a Band of Sisters: Class and Domesticity in the Washingtonian Temperance Movement, 1840–1850," *Journal of American History*, 75 (1988), 763–785; on working-class entertainments in New York see Wilentz, *Chants Democratic*, 257–271; Madeleine B. Stern, "Dick and Fitzgerald," in Madeleine B. Stern, ed., *Publishers for Mass Entertainment in Nineteenth-Century America* (Boston, 1980), 103–106; on parlor entertainments see Halttunen, *Confidence Men and Painted Women*, 153–190.
38. Green, *Gambling Unmasked*, 191.
39. J. H. Green, *The Gambler's Mirror* (Baltimore, Md., 1844), 1. On the dangers of reading fiction see Joseph P. Thompson, *Vice Progressive: A Sermon to Young Men; Preached in the Broadway Tabernacle August 2nd, 1846* (New York, 1846), 10–14; R. W. Pomeroy, *The Young Merchant* (Philadelphia, 1839), 92, 201; and Cathy Davidson, *Revolution and the Word* (New York, 1987), 38–54.
40. Richards, "Discourse on Gambling," 11; Charles Caldwell, *An Address on the Vice of Gambling Delivered to the Medical Pupils of Transylvania University, November 4, 1834* (Lexington, Ky., 1834), 4; Caldwell, *A Discourse on the Vice of Gambling Delivered by appointment, to the Anti-Gambling Society of Transylvania University, November 2d and 3rd, 1835* (Lexington, Ky., 1835), 3, 11.
41. Green, *Arts and Miseries*, 264.
42. Green, *Arts and Miseries*, 262–264. Caldwell had also proposed that the Kentucky legislature prohibit "traffic in playing cards," in "A Discourse on Gambling," 30–31; see also Catherine Perry Hargrave, *A History of Playing Cards and a Bibliography of Cards and Gaming* (Boston, 1930).
43. Green, *Twelve Days in the Tombs*, 182; Green, *Arts and Miseries*, 267–269; John O'Connor [John Morris], *Wanderings of a Vagabond* (New York, 1873), 348.
44. Michael Denning, *Mechanic Accents: Dime Novels and Working-Class Culture in America* (London, 1987), 100, 87–103. On the middle class and fictions of reform see Alan Trachtenberg, *The Incorporation of America: Culture and Society in the Gilded Age* (New York, 1982), 103–105.
45. Green, *Arts and Miseries*, 10; Jonathan Harrington Green, *The Secret Band of Brothers; or, The American Outlaws* (Philadelphia, 1847), 3.
46. J. H. Green, "A Short Address to All," *American Journal of Phrenology*, 8 (1846), 50.
47. Green, *Arts and Miseries*, 9–10. Green later revealed that the task of revising his manuscript was a commercial transaction and one, like so many of his transactions, that ended on a sour note. He wrote his first book at Augusta College in Kentucky, and the president of the college took on the task of revising it, "for which he charged *three hundred dollars!*" Green, *Twelve Days in the Tombs*, 17.

48. Green, *Arts and Miseries*, 8.

49. Green, *Arts and Miseries*, 172.

50. Green, *Arts and Miseries*, 178, 181, 194–196, 202.

51. J. H. Green, *The Gambler's Mirror*, 1.

52. John Tebbel, *A History of Book Publishing in the United States* (New York, 1972), *The Creation of an Industry, 1630–1865*, 1:245. As evidence of Green's appeal to northern working-class audiences, see advertisements for Green's books run by his publisher, G. B. Zeiber, in the spring of 1847 in the *National Police Gazette* under the headline "A Most Fearful and Startling Record of Crime." See issues for March 13, March 20, April 3, April 10, and April 17, 1847.

53. Rev. B. Kurtz, D. D., "Gambling Unmasked. By J. H. Green," *Baltimore Lutheran Observer*, reprinted in *Gambling Unmasked*, 300–301.

54. Green, *Secret Band of Brothers*, 4; see also David Brion Davis, "Some Aspects of Countersubversion: An Analysis of Anti-Masonic, Anti-Catholic, and Anti-Mormon Literature," *Mississippi Valley Historical Review*, 47 (September 1960), 205–224. The phrase "literary proletariat" is from Robert Darnton, "The High Enlightenment and the Low-Life of Literature in Pre-Revolutionary France," *Past and Present*, 51 (1970), 112.

55. Green, *Secret Band of Brothers*, 79–80, 90, 99–101.

56. Bertram Wyatt-Brown, *Lewis Tappan and the Evangelical War against Slavery* (Cleveland, Ohio, 1969), 233.

57. Green, *Secret Band of Brothers*, 73, 112, 107–110.

58. Green, *Secret Band of Brothers*, 3–4, 115. On business frauds see P. T. Barnum, *Humbugs of the World* (New York, 1866), 150–170.

59. In the 1850s T. B. Peterson published four books by Green, reprints of books published earlier by other houses and under other titles. They included: *The Gambler's Life; or, The life adventure and personal experiences of J. H. Green written by himself* (1857); *Gambling Exposed* (1857); *The Reformed Gambler; or, The history of the later years of the game of thimbles; diamond cut diamond, or, the gentleman's game* (1858); and *The Secret Band of Brothers* (1858). On T. B. Peterson see Marie E. Korey, "T. B. Peterson," in Stern, ed., *Publishers for Mass Entertainment*, 229–230. In 1862 Green tried his hand at one more publishing venture. Adding military rank, "Captain J. H. Green, U.S.A.," to his title-page sobriquet "the reformed gambler," Green took the confession of a Union soldier who was to be executed for murder. He wrote a brief preface explaining how he had encountered so desperate a villain, and published the confession himself. Green billed himself as "the author of various works on gambling" and asserted that his twenty years of authorship had made him into an expert on tales of villainy. The book was reprinted as *A Desperado in Arizona, 1858–1860; or, The Life, Trial, Death and Confession of Samuel H. Calhoun, the Soldier-Murderer* (Santa Fe, N.M., 1964).

60. Green, *Twelve Days in the Tombs*, 10.

61. Green, *Twelve Days in the Tombs*, 145. See also Walter Benjamin, "The Storyteller," in *Illuminations*, trans. H. Zohn (New York, 1969), 106; Keith Thomas, *Religion and the Decline of Magic* (New York, 1971), 234–237; and Alan

Notes

Taylor, "The Early Republic's Supernatural Economy: Treasure Seeking in the American Northeast, 1780–1830," *American Quarterly*, 38 (Spring 1986), 6–34; Reynolds, *Beneath the American Renaissance*, 55.

62. *Broadway Journal*, 1 (March 1, 1845), 133–134; reprinted in Green, *Twelve Days in the Tombs*, 188.

63. Reprinted in Green, *Twelve Days in the Tombs*, 187, 189.

64. "William Wilson" was first published in *Burton's Gentleman's Magazine* in 1839 and reprinted in the *Broadway Journal*, August 30, 1845. While David Reynolds asks us to expand the cultural field from which Poe, Emerson, Hawthorne, Melville, and other writers drew and to see them as embracing a multiplicity of voices rather than writing in simple dissent from the shallow optimism of the antebellum United States, I would temper this reading of the relations between Poe and Green with a caution. While Green may have been a part of the popular cultural discourse that fertilized Poe's imagination, I do not intend to reduce texts like Green's to canon fodder for the more complex (and therefore more important) literary productions of the American Renaissance. They deserve to be read in their own troubled complexity. See *Beneath the American Renaissance*, 60, 70–72. As a counterexample see Michael Denning's reading of George Lippard in *Mechanic Accents*, 85–117.

65. Green, *Gambling Unmasked*, 227–228. For a close reading of Adam Smith's *Theory of Moral Sentiments* and the problem of sympathy see Agnew, *Worlds Apart*, 177–188.

66. Robert M. Coates, *The Outlaw Years: The History of the Land Pirates of the Natchez Trace* (New York, 1930); Thomas D. Clarke, *The Rampaging Frontier: Manners and Humors of Pioneer Days in the South and Middle West* (Indianapolis, Ind., 1939); Rothert, *The Outlaws of Cave-In-Rock;* Green, *Arts and Miseries*, 108. On treasure seekers as tale tellers see Taylor, "Supernatural Economy," 13.

67. Green, *Gambling Unmasked*, 230–237, 277–278; Green, *Arts and Miseries*, 171, 178, 181, 194–196, 202; Neil Harris, *Humbug: The Art of P. T. Barnum* (Chicago, 1973), 57, 61–89; Dan Schiller, *Objectivity and the News: The Public and the Rise of Commercial Journalism* (Philadelphia, 1981).

68. Philip Fisher, *Hard Facts: Setting and Form in the American Novel* (New York, 1985), 108.

69. Burdett, *The Gambler; or, The Policeman's Story*, 22–23; see also Osgood Bradbury, *The Gambler's League; or, The Trials of a Country Maid* (New York, 1857); for a survey of gambling fiction see Clarence E. Brown, "The American Gambler Story in the Sentimental Tradition, 1794–1870," (Ph.D. diss., Michigan State University, 1970).

70. Burdett, *The Gambler*, vi.

71. On imitation among the Virginia gentry see Lawrence Stone, review of T. H. Breen, *Puritans and Adventurers*, in the *New York Review of Books* (February 1981), 5. One could make a similar argument about the evocation of the nineteenth-century frontier in twentieth-century Las Vegas. See John Findlay, *People of Chance: Gambling in America from Jamestown to Las Vegas* (New York, 1986), 127–128.

72. Green, *Arts and Miseries,* 20–56.

73. In their recent study of class, gender, and the middle-class family in early nineteenth-century Birmingham, Leonore Davidoff and Catherine Hall argued that the "purpose of business was not the avid pursuit of profit, but the provision of a 'modest competency' so that [the] family could live in a simple but comfortable way." For Green it was just such backward-looking ambition that left youths ill prepared to cope with the wiles of sophisticates. *Family Fortunes,* 16. See also James A. Henretta, "Families and Farms: *Mentalité* in Pre-Industrial America," *William and Mary Quarterly,* 3d ser., 35 (January 1978), 3–32.

74. Green, *Gambling Unmasked,* 207; see also Timothy Shay Arthur, *Ten Nights in a Bar-Room and What I Saw There* (Cambridge, 1964 [1854]), 101.

75. Green, *Arts and Miseries,* 20–56.

76. Like the drunks who imbibed at the heart of so many temperance tales, gamblers destroyed their families. Temperance tales, however, appealed to emotions already lost in Green's world of greed and chicanery. On temperance tales see William Breitenbach, "Sons of the Fathers: Temperance Reformers and the Legacy of the American Revolution," *Journal of the Early Republic,* 3 (1983), 69–82; and Blumin, *The Emergence of the Middle Class,* 200–203.

77. Orville Dewey, *Moral Views of Commerce, Society and Politics in Twelve Discourses* (New York, 1838), 113–114.

78. Barbara Leslie Epstein, *The Politics of Domesticity: Women, Evangelism, and Temperance in Nineteenth-Century America* (Middletown, Conn., 1981), 71–72. On the education of sons, see Ryan, *Cradle of the Middle Class,* 145–185.

79. One crooked faro dealer who worked at the end of the nineteenth century remembered winning money from a railroad brakeman, but he supported the logic of off-limit wages by returning the brakeman's money with a lecture: "You are a working man and any man who works for his money cannot afford to gamble, for while you are earning your money the gambler is practising methods of deception and fraud how to steal your money from you," John Philip Quinn, *Gambling and Gambling Devices* (Canton, Ohio, 1912), 7. On the rhetoric of work see Daniel Rodgers, *The Work Ethic in Industrial America, 1850–1920* (Chicago, 1974), 1–29, 210–232. George Devol, the Mississippi Sport, gave up his work as a ship calker to become a fulltime gambler. He kicked his tools into the river in a grand gesture of defiance. *Forty Years a Gambler on the Mississippi* (New York, 1892), 14.

80. *Philadelphia Sunday Courier,* April 1847, quoted in J. H. Green, *Twelve Days in the Tombs,* 229.

81. Agnew, *Worlds Apart,* 193; J. H. Plumb, *The Commercialization of Leisure in Eighteenth-Century England* (Reading, 1974).

82. On the dangers of misspent leisure see, for example, Pomeroy, *The Young Merchant,* 96–98, 102–103; on the twentieth-century development of the utilitarian defense of gambling see Findlay, *People of Chance,* 136–170.

83. Green, *Twelve Days in the Tombs,* 51–72.

84. Quoted in Green, *Twelve Days in the Tombs,* 79–80.

85. New York Association for the Suppression of Gambling, *First Annual*

Report (New York, 1851), 1. On the importance of numbers, statistics, and facts in early nineteenth-century America and their use by moral reformers see Patricia Cline Cohen, *A Calculating People: The Spread of Numeracy in Early America* (Chicago, 1982), 116–117, 169–173, 207–211. Cohen's argument about the cultural importance of calculation goes far beyond the scope of Green's feeble efforts to create a gambling-reform association, but she suggests that in the 1830s and 1840s moral reformers, abolitionists, and temperance advocates all relied on combinations of statistics and sentiment. Green's mistake was not so much his turn to statistics and facts but rather his contention that gambling reform would do nothing to protect the country from the expansion of the selfish relations of the market.

86. *Green's Report number 1 on Gambling and Gambling Houses in New York* (1851), 48.

87. *Green's Report number 1,* 23; James F. Richardson, *The New York Police: Colonial Times to 1901* (New York, 1970), 27; National Institute of Law Enforcement, *Development of the Law of Gambling* (Washington, D.C., 1977), 152–156.

88. New York Association for the Suppression of Gambling, *Constitution and Bye-Laws* (New York, 1850), 2; Allan Stanley Horlick, *Country Boys and Merchant Princes: The Social Control of Young Men in New York* (Lewisburg, Pa., 1975), 245.

89. Association for the Suppression of Gambling, *First Annual Report,* 6.

90. Green, *First Annual Report,* 28.

91. Horlick, *Country Boys and Merchant Princes,* 242–250.

92. The evolution of the figure of Virgil Stewart, the man who captured John Murrell, the "great western land pirate," illustrates well the plight of the informer. When Stewart first told his tale in the 1830s he painted himself as a clever and brave hero who had outwitted the villain by infiltrating his band, but subsequent versions suggested ambiguities in the detective hero. Virgil A. Stewart, [Augustus Q. Walton], *A History of the Detection, Conviction, Life and Designs of John A. Murel, the Great Western Land Pirate* (Cincinnati, Ohio, 1835). A long version of Murrell's saga appeared in the *National Police Gazette* between September 1846 and April 1847; see also Henry S. Foote, *Casket of Reminiscences* (Washington, D.C., 1874).

93. Green, *Arts and Miseries,* 14.

94. On Tappan see Wyatt-Brown, *Lewis Tappan,* 226–244; see also Lawrence J. Friedman, *Gregarious Saints: Self and Community in American Abolitionism, 1830–1870* (New York, 1982), 68–95.

95. *Green's Report number 1,* 33; *Constitution and Bye-Laws,* 15–16.

96. *First Annual Report,* 6; Wyatt-Brown, *Lewis Tappan,* 232.

97. *First Annual Report,* 5; the phrase in the *Report* actually appeared as "nervousness awakened or simulated lest we trench on individual rights." However, a reporter for the *New York Tribune* (May 10, 1851, 9) was more careful.

98. *New York Tribune,* May 8, 1851, 1.

99. *First Annual Report,* 14.

100. A story reported in the *New York Times* in the late 1860s and early 1870s illustrated how just such an antigambling association as they had devised could serve as cover for fraud and blackmail. A brief announcement appeared on May 4, 1868, heralding the opening of an office of a Society for the Suppression of Gambling. On January 9, 1869, the society issued an annual report and claimed receipts worth $23,975. They had paid out money for rent and salaries, by far the largest sum, $19,720, to a detective who had found 1,034 employees frequenting gambling houses. With his help, they had closed, they said, 317. But on June 25, 1870, a "serious charge" was brought against the officers of the society by a woolen merchant who had been led to believe that his partner was frequenting gambling houses and that "his interests were thus jeopardized." Rowland West, the president of the society, offered to exchange information he had gathered for a "money consideration," and Albert G. Hyde, the merchant, paid him a twenty-five-dollar fee. A few days later the detective demanded another fifty dollars to furnish him with the damning particulars. The charges proved "false and malicious slanders" and Hyde succeeded in obtaining a warrant for the arrest of the society's officers for obtaining money under "fraudulent representations." They were all brought to trial in September, where they defended themselves saying they offered a service and gave information only to paid subscribers. *New York Times,* September 20, 1870. Those who pretended to oppose gambling proved as adept at fraud as those who pretended to gamble.

101. Wyatt-Brown, *Lewis Tappan,* 235–237.

102. Harris, *Humbug,* 68, 78.

103. Schiller, *Objectivity and the News,* 76, 142.

104. See for example the report on the 35th Anniversary Meeting of the New York Bible Society, *New York Herald,* May 9, 1851.

105. *New York Daily Tribune,* May 10, 1851, 9; see also *New York Herald,* May 13, 1851.

106. Fisher, *Hard Facts,* 102–105; Halttunen, *Confidence Men and Painted Women,* 153, 157, 186–187.

Chapter 3. *Gambling on the Color Line*

1. James Weldon Johnson, *The Autobiography of an Ex-Coloured Man* (New York, 1986 [1912]), 190, 193.

2. Johnson, *The Autobiography,* 103–109; James Weldon Johnson, *Black Manhattan* (New York, 1968 [1930]), 75–77.

3. Johnson, *The Autobiography,* 89, 110, 89.

4. Johnson, *The Autobiography,* 196, 194, 197.

5. Johnson, *The Autobiography,* 194.

6. Johnson, *The Autobiography,* 211. On the importance of the independence of African-American economic identity, albeit in a different context, see Elizabeth Fox-Genovese and Eugene D. Genovese, "Poor Richard at Work in the Cotton

Notes

Fields," in their *Fruits of Merchant Capital: Slavery and Bourgeois Property in the Rise and Expansion of Capitalism* (New York, 1983), especially 105, 133. On artistic creativity and its basis in the economy of gifts see Lewis Hyde, *The Gift: Imagination and the Erotic Life of Property* (New York, 1983).

7. See, for example, Walter A. Wyckoff, *The Workers: An Experiment in Reality* (New York, 1899); Annie M. MacLean, "Two Weeks in Department Stores," *American Journal of Sociology*, 4 (May 1899), 721–741; Jack London, "South of the Slot," *Saturday Evening Post*, 181 (May 22, 1909), 3–4, 36–38.

8. On the logic of exchange see Marcel Mauss, *The Gift: Forms and Functions of Exchange in Archaic Societies*, trans. Ian Cunnison (New York, 1967 [1925]).

9. The connection is oblique, but I am building on the idea of Johan Huizinga that the origin of culture lies in play. *Homo Ludens: A Study of the Play Element in Culture*, trans. R.F.C. Hull (Boston, 1955 [1944]).

10. "Lottery Policy Gambling," *National Police Gazette*, October 4, 1844, 44; John Samuel Ezell, *Fortune's Merry Wheel: The Lottery in America* (Cambridge, Mass., 1960), 95, 189–190; Herbert Asbury, *Sucker's Progress: An Informal History of Gambling in America from the Colonies to Canfield* (New York, 1938), 72–106.

11. Ezell, *Fortune's Merry Wheel*, 17–18, 29–53. For lists of beneficiaries of lotteries see Job R. Tyson, *Brief Survey of the Great Extent and Evil Tendencies of the Lottery System as Existing in the United States* (Philadelphia, 1833), 6, and Thomas Doyle, *Five Years in a Lottery Office; or, An Exposition of the Lottery System in the United States* (Boston, 1841), 12. For an estimate on the frequency of lotteries see National Institute of Law Enforcement and Criminal Justice, *The Development of the Law of Gambling, 1776–1976* (Washington, D.C., 1977), 660–667, and Ezell, *Fortune's Merry Wheel*, 136. Keith Thomas traced the changing attitudes toward the use of lots in early modern Europe. "There were thus," he wrote, "three types of attitude to the use of lots. The first was to regard them as a readily available instrument for settling daily problems with God's aid; hence the extensive use of ordeals in medieval times. The second was the growing conviction that it was irreverent and sinful to invoke God's aid on every trivial occasion; hence the prohibitions of medieval canonists and . . . sweeping Tudor condemnations of 'lusory' lots . . . . The third stage brings us into the modern world, for it involved the denial that a lot was a divine providence at all; or rather the denial that it was any more providential than any other event." *Religion and the Decline of Magic* (New York, 1971), 122.

12. Ezell, *Fortune's Merry Wheel*, 20, 79–87, 97–100.

13. Arguments on the public interest in the means as well as the ends of finance were widespread. One witness concluded, for example, that it was pointless "to support public treasuries at the expense of public and private morality and happiness." *Lotteries Exposed; or, An Inquiry into the Consequences Attending Them in a General and Individual Point of View By a Foe to Deception* (Philadelphia, 1827), 18. See also Pennsylvania, House of Representatives, *Report of the Committee of the House of Representatives of Pennsylvania to whom were referred the message of the*

Governor and sundry memorials relating to the Abolition of Lotteries. Read February 10, 1832 by Mr. Dunlop, Chairman (Harrisburg, Pa., 1832), 35. On the social construction of reason see Martin Hollis and Edward J. Nell, *Rational Economic Man* (London, 1975), 51–54.

14. Ezell, *Fortune's Merry Wheel*, 209–211, 221.

15. Daniel Rogers, *Report of the Trial of Charles N. Baldwin for a Libel, in Publishing Charges of Fraud and Swindling against the Managers and Submanagers of the Medical Society Lottery* (New York, 1818); Doyle, *Five Years in a Lottery Office*, 14–16; Ezell, *Fortune's Merry Wheel*, 187–189.

16. Henrietta M. Larson, "S. & M. Allen—Lottery, Exchange, and Stock Brokerage," *Journal of Economic and Business History*, 3 (May 1931), 431n.

17. Viviana Zelizer, *Morals and Markets: The Development of Life Insurance in the United States* (New York, 1979), xiii, 73–78. On benefits that did not run back to poor communities, see Tyson, *Brief Survey*, 87.

18. John Pintard, *Letters from John Pintard to His Daughter Eliza Noel Pintard Davidson, 1816–1833* (New York, 1940), 1:153–154, 173–174, 3:1; on his own successful lottery speculations see 1:88–89.

19. Tyson, *Brief Survey*, 85–86. On revelations of corruption see Doyle, *Five Years in a Lottery Office*, 22–26; on the folly of the masses see *Lotteries Exposed*, 13, 20, 22–23; on the rise of common arithmetic and its importance for early nineteenth-century constructions of democracy, commerce, and gender see Patricia Cline Cohen, *A Calculating People: The Spread of Numeracy in Early America* (Chicago, 1982), 116–149.

20. Doyle, *Five Years in a Lottery Office*, 18, 43; Tyson, *Brief Survey*, 10, 23; Thomas Man, *Picture of a Factory Village: To which are annexed, remarks on lotteries. By Sui Generis* (Providence, R.I., 1833), 119.

21. *Lotteries Exposed*, 7. On the limits of economic rationality and market incentives see Eric Foner, *Reconstruction: America's Unfinished Revolution, 1863–1877* (New York, 1988), 132–133.

22. Tyson, *Brief Survey*, 85; *Lotteries Exposed*, 9.

23. Eric Foner, *Free Soil, Free Labor, Free Men: The Ideology of the Republican Party before the Civil War* (New York, 1970), 11–18, 25; Daniel T. Rodgers, *The Work Ethic in Industrial America, 1850–1920* (Chicago, 1974), 223–224. Idleness had a rich history long before the nineteenth century. "If it is true," Michel Foucault wrote, "that labor is not inscribed among the laws of nature, it is enveloped in the order of the fallen world. This is why idleness is rebellion—the worst form of all, in a sense: it waits for nature to be generous as in the innocence of Eden, and seeks to constrain a Goodness to which man cannot lay claim since Adam. Pride was the sin of man before the Fall; but the sin of idleness is the supreme pride of man once he has fallen, the absurd pride of poverty." *Madness and Civilization: A History of Insanity in the Age of Reason*, trans. Richard Howard (New York, 1973), 56. I am deeply indebted here to Kristin Ross's inspired reading of Paul Lafargue's *Le droit à la paresse* in *The Emergence of Social Space:*

Notes

Rimbaud and the Paris Commune (Minneapolis, Minn., 1988), 47–74. Laziness might be read as oppositional culture. As she put it, it is "the antibourgeois value par excellence." 53.

24. Tyson, *Brief Survey*, 12, 67, 72; see also *Lotteries Exposed*, 5.

25. Doyle, *Five Years in a Lottery Office*, 38; Job R. Tyson, *The Lottery System in the United States* (Philadelphia, 1837), 99.

26. Tyson, *The Lottery System*, 69; Tyson, *Brief Survey*, 33–36, 46. The religious reformer J. R. McDowell gave Tyson's position sentimental form in his novel, *Henry Wallace; or, The Victim of Lottery Gambling. A Moral Tale* (New York, 1832). A prize of $20,000 "seal[ed] the fate of poor Henry." Lottery dealers then swindled him out of it and lured him away from his upstanding Scottish family in New York. He followed the dealers to Havana to recover his money but they stabbed the poor boy when he tried to escape in a crowd of Catholics coming out of High Mass. McDowell concluded with the hope that his text would awaken the public mind against the lottery and that with heightened public sentiment the "Babel of moral corruption shall be prostrate, and the language of its builders utterly confounded." Pp. 25, 108.

27. George Brewster, *An Oration on the Evils of Lotteries* (Brooklyn, N.Y., 1828), 18.

28. *Lotteries Exposed*, 5, 8; Man, *Picture of a Factory Village*, 136.

29. Tyson, *Brief Survey*, 101.

30. Man, *Picture of a Factory Village*, 124–125.

31. George Gordon, *Lecture Before the Boston Young Men's Society on the subject of Lotteries, March 12, 1833* (Boston, 1833), 38, 39, 40.

32. Tyson, *Brief Survey*, 36; Brewster, *An Oration*, 12; and *Lotteries Exposed*, 4, 19, 10. Doyle also described exhausted speculators. See *Five Years in a Lottery Office*, 31. On the representation of desire and visual pleasures of the streets see Blumin, *The Emergence of the Middle Class*, 98, and for a discussion of a later period Kathy Peiss, *Cheap Amusements: Working Women and Leisure in Turn-of-the-Century New York* (Philadelphia, 1986), 56–87. For warnings on dangerous street seductions, see [Henry William Herbert], *The Tricks and Traps of New York City* (Boston, 1857).

33. *Lotteries Exposed*, 20; Tyson, *Brief Survey*, 36, 22; see also Doyle, *Five Years in a Lottery Office*, 38.

34. Tyson, *Brief Survey*, 11; Doyle, *Five Years in a Lottery Office*, 29.

35. J. A. Powers, *The Lottery Exterminator containing an Exposition of the Enormous Frauds incident to the modern system of Lottery Gaming with simple methods of detecting them; frauds and artifices of managers and vendors; plain methods of analyzing schemes, of calculating the number of tickets, the number of blanks, &c. comprising also. Remarks on the Progress of Lottery Gaming in the United States; moral and political effects of the system* (New York, 1842), 6; see also Brewster, *An Oration on the Evils of Lotteries*, 8. Lottery adventurers and policy players were often represented as a "swarm," and following Kristin Ross, such figures link bettors closely to anarchic powers of desire. "The greatest danger to the 'friends of order,' " she has written,

"is not in the masses; it is in their decomposition . . ., the swarm." *The Emergence of Social Space*, 20; see also 100–125.

36. Promotional Letters from Emory & Co. (n.d.) and Colvin & Co. (April 1853) in Bella C. Landauer Collection, New-York Historical Society. On occasion fortune crept back into promotional letters. A letter produced by J. Marshall & Co. (May 14, 1860) was printed on a letterhead illustrated with Dame Fortune lying amid coins spilling from a cornucopia, and in March 1861 Smallwood & Co. introduced readers to "Old Dame Fortune." But in October 1864 Egerton Bros., calling themselves "Egerton Bros. Lucky Office," sold lottery tickets under an engraving of farmers loading an abundant hay crop.

37. The greatest of the nineteenth-century lotteries was the famous Louisiana lottery, conceived in the aftermath of the Civil War and running with state charter until 1895. In the 1890s opponents constructed opposition along different lines from those of their ancestors in the 1830s. They worried more about the power and profits of managers than the superstition and idleness of bettors. They attacked the lottery for its undue influence, for its advertisements in newspapers throughout the nation, and for its ability, therefore, to raise money from people who had never set foot in Louisiana. Its opponents succeeded in labeling it a corrupt and immoral monopoly. See Ezell, *Fortune's Merry Wheel*, 242–268; G. W. McGinty, "The Louisiana Lottery Company," *Southwestern Social Science Quarterly*, 20 (March 1940), 329–348.

38. Tyson, *Brief Survey*, 50–59. Tyson's list of unfortunate winners was reprinted by Gordon, *Lecture Before the Boston Young Men's Society*, 56–62, and again in Tyson, *The Lottery System*, 69–79. See also Powers, *The Lottery Exterminator*, 16; *Lotteries Exposed*, 8.

39. Michael P. Johnson and James L. Roark, *Black Masters: A Free Family of Color in the Old South* (New York, 1984), 37–42; Eugene D. Genovese, *Roll, Jordan, Roll: The World the Slaves Made* (New York, 1976), 593–597. On the Charleston lottery to support work on East Bay Street see Ezell, *Fortune's Merry Wheel*, 111–112. On the role of conjure in slave insurrections see Albert J. Raboteau, *Slave Religion: The "Invisible Institution" in the Antebellum South* (New York, 1978), 283–284, 370–371n.

40. When today's lottery millionaires insist they will keep their jobs, however dull, they seem to be trying to quiet the doubts about idleness we may have inherited from our older moral economy. Could we tolerate a lottery that openly promoted idleness? On the racist assertions about the work ethic see Gerald David Jaynes, *Branches without Roots: Genesis of the Black Working Class in the American South, 1862–1882* (New York, 1986), 58–61, and Foner, *Reconstruction*, 124–175. Well-known examples of the power of literacy can be found in Frederick Douglass, *My Bondage and My Freedom*, ed. William L. Andrews (Urbana, Ill., 1987 [New York, 1855]), 96–102; on perceived dangers of slaves learning to calculate and working as clerks see J. H. Harmon, Jr., Arnett G. Lindsay, and Carter G. Woodson, *The Negro as a Business Man* (College Park, Md., 1969 [1929]), 1.

41. George Fitzhugh, "Freedmen and Free Men," *DeBow's Review*, 1 (June

Notes

1866), 416–417. Discussions of the freed people's constructions of freedom inform much of Eric Foner's recent work. See his essays on the Caribbean and South Carolina collected in *Nothing but Freedom: Emancipation and Its Legacy* (Baton Rouge, La., 1983).

42. Genovese, *Roll, Jordan, Roll*, 285–324; see also Roger L. Ransom and Richard Sutch, *One Kind of Freedom: The Economic Consequences of Emancipation* (New York, 1977), 19–22; Ransom and Sutch entered the lists against Robert W. Fogel and Stanley L. Engerman's claims to have discovered a Protestant work ethic in slave communities. *Time on the Cross*, 2 vols. (Boston, 1974).

43. Jaynes, *Branches without Roots*, 71.

44. "The South as It Is," *Nation*, December 25, 1865, 779. The most thorough study of the Freedman's Bank is Carl R. Osthaus's *Freedmen, Philanthropy, and Fraud: A History of the Freedman's Savings Bank* (Urbana, Ill., 1976), 2.

45. U.S. Congress, House of Representatives, *Freedman's Bank*, House Report No. 502, 44th Cong., 1st sess., 1876, i–ii; Osthaus, *Freedmen, Philanthropy, and Fraud*, 2–8; on Alvord see Osthaus, 12–14. See also Abram L. Harris, *The Negro as Capitalist: A Study of Banking and Business among American Negroes* (New York, 1969 [1936]), 32.

46. Osthaus, *Freedmen, Philanthropy, and Fraud*, 44; Walter L. Fleming, *The Freedmen's Savings Bank: A Chapter in the Economic History of the Negro Race* (Westport, Conn., 1970 [1927]), 35–44.

47. Frederick Douglass, *Life and Times of Frederick Douglass Written by Himself* (London, 1969 [New York, 1892]), 401; on his stint as president see *Life and Times*, 400–405 and his testimony before the Bruce Committee in U.S. Congress, Senate, *Report of the Select Committee to Investigate the Freedman's Savings and Trust Company*. Senate Report No. 440, 46th Cong., 2d sess., 1880, 236–241, Appendix, 42–46.

48. Although there is little overt discussion of suffrage in the literature surrounding the Freedman's Savings Bank, clearly white property owners perceived a relationship between the achievement of economic rationality, taught by careful accumulation, and earning the right to vote. Joyce Appleby argued for an earlier period that a belief in "universal" "self-interest" which "gave to all men the capacity for rational decisions directed to personal ends" stood behind the Republicans' extension of suffrage to white males, regardless of property holdings. *Capitalism and a New Social Order: The Republican Vision of the 1790s* (New York, 1984), 97, 101. It is impossible to argue that prosperity would have provided a defense against the limitations imposed on black suffrage, but steady accumulations by freedpeople deposited in a prosperous public institution would have provided rich evidence of the behavior whites dubbed economic rationality. Writing in the beginning of the twentieth century Booker T. Washington asserted that black banks opened in Virginia in the 1890s had all "been started since the passage of new suffrage laws requiring Negro voters in Virginia to be property owners, or to be educated, or to be war veterans." And this is in spite of the fact that "members of the Legislature looked upon a Negro bank as a joke, and granted

the charter in a spirit of fun, never expecting to see a real Negro savings institution in operation in Virginia." *The Story of the Negro: The Rise of the Race from Slavery* (New York, 1909), 2:215–216.

49. A black paper in New Orleans, *The Louisianan,* advertised the bank as an "institution which gives colored men who know how to do business the chance to be useful; it is a good school for worthy, but inexperienced colored men to learn something of financiering; while on the other hand it helps our race to lay by something for a rainy day." In Osthaus, *Freedmen, Philanthropy, and Fraud,* 48–49, 79. See also Foner, *Reconstruction,* 97, and Fleming, *The Freedmen's Savings Bank,* 145.

50. "The Amendment of 1870" and "Act of June 20, 1874," reprinted in Fleming, *The Freedmen's Savings Bank,* 136–137.

51. W.E.B. Du Bois, *Souls of Black Folk* (New York, 1969 [1903]), 75. For other assessments of the bank and the meaning of its collapse see W. E. B. Du Bois, *Black Reconstruction in America* (New York, 1962 [1935]), 599–600; and Washington, *The Story of the Negro,* 211–214.

52. Quoted in Fleming, *The Freedmen's Savings Bank,* 159–160.

53. Osthaus, *Freedmen, Philanthropy, and Fraud,* 52–53; Martin Abbott, *The Freedmen's Bureau in South Carolina, 1865–1872* (Chapel Hill, N.C., 1967), 111.

54. Samples of the literature produced by the Freedman's Savings Bank are reprinted in Fleming, *The Freedmen's Savings Bank,* 144–150.

55. Fleming, *The Freedmen's Savings Bank,* 147. That black communities saved with their own interests and intentions in mind is clear in saving associations and burial societies that were part of fraternal orders. Savings institutions begun after the collapse of the Freedman's Savings Bank most often had their origins in fraternal societies. Washington, *The Story of the Negro,* 215.

56. From "A Few Words, Colored People" (1867), in Fleming, *The Freedmen's Savings Bank,* 147–148.

57. *Freedman's Bank,* House Report No. 502, vi, viii.

58. Minutes of the Agency Committee, Book A, August 12, 1869, 119. Freedman's Savings and Trust Co., National Archives, Record Group 101, in Osthaus, *Freedmen, Philanthropy, and Fraud,* 133.

59. Douglass, *Life and Times,* 401.

60. U.S. Congress, *Freedman's Bank,* House Report No. 502, 93.

61. Harris, *The Negro as Capitalist,* 177.

62. Quoted in Junius B. Wood, *The Negro in Chicago: How He and His Race Kindred Came to Dwell in Great Numbers in a Northern City; How He Lives and Works; His Successes and Failures; His Political Outlook* (Chicago, 1916), 28.

63. Charles White, *De Witt's Ethiopian and Comic Drama: The Policy Players; an Ethiopian Sketch in one Scene* (New York, 1847), 4. Ralph Ellison suggested something similar when the Invisible Man was given a name and hailed on the streets as "Rinehart, the runner." *Invisible Man* (New York, 1972 [1947]), 468–501. Richard Wright included a detailed description of policy in *Lawd Today* (Boston, 1986 [1963]), 41–48.

Notes

64. Mauss, *The Gift,* and Georges Bataille, "The Notion of Expenditure," in *Visions of Excess: Selected Writings, 1927–1939,* ed. and trans. Allan Stoekl (Minneapolis, Minn., 1985), 116–129; Thorstein Veblen, *The Theory of the Leisure Class: An Economic Study of Institutions* (New York, 1953 [1899]), 78–80; Raboteau, *Slave Religion,* 3–42; Lawrence W. Levine, *Black Culture and Black Consciousness: Afro-American Folk Thought from Slavery to Freedom* (New York, 1977), 3–80.

65. *National Police Gazette,* October 4, 1845, 44.

66. *National Police Gazette,* October 4, 1845, 44; October 11, 1845, 54; May 9, 1846, 301; May 30, 1846, 324.

67. *National Police Gazette,* October 11, 1845, 54.

68. Doyle, *Five Years in a Lottery Office,* 45–46.

69. *New York Times,* April 26, 1856.

70. *New York Times,* April 26, 1856. James D. McCabe wrote in 1879, "The negroes are not the only purchasers of [dream books]. Even men accounted 'shrewd' on Wall Street are among the number. Indeed Wall Street furnishes some of the most noted policy players in the city." *Lights and Shadows of New York Life* (Philadelphia, 1879), 729.

71. W. E. B. Du Bois, *The Philadelphia Negro: A Social Study* (New York, 1899), 310–311, 319, 265–266.

72. In the 1870s the *New York Times* often reported the arrests of individual policy dealers and raids on policy shops. See, for example, March 13, 1873; March 19, 1873; March 20, 1873; December 16, 1873; December 27, 1873; and December 28, 1873. Asbury, *Sucker's Progress,* 88–105.

73. James F. Richardson, *The New York Police: Colonial Times to 1901* (New York, 1970), 240, 236–242.

74. New York State, Senate [Lexow Commission], *Report and Proceedings of the Senate Committee appointed to investigate the Police Department of the City of New York* (Albany, N.Y., 1895), 3243.

75. For descriptions of New York's "policy kings" see Asbury, *Sucker's Progress,* 88–105. The best description of how policy operated is in [Lexow Commission], *Report and Proceedings,* 3134–3136, 3235–3257.

76. [Lexow Commission,], *Report and Proceedings,* 2416, 3246. Patricia Cline Cohen argued that "quantification as a method for ordering reality was born in an era marked by disorder and sometimes by outright chaos." *A Calculating People,* 45. On the late nineteenth-century search for certainty see Edward C. Kirkland, *Dream and Thought in the Business Community, 1860–1900* (Ithaca, N.Y., 1956), 17, 116; or more generally Robert H. Wiebe, *The Search for Order, 1877–1920* (New York, 1967).

77. [Lexow Commission], *Report and Proceedings,* 3246. Another witness told them, "Everybody has a dream and next morning they come in and tell them to the policy writer, and the policy writer gives then a gig for it." If the writer should be at a loss "there is a book for it; the dream-book, that tells you what the dreams are." Pp. 2417–2420. In 1827 the "Foe to Deception" had found lottery bettors following their dreams, but they dreamed numbers, not narratives to be

reinterpreted as numbers: "Perhaps he is . . . endeavouring to obtain a certain number, which himself, or a relation, or some other farsighted being has had a most singular dream about, and all the wild and formless ideas of a superstitious imagination are called in to aid him in the belief that he is very shortly to become the independent lord of thousands; and already has he formed some very laudable projects for rewarding the kind dreamer for his fortunate prescience." *Lotteries Exposed*, 6. In 1841 Doyle had also found a lottery broker, involved in a scam, who offered as his excuse for backing a certain number "that he had dreamed twice of that number during the preceding night." *Five Years in a Lottery Office*, 16. By the end of the century it was no longer necessary to dream precise numerical figures.

78. Harry B. Weiss, "Oneirocritica Americana," *Bulletin of the New York Public Library*, 48 (June 1944), 519–539; S.R.F. Price, "The Future of Dreams: From Freud to Artemidorus," *Past and Present*, 113 (November 1986), 13, 32. In the early part of the nineteenth century Charles Mackay had found the demand in England and France for "dream-books, and other trash of the same kind" "quite astonishing." "It is stated on the authority of one who is curious in these matters, that there is a demand for these works, which are sold at sums varying from a penny to sixpence, chiefly to servant girls and imperfectly-educated people, all over the country of upwards of eleven thousand annually; and that at no period during the last thirty years has the average number sold been less than this. The total number during this period would thus amount to 330,000." *Memoirs of Extraordinary Popular Delusions and the Madness of Crowds* (London, 1841), 3:268–269n. Thomas, *Religion and the Decline of Magic*, 129–130. For a survey of American interpretations see Merle Curti, "The American Exploration of Dreams and Dreamers," *Journal of the History of Ideas*, 27 (1966), 391–416; and on the prevalence of books on astrology and persistence of magical beliefs in eighteenth-century America see Jon Butler, "Magic, Astrology, and the Early American Religious Heritage, 1600–1760," *American Historical Review*, 84 (April 1979), 317–346. Like most oracles, dream interpretations, right or wrong, never challenged the system; one consulted another book, a rival oracle. See E. E. Evans-Pritchard, *Witchcraft, Oracles and Magic among the Azande* (Oxford, 1937), 355; and Robin Horton, "African Thought and Western Science," in Bryan R. Wilson, ed., *Rationality* (Oxford, 1979), 162–163.

79. Albert Raboteau explained conjure as "a theory which made sense of the mysterious and inexplicable occurrences of life." It "was a method of control: first, the control which comes from knowledge—being able to explain crucial phenomena, such as illness, misfortune and evil; and second, the control which comes from the capacity to act effectively . . . ; third, a means of control over the future through reading the 'signs'; fourth, an aid to social control because it supplied a system whereby conflict, otherwise stifled, could be aired." *Slave Religion*, 276, 286.

80. Raboteau, *Slave Religion*, 282–284. On urban fortunetellers, see Philander Doesticks [Mortimer Thomson], *The Witches of New York* (New York, 1858).

Notes

Newbell Niles Puckett has discussed traditional interpretations of dream content in *Folk Beliefs of the Southern Negro* (Chapel Hill, N.C., 1926), 496–505. The ideal dime-novel incarnation of the Mississippi River gambler, Fred Henning, better known as "Flush Fred," was one of many "superstitious" white men to consult "Aunt Cynthy, the voodoo Queen." Edward Willett, *Flush Fred, the Mississippi Sport; or, Tough Times in Tennessee* (New York, 1884), 6. See *Old Aunt Dinah's Policy Player's Sure Guide to Lucky Dreams and Lucky Numbers* (Baltimore, n.d.); Uriah Konje, *The Lucky Star Dream Book* (White Plains, N.Y., 1928); *Gypsy Witch Dream Book and Policy Player's Guide* (Chicago, 1903); *Old Gypsy Madge's Fortune Teller and Witches Key to Lucky Dreams* (Baltimore, 1889); *Aunt Sally's Policy-Player's Dream Book and Wheel of Fortune* (New York, 1889). Lawrence Levine has a powerful reading of superstition and its importance for the powers of interpretation which helped maintain sanity in slave communities. *Black Culture and Black Consciousness*, 56–59.

81. Dream books designed as promotions include *Egyptian Dream Book,* offered "Compliments of Dr. V. M. Pierce, Pres. Invalids Hotel, Buffalo, N.Y." [n.d.]. Pierce also gave out *Dream Book Bridal Superstitions.* Later, in the mid 1930s, Dr. Kilmer & Co., Binghamton, N.Y., used a *Swamp-Root Almanac Dream Book* (presented on the cover by a beautiful young Indian maiden and by Indians portraying the signs of the zodiac) to sell his "Diuretic to the Kidneys." George Monroe offered Irish interpretations tied in with his role in the "musical farce comedy" *Widow Dooley's Dream. Widow Dooley's Dream book compiled Geo. W. Monroe.* In the 1850s Wm. H. Murphy, a printer and publisher in New York, promoted himself with *The Gipsy Dream Book* and *Old Aunt Dinah's Policy Dream Book.* White couples grace the cover of *Lucky Number Policy Player's Dream Book Including Napoleon's Oraculum.*

82. Levine, *Black Culture and Black Consciousness,* 59. For a discussion of the rationality of the eighteenth century and its limits as an explanatory force see Robert Darnton, *Mesmerism and the End of the Enlightenment in France* (Cambridge, Mass., 1968), 83, 107–127.

83. To return to *Invisible Man:* " 'Yes, these old folks had a dream book, but the pages went blank and it failed to give them the number. It was called the Seeing Eye, The Great Constitutional Dream Book, The Secrets of Africa, The Wisdom of Egypt—but the eye was blind, it lost its luster. It's all cataracted like a cross-eyed carpenter and it doesn't saw straight. All we have is the Bible and this Law here rules that out. So where do we go? Where do we go from here, without a pot—' " Ellison, *Invisible Man,* 273.

84. *Gypsy Witch Dream Book and Policy Player's Guide,* 4–5.

85. Carleton B. Case, ed., *Gypsy Witch Dream Book and Policy Players Guide by the Queen of the Romanies* (Chicago, 1930), 10.

86. J. H. Green, *Report on Gambling in New York* (New York, 1851), 45. Song and Toy Book Depot, an arm of "Wm. H. Murphy, Printer, Publisher, Bookseller and Stationer" of 384 Pearl Street, published a version of *Old Aunt Dinah's Policy Dream Book* (New York, n.d.) illustrated with woodcuts of thick-

lipped black figures. The book opened with two coy poses of Aunt Dinah and closed with two African-American men in the fields of a plantation, one leaning on a shovel but in animated conversation with a wise-looking character smoking a pipe. The book mocked the African-American tradition in the interpretation of dreams, presenting it as just another aspect of minstrelsy. The Franklin Book Store, located at the same address on Pearl Street, published *The Gipsy Dream Book; or, The Science of Foretelling Future Events by Dreams* in 1854. The cover is illustrated with a sleeping woman surrounded by dream images. These include three mysterious vessels in a box, a dove with an olive branch, a three-windowed coach, a soldier gesturing with an open hand, and a very swarthy woman holding a cup and pointing a menacing dagger at the sleeper. The alphabetical list of dreams contains no numbers, and interpretations most often concern business ventures, the fate of love and friendship, and the outcome of lawsuits.

87. The reduction of dreams to numbers was complete in the *Harlem Pete Dream Book* (Philadelphia, 1949), which was nothing but a list of words matched with numbers. The cover was illustrated with a turbaned snake charmer and a serene cobra. A to Z Dale Publications, Inc., also produced "Three Figures Interpretation" by "Rajah Rabo" and "Policy Pete."

88. *Policy Player's Lucky Number Dream Book and Napoleon's Oraculum* (n.p., n.d.), 24.

89. James Monroe, *The Dream Investigator and Oneirocritica* (Peoria, Ill., 1884), 8, 12–13, 156, 311, 256.

90. Monroe, *The Dream Investigator*, 222.

91. *Lucky Number Policy Player's Dream Book including Napolean's Oraculum* (n.p., n.d.), 115, 23; *Gypsy Witch Dream Book and Policy Player's Guide*, 120. *Aunt Sally's Policy-Players' Book*, 23.

92. *Old Aunt Dinah's Policy Player's Sure Guide;* Professor de Herbert, *The Success Dream Book* (White Plains, N.Y., 1931); Knoje, *The Lucky Star Dream Book.*

93. Doyle, *Five Years in a Lottery Office*, 45–46. Freud acknowledged the popular superstitions attached to dreams of number, but for him calculations, another of the "peculiar or unusual modes of representation in dreams," were versions of the dream work of analysis. Policy players were content to arrive at the numbers with which Freud obviously began. See "Calculations in Dreams," in *The Interpretation of Dreams*, trans. James Strachey (New York, 1965 [1900]), 440, 449–461.

94. Daniel Calhoun, *The Intelligence of a People* (Princeton, N.J., 1973), 342.

95. Brewster, *An Oration on the Evils of Lotteries*, 19–20; A. O. Stansbury, "Considerations on the Lawfulness of Lotteries and the Propriety of Christians Holding Tickets. Addressed to the Assistant New-York Missionary Society, at a Meeting January 11, 1813" (New York, 1813), 6–7.

96. Veblen, *The Theory of the Leisure Class*, 184–193, 195.

97. Veblen, *The Theory of the Leisure Class*, 210.

98. Clemens J. France, "The Gambling Impulse," *American Journal of Psychol-*

ogy, 12 (1902), 397. William I. Thomas argued that an interest in precarious situations was bred in all normal persons. One had, however, to "discriminate between its applications." "The Gambling Instinct," *American Journal of Sociology*, 6 (1901), 750–763. There were those who used the language of evolution to argue against gambling. Gambling, one minister argued, had to be "treated quite apart from the question of religion, regarded simply as one of the actions which tend to the disadvantage of the community in the struggle for existence, which discredit industry, promote poverty and foster vice." Henry A. Stimson, *A Comfort to Sodom: A Sermon on Gambling Preached at Union Congregational Church* (Worcester, Mass., 1883), 7.

99. *Harlem Pete Dream Book* (Philadelphia, 1949), 2.

Chapter 4. *Devils in Their Gambling Hells*

1. *Fictitious Dealing in Agricultural Products*, U.S. Congress, House Committee on Agriculture, 52nd Cong., 3d sess. (Washington, D.C., 1892), 306–307.

2. *Fictitious Dealing*, 308, 332. A St. Louis pork merchant who supported the agrarian criticism of the commodities exchanges told the story of two men who had been broken by their encounters with this world of "unmitigated" evil and reminded his congressional audience that "the devil always tolls a fellow." *Fictitious Dealing*, 146–147. A cotton farmer from Russellville, Arkansas, complained that the "men who are engaged in this business . . . argue that options dealing enhances values, though it would be, in my mind, as reasonable and as true to assert that a probation in hell would fit a man for heaven." *Fictitious Dealing*, 319. With more literary grace, but to the same political ends, Henry Demarest Lloyd used Dante's entrance into hell to describe the threshold of the exchanges. See "Making Bread Dear," *North American Review*, 137 (1883), 131–132. Lloyd also described the psyche of the railroad shareholder possessed by devils. "He has become within himself the battle-ground of a troop of warring devils of selfishness; his selfishness as a stockholder clutched at the throat by his selfishness as a parasite, in some 'inside deal,' feeding on the stockholder; some rebate arrangement, fast-freight line, sleeping-car company, or what not. And, as like as not, upon this one's back is another devil of depredation from some inner ring within a ring. Torn at the vitals, the enlightened swinishness of our *leit-motif* is hastening to throw itself into the sea." *Wealth against Commonwealth* (New York, 1895), 510.

3. Cedric B. Cowing, *Populists, Plungers, and Progressives: A Social History of Stock and Commodity Speculation, 1890–1936* (Princeton, N.J., 1965), 5–8.

4. Henry Crosby Emery, *Speculation on the Stock and Produce Exchanges of the United States* (New York, 1896), 38–42; Jonathan Lurie, *The Chicago Board of Trade, 1859–1905: The Dynamics of Self-Regulation* (Urbana, Ill., 1979), 53–54; Henrietta M. Larson, *The Wheat Market and the Farmer in Minnesota, 1858–1900* (New York, 1926); Thorstein Veblen, "The Price of Wheat since 1867," *Journal*

of Political Economy, I (1893), 68–103; Edward W. Bemis, "The Discontent of the Farmer," *Journal of Political Economy,* I (1893), 193–213; C. Wood Davis, "Why the Farmer Is not Prosperous," *The Forum,* 9 (1890), 221–241; see also Richard Hofstadter, *The Age of Reform* (New York, 1955), 23–130. Howard Horwitz found in these same debates discussions of value which extended from markets to literature; see his excellent essay " 'To Find the Value of X': *The Pit* as a Renunciation of Romance," in Eric J. Sundquist, ed., *American Realism: New Essays* (Baltimore, Md., 1982), 215–237.

5. Michael T. Taussig, *The Devil and Commodity Fetishism in South America* (Chapel Hill, N.C., 1980), 97, 37, 13–38; see also George M. Foster, "Treasure Tales, and the Image of a Static Economy in a Mexican Peasant Community," *Journal of American Folklore,* 77 (January–March 1964), 39–44. On the cultural struggle implicit within the language of agrarian reform see Lawrence Goodwyn, *Democratic Promise: The Populist Moment in America* (New York, 1976), 359–367; on the importance of maintaining the connection between religious language and economic ends see 666–667; on religious imagery in the rhetoric of southern Populists see Bruce Palmer, *"Man over Money": The Southern Populist Critique of Capitalism* (Chapel Hill, N.C., 1980), 22–26.

6. Taussig, *The Devil and Commodity Fetishism,* 118, 135.

7. This sort of "meta-fetishization" has provoked considerable theoretical interest. See, for example, Arjun Appadurai, *The Social Life of Things* (Cambridge, 1986), 48–51; Jean Baudrillard, *The Mirror of Production,* trans. Mark Poster (St. Louis, Mo., 1975), and Baudrillard, *For a Critique of the Political Economy of the Sign,* trans. Charles Levin (St. Louis, Mo., 1981), 88–101.

8. Taussig, *The Devil and Commodity Fetishism,* 38.

9. Jacques Le Goff, *Your Money or Your Life: Economy and Religion in the Middle Ages,* trans. Patricia Ranum (New York, 1988), 93.

10. Le Goff, *Your Money or Your Life,* 70–74. It also obviously opened the profession of moneylending to Christians. See Benjamin Nelson, *The Idea of Usury: From Tribal Brotherhood to Universal Otherhood* (Chicago, 1969), 73–108. The long association perhaps explains what Richard Hofstadter called the "slight current of anti-Semitism" in Populist rhetoric; see his *The Age of Reform,* 77, 78–79.

11. See Harry Braverman, *Labor and Monopoly Capital: The Degradation of Work in the Twentieth Century* (New York, 1974), 411–412. I do not intend to reduce the Populist protests to a struggle over meaning. I argue rather that the struggle over definitions of exactly what was right, moral, and just was yet another manifestation of the political and economic struggles that lay behind farmers' grievances. Daniel Rodgers found both radicals and conservatives sharing the language of work and idleness, but using it to different ends. *The Work Ethic in Industrial America, 1850–1920* (Chicago, 1974), 225–232; he mentions the agrarian attack on short selling on 230.

12. Taussig, *The Devil and Commodity Fetishism,* 121; Walter Benn Michaels, "Dreiser's *Financier:* The Man of Business as a Man of Letters," in Sundquist, ed.,

American Realism, 281–284. See also Michaels, "The Gold Standard and the Logic of Naturalism," in his *The Gold Standard and the Logic of Naturalism* (Berkeley, Calif., 1987), 139–180, especially 177–180; Steven Knapp and Walter Benn Michaels, "Against Theory," *Critical Inquiry,* 8 (Summer 1982), 723–742; and Knapp and Michaels, "Against Theory 2: Hermeneutics and Deconstruction," *Critical Inquiry,* 14 (Autumn 1987), 49–68. Michaels's "new historicist" reading of the "logic of naturalism" and its relation to speculative markets, however luminous and playful, seems to warrant caution on the part of historians. Michaels's readings, substitutions, and transformations risk abandoning history in a hall of mirrors. However strong his sense of ties between the language of fiction and that of the market, his synchronous interplay of texts makes it hard to see how meaning itself might have been contested terrain. I have tried here to follow the language of farmers and producers back to efforts to resist transformations in their economic lives. That they failed or that language failed them does not mean they were exactly complicit in the triumph of speculative markets or that they were left with only the "terms of evaluation" provided by a prolific marketplace, as Michaels argues. The farmer's invocation of the devil suggests a more dialectical view of cultural criticism than Michaels allows, and I would argue that they tried to use the powers of contradiction to obstruct the advance of abstracted markets. By working within the political culture of Populism one can mark the farmers as dissenters without falling into the assumptions of "oppositional criticism" to which Michaels so strenuously objects. *The Gold Standard,* 18.

13. On the diabolical nature of money that reproduces itself see Le Goff, *Your Money or Your Life,* 18–29; see also Marc Shell, *Money, Language, and Thought: Literary and Philosophical Economies from the Medieval to the Modern Era* (Berkeley, Calif., 1982), 14. On wheat's relation to money see the opinion of Oliver Wendell Holmes, Jr., in *Board of Trade of the City of Chicago* v. *Christie Grain and Stock Company,* 198 U.S. 250 (1905).

14. Appadurai, *The Social Life of Things,* 50. For the most compelling discussion of the long and complicated history of the intellectual evolution of market culture see Jean-Christophe Agnew, *Worlds Apart: The Theater and the Market in Anglo-American Thought, 1550–1750* (New York, 1986).

15. Emery, *Speculation on the Stock and Produce Exchanges,* 98–101.

16. Henry Ward Beecher, *Seven Lectures to Young Men* (Indianapolis, Ind., 1844). See also Wm. Alcott, *The Young Man's Guide* (Boston, 1834); O. B. Frothingham, "The Ethics of Gambling," *North American Review,* 135 (1882), 162–174.

17. Sean Wilentz, *Chants Democratic: New York City and the Rise of the American Working Class, 1788–1850* (New York, 1984), 219; Irwin Unger, *The Greenback Era: A Social and Political History of American Finance, 1865–1879* (Princeton, N.J., 1964), 30–31; on side bets see Clifford Geertz, "Notes on the Balinese Cockfight," in his *The Interpretation of Cultures* (New York, 1973), 426–432. Bear speculators seemed to profit from human misery. Thomas Gibson described a scene on Wall

Street: "In the cholera scare of 1892, when the 'yellow flag' indicating cholera on board was shown outside the New York harbor, an excited bear rushed upon the floor of the Exchange, shouting 'Hurrah, hurrah, the cholera is here.' He was suspended." *The Pitfalls of Speculation* (New York, 1906), 38n.

18. *The Oxford English Dictionary* (New York, 1971), 2:2952; Adam Smith, *An Inquiry into the Nature and Causes of the Wealth of Nations* (London, 1880 [1776]), 1:11–12, 119.

19. Timothy Dwight, *Travels in New England* (New Haven, Conn., 1821), 1:218; *Tait's Magazine*, 1 (1834), 408. For Raymond Williams changes in the use of *"industry, democracy, class, art and culture"* in the last decades of the eighteenth century and in the first half of the nineteenth "bear witness to a general change in our characteristic ways of thinking about our common life: about the purposes which these institutions are designed to embody; and about the relations to these institutions and purposes of our activities in learning, education and the arts." During this period, he adds, speculator (financier), along with a number of other words, acquired modern meanings. *Culture and Society, 1780–1950* (New York, 1958), xi, xv.

20. Lydia Maria Child, *Letters from New York* (New York, 1849), 47–49.

21. Child, *Letters from New York*, 53, 111–112.

22. Hofstadter, *The Age of Reform*, 47, 24–33, 39–59. My reading of the farmers' discourse at the end of the century suggests that Hofstadter's description of the "dual character" of the American farmer—a " 'soft' side" based on the idea of the virtuous yeoman and a " 'hard' side" derived from the embrace of business methods—ignored more subtle nuances in farmers' conceptions of their relations to agricultural markets. They not only suffered from a decline in power relative to rhetorical descriptions of their worth, but they envisioned, as well, the development of marketing structures controlled by individuals whose interests were antithetical to their own. Agrarian views of speculation and the movement of goods on speculative markets were thus far from naive.

23. Wilentz, *Chants Democratic*, 92–94.

24. Steven Watts, *The Republic Reborn: War and the Making of Liberal America, 1790–1820* (Baltimore, Md., 1988), 220, 251; see also Karen Halttunen, *Confidence Men and Painted Women: A Study of Middle-Class Culture in America, 1830–1870* (New Haven, Conn., 1982), 16–18.

25. Wilentz, *Chants Democratic*, 102, 95; see also David Montgomery, "Labor and the Republic in Industrial America, 1860–1920," *Le Mouvement Social*, 110 (1980), 201–215.

26. Joyce Appleby, *Capitalism and a New Social Order: The Republican Vision of the 1790s* (New York, 1984), 31.

27. See Halttunen, *Confidence Men and Painted Women*, 8–10. For a complicated portrait of a gamblers' conspiracy to disrupt the election of 1844 see David Francis Bacon, *Mystery of Iniquity: A Passage of the Secret History of American Politics* (New York, 1845).

28. Allan Nevins, ed., *The Diary of Philip Hone, 1828–1851* (New York, 1927), 111, 180.

29. Thomas Gibson, *The Cycles of Speculation* (New York, 1909), 6.

30. Appleby, *Capitalism and a New Social Order*, 34–35; see also Gordon S. Wood, *The Creation of the American Republic, 1776–1788* (Chapel Hill, N.C., 1969), 52–114. There is a strong Weberian component to this argument, but in studying the rise of economic rationality I am trying to locate contests between rationality and nonrationality, as well as contests between the virtues constructed by the Protestant ethic and the vices on which those virtues were based. See Max Weber, *The Protestant Ethic and the Spirit of Capitalism*, trans. Talcott Parsons, (New York, 1958).

31. J. E. Crowley, *This Sheba, Self: The Conceptualization of Economic Life in Eighteenth-Century America* (Baltimore, Md., 1974).

32. William Harbutt Dawson, *The Unearned Increment; or, Reaping without Sowing* (London, 1910), 63–64, quoted in Robert P. Swierenga, "Land Speculation and Its Impact on American Economic Growth and Welfare: A Historiographic Review," *Western Historical Quarterly,* 8 (July 1977), 287–288.

33. Benjamin Horace Hibbard, *Public Land Policies,* quoted in Swierenga, "Land Speculation," 288.

34. Paul Wallace Gates, "The Role of the Land Speculator in Western Development," *Pennsylvania Magazine of History and Biography,* 66 (1942), 327, 331–332; for a classic statement of his argument see also "The Homestead Law in an Incongruous Land System," *American Historical Review,* 41 (July 1936), 652–681.

35. Gates, "The Role of the Land Speculator," 327.

36. Richard T. Ely, "Land Speculation," *Journal of Farm Economics,* 2 (July 1920), 121–135. See also William P. Yohe's recent "An Economic Appraisal of the Sub-Treasury Plan," in Goodwyn, *Democratic Promise,* 581.

37. See Allan G. Bogue and Margaret Beattie Bogue, " 'Profits' and the Frontier Land Speculator," *Journal of Economic History,* 17 (1957), 1–24. The Bogues criticized a number of historians who had argued that land speculators made little profit. With considerable moderation they concluded that one could not say with any certainty that frontier land speculation in the United States was either "generally well rewarded or generally unremunerative." See also James W. Silver, "Land Speculation Profits in the Chickasaw Cession," *Journal of Southern History,* 10 (February 1944), 84–92; Swierenga, "Land Speculation," 293–299.

38. Ray Allen Billington, "The Origin of the Land Speculator as a Frontier Type," *Agricultural History,* 19 (October 1945), 204–212.

39. On the political uses of the false dichotomy between speculators and settlers see Daniel Feller, *The Public Lands in Jacksonian Politics* (Madison, Wisc., 1984), 30–31, 195–198. The quotation is found on 197.

40. Swierenga, "Land Speculation," 302; Edward H. Rastatter, "Nineteenth-Century Public Land Policy: The Case for the Speculator," in *Essays in Nineteenth-Century Economic History: The Old Northwest,* ed. David C. Klingaman and Richard K. Vedder (Athens, Ohio, 1975), 135; see also Robert W. Fogel and Jack L.

Rutner, "The Efficiency Effects of Federal Land Policy, 1850–1900: A Report of Some Provisional Findings," *The Dimensions of Quantitative Research in History,* ed. William Aydelotte, Allan Bogue, and Robert Fogel (Princeton, N.J., 1972), 390–418.

41. Frank Norris, *The Pit: A Story of Chicago* (New York, 1903), 419; see also James H. Gannon, Jr., " 'Smith, Debtor': A Bucket Shop Idyll," *Everybody's Magazine,* 15 (September 1906), 358–364. On the importance of tangible reality to Norris see Michaels, "Dreiser's *Financier,*" 286; on Norris's confusion about short selling see Horwitz, " 'To Find the Value of X,' " 224, 229–230.

42. Frank Norris, "A Deal in Wheat," *Everybody's Magazine,* 11 (July 1902), 173–180.

43. W. G. Nichols, *Cold Facts about Bucket Shops* (Chicago, 1887), 4; *Fictitious Dealing,* 289, 271, 152.

44. C. C. Christie, "Bucket-Shop vs. Board of Trade," *Everybody's Magazine,* 15 (December 1906), 710.

45. Merrill A. Teague, "Bucket-Shop Sharks," pt. 1, *Everybody's Magazine,* 14 (June 1906), 726; *Fictitious Dealing,* 77–78.

46. John Philip Quinn, *Fools of Fortune; or, Gambling and Gamblers* (Chicago, 1890), 34–66, 578; Quinn, *Gambling and Gambling Devices* (Canton, Ohio, 1912), 3–24; Quinn, *19th Century Black Art; or, Gambling Exposed* (Chicago, 1891); Quinn, *The Highway to Hell* (Chicago, 1895); Quinn, *Why Gamblers Win* (New York, n.d.).

47. "The Race Track and Social Gambling," *New York Times,* May 22, 1893, 6; "No Chance with Gamblers," *New York Times,* June 6, 1892, 9.

48. "Evangelist Goff's Daughter Elopes," *New York Times,* Feb. 7, 1894, 5; "Will Forgive Elopers," *New York Times,* Feb. 8, 1894, 9; "Evangelist Quinn and Bride Return," *New York Times,* Feb. 9, 1894, 5.

49. Quinn, *Fools of Fortune,* 601. Reformed gamblers frequently compared the behavior of successful speculators to their own and used hypocrisy as a defense. See, for example, Mason Long, *The Life of Mason Long, the Converted Gambler* (Chicago, 1878), 133; and George Devol, *Forty Years a Gambler on the Mississippi* (Cincinnati, Ohio, 1887), 298.

50. Quinn, *Fools of Fortune,* 69.

51. "Statement of Dr. C. W. Macune, Representing the Farmer's National Alliance," in *Fictitious Dealing,* 254, 251. According to Lawrence Goodwyn, Macune "understood the nation's economy better than most Gilded Age economists"; see *Democratic Promise,* 562. By the spring of 1892, when he testified before Congress on the Hatch bill, Macune's influence in the National Farmers Alliance was already waning. He continued to edit the movement's national journal, but Alliance leadership had gone to William Lamb, L. L. Polk, and others who were directly committed to the People's Party. Less than two weeks after he testified in Washington, Macune would watch the Alliance move into third-party politics. For Goodwyn, Macune represents the abiding ironies of Populism. Macune, "the boldest single theorist of the agrarian revolt," devised the subtreasury plan and it

was his subtreasury plan that pushed agrarian reformers into a third party. But Macune himself remained deeply ambivalent about committing the movement to politics. He hesitated, wavered, and finally returned to the Democrats. He ended his career as a Methodist pastor working among the rural poor in Texas. Goodwyn concludes, "While he was an orthodox, even a reactionary social philosopher, and still a political traditionalist, C. W. Macune was an economic radical." His "sub-treasury system for the 'whole class' was one of the boldest and most imaginative economic ideas suggested in nineteenth-century America." *Democratic Promise*, 564, 149, 563, also 146–152, 232–243, 267–268, 562–564. See also Steven Hahn, *The Roots of Southern Populism: Yeoman Farmers and the Transformation of the Georgia Upcountry, 1850–1890* (New York, 1983), 73–84, 192, 282; on farmers as moral producers see Palmer, *"Man over Money,"* 15.

52. *Fictitious Dealing*, 199, 187–198. Bruce Palmer has argued that the emphasis on tangible reality along with a belief in the paramount importance of personal relations were the guiding principles of Southern Populist thought. See *"Man over Money,"* 3–5, 11.

53. On farmers, commerce, and capitalism see James A. Henretta, "Families and Farms: Mentalité in Pre-Industrial America," *William and Mary Quarterly*, 3d ser., 35 (January 1978), 3–32; Michael Merrill, "Cash Is Good to Eat: Self-Sufficiency and Exchange in the Rural Economy of the United States," *Radical History Review*, 3 (Winter 1977), 42–71; Ralph Lerner, "Commerce and Character: The Anglo-American as New-Model Man," *William and Mary Quarterly*, 3d ser., 36 (January 1979), 3–26; see also Hofstadter, *The Age of Reform*, 23–59. I am trying to draw a distinction here between farmers' participation in a commercial economy and the nature of their labor in the age of industrial capitalism; see Braverman, *Labor and Monopoly Capital*, 411–412.

54. Emery, *Speculation on the Stock and Produce Exchanges*, 219–221; the argument runs through Lurie, *The Chicago Board of Trade*. On the Hatch bill see also William G. Ferris, *The Grain Traders: The Story of the Chicago Board of Trade* (East Lansing, Mich., 1988), 89–93.

55. Charles W. Smith, *Commercial Gambling: The Principal Causes of Depression in Agriculture and Trade* (London, 1893), 8–10. Whether or not commodities speculators actually manipulated markets is beside the point. What troubled farmers was that markets could be manipulated and that it was often in a speculator's self-interest to do so.

56. *Fictitious Dealing*, 319–320, 276–277; Goodwyn, *Democratic Promise*, 114; Quinn, *Fools of Fortune*, 588.

57. Goodwyn, *Democratic Promise*, 126.

58. *Fictitious Dealing*, 249; "Ocala Demands," reprinted in John D. Hicks, ed., *The Populist Revolt: A History of the Farmers' Alliance and the People's Party* (Lincoln, Neb., 1961), 430–431. Except for a brief mention in his discussion of the Cleburne demands, Lawrence Goodwyn, the most astute chronicler of the politics and economics of Populism, largely ignored the problem of speculation in commodity futures. His summary of the Ocala demands lists "the abolition of the national

banking system, the substitution of legal tender treasury notes, an increase in circulating currency to a level of 'not less than $50 per capita,' establishment of the subtreasury plan, free and unlimited coinage of silver, a graduated income tax, removal of the protective tariff . . . , and direct election of United States Senators." He also notes that the alliance called for the "rigid regulation of public communication and transportation," but he left out the second plank on commodities speculation. *Democratic Promise*, 79–81, 230.

59. *Fictitious Dealing*, 261–262.

60. *Fictitious Dealing*, 250.

61. *Fictitious Dealing*, 254, 261. One of the most powerful indictments of society constructed on selfishness disguised as self-interest appears in the last chapters of Henry Demarest Lloyd's *Wealth against Commonwealth*, 494–536.

62. Goodwyn, *Democratic Promise*, 167.

63. See "Report of the Committee on the Monetary System," *National Economist*, 2 (Dec. 21, 1889), 216–217.

64. Harry Tracy, "The Sub-Treasury System," reprinted in James H. Davis, *A Political Revelation in which the Principles of this Government, the Teachings of its Founders, and the Issues of Today are Brought to a Fair and Just Comparison with each other, by means of a rigid analysis; a full and true description, and many happy illustrations* (Dallas, Tex., 1894), 351, 380.

65. The lines of this argument are contained in Hofstadter, *The Age of Reform*, 23–130; Hahn, *The Roots of Southern Populism*, especially 1–11, 170–203; and run through Goodwyn, *Democratic Promise*; and Palmer, "*Man over Money*"; see also Unger, *The Greenback Era*, 195–212.

66. "Omaha Platform, July 1892," reprinted in Hicks, *The Populist Revolt*, 439–444; see also Goodwyn, *Democratic Promise*, 354–358.

67. *Fictitious Dealing*, 293.

68. "Statement of Mr. H. H. Aldrich," *Fictitious Dealing*, 19–29.

69. *Fictitious Dealing*, 19, 297, 148, 312.

70. *Fictitious Dealing*, 190, 189.

71. Quoted in Goodwyn, *Democratic Promise*, 271; see also Clanton, *Kansas Populism*, 79.

72. *Workingman's Advocate* (Chicago), April 21, 1866, quoted in Walter T. K. Nugent, *Money and American Society*, 5; and in Goodwyn, *Democratic Promise*, 14.

73. Concord (N.C.) *Standard* in Salisbury (N.C.) *Watchman*, Oct. 29, 1891, cited in Palmer, "*Man over Money*," 105.

74. One witness introduced into the record a passage from a California paper. The writer used language that made explicit the connection between the debate over the reality of wheat and the currency question. "If legislation can stop selling of *fiat wheat* it is to be hoped that an adequate law will be passed. The gamblers who use bushels of wheat as counters in their game should be compelled to turn attention to other channels. If they were retired to Monte Carlo the country could well spare them." "Dealings in 'Wheat Futures,' " *Fictitious Dealing*, 54 (emphasis added). Jeffrey Williams has recently argued that futures markets are best under-

stood as analogous to money markets, not insurance. "Economists should approach firms' use of futures markets with the tools they have developed to study financial intermediation rather than the tools they have developed to study risk aversion." *The Economic Function of Futures Markets* (New York, 1986), 2.

75. Taussig, *The Devil and Commodity Fetishism*, 129–132; Eric Roll, *A History of Economic Thought* (London, 1973), 33.

76. For the significance of self-regulation see Lurie, *The Chicago Board of Trade;* on the incidental nature of speculative evil, Lurie quotes an editorial from the *Chicago Tribune,* April 1, 1890, 4, in *The Chicago Board of Trade,* 144–145.

77. James E. Boyle, *Speculation and the Chicago Board of Trade* (New York, 1920), 89.

78. Nichols, *Cold Facts,* 9.

79. John Hill, Jr., *The Gold Bricks of Speculation* (Chicago, 1904), 39; *The Oxford English Dictionary,* 1:288; Quinn, *Fools of Fortune,* 597; Charles H. Baker, *Life and Character of William Taylor Baker* (New York, 1908), 115–116. An Illinois statute of June 6, 1887, defined bucket shops as "places wherein is permitted the pretended buying and selling of grain, etc., without any intention of receiving and paying for the property so bought, or of delivering the property so sold"; cited in *Board of Trade of the City of Chicago* v. *Christie Grain and Stock Company,* 198 U.S. 246 (1904). See Merrill A. Teague, "Bucket-Shop Sharks," pt. 1: 731–735; pt. 2: 15 (July 1906), 33; Ferris, *The Grain Traders,* 117–118.

80. Lurie, *The Chicago Board of Trade,* 201.

81. Statement of the representative of the Minneapolis Exchange is reprinted in *Fictitious Dealing,* 280; see also a letter from Andrew Van Bibber in *Fictitious Dealing,* 306. Christie, "Bucket-Shop vs. Board of Trade," 707.

82. Nichols, *Cold Facts,* 7; Teague, "Bucket-Shop Sharks," pt. 1: 731–735; also pt. 2.

83. Boyle, *Speculation,* 90; Harry C. Vrooman, "Methods and Devices," in "Gambling and Speculation: A Symposium," *Arena,* 11 (February 1895), 421; Nichols, *Cold Facts,* 5; *Christie-Street Commission Co.* v. *Board of Trade and Western Union Telegraph Co.,* no. 20453, Circuit Court, Cook County, Ill., 1900, cited in Ferris, *The Grain Traders,* 123. In New York bucket shops traded in differences in stock prices rather than in prices for agricultural commodities. See James H. Gannon, " 'Smith, Debtor': A Bucket-Shop Idyll," *Everybody's Magazine,* 15 (September 1906), 359.

84. Nichols, *Cold Facts,* 6; Cowing, *Populists, Plungers, and Progressives,* 27–28; Lurie, *The Chicago Board of Trade,* 76–78, 159–160, 200; Teague, "Bucket-Shop Sharks," pt. 2:36; pt. 1:731; Quinn, *Fools of Fortune,* 584, 597; Hill, *Gold Bricks,* 21; Baker, *Life and Character of William Taylor Baker,* 115–116.

85. Patton Thomas, "The Bucket Shop in Speculation," *Munsey's Magazine,* 24 (October 1900), 68; Teague, "Bucket-Shop Sharks," pt. 2:43; Cowing, *Populists, Plungers, and Progressives,* 28; Vrooman, "Methods and Devices," 422.

86. Teague, "Bucket-Shop Sharks," pt. 2:34–35, 40; pt. 4; *Everybody's Magazine,* 15 (September 1906), 402; Hill, *Gold Bricks,* 43; Thomas, "The Bucket

Shop," 68. In his short story " 'Smith, Debtor': A Bucket-Shop Idyll" published in 1906, James H. Gannon describes a bucket shop ruined by an extended bull market but whose offices then filled with the "firm's friends" who played poker and fan-tan while resting their feet on the mahogany tables. Whenever someone appeared who might have been willing to buy the business the gamblers instantly transformed themselves into customers. They reverted to gambling once the prospect disappeared. Gannon's point was that the metamorphoses were facile transformations. See 359–360.

87. Nichols, *Cold Facts*, 4.

88. Thomas, "The Bucket Shop," 68–69; Nichols, *Cold Facts*, 4.

89. Nichols, *Cold Facts*, 2–5.

90. Rodgers, *The Work Ethic*, 27–28.

91. Michaels, "Dreiser's *Financier*," 287.

92. Hill, *Gold Bricks*, 45; Nichols, *Cold Facts*, 4–6.

93. Hill, *Gold Bricks*, 44–45; Teague, "Bucket-Shop Sharks," pt.1:728, 731; pt.2:33, 36; pt. 4:400; Harrison H. Brace, *The Value of Organized Speculation* (New York, 1913), 184, 242; Burton Bledstein, *Culture of Professionalism: The Middle Class and the Development of Higher Education in America* (New York, 1976), 80–120; the accusation of anarchy is from an 1895 Board of Trade handout in Lurie, *The Chicago Board of Trade*, 159–160; for a sample of antibucket shop statutes see T. Henry Dewey, *Legislation against Speculation and Gambling in the Forms of Trade* (New York, 1905). A similar dismissive attitude, complete with abusive language, characterized the portrait of Populism in the metropolitan press. See Goodwyn, *Democratic Promise*, 362–367.

94. C. Baker, *The Life of William T. Baker*, 121–128, 144–145; on John Hill, Jr.'s crusade see Ferris, *The Grain Traders*, 120–121.

95. Lurie, *The Chicago Board of Trade*, 201–205.

96. On journalism see Cowing, *Populists, Plungers, and Progressives*, 27–29; see also Lurie, *The Chicago Board of Trade*, 204–205; Nichols, *Cold Facts;* Teague, "Bucket-Shop Sharks," pt.1:731–735; pt.2; pt.3:15 (August 1906); pt.4; Thomas, "The Bucket Shop in Speculation," *Munsey's Magazine*, 24 (October 1900).

97. Emery, *Speculation on the Stock and Produce Exchanges*, 10, 99–100, 103–108, 167.

98. Emery, *Speculation on the Stock and Produce Exchanges*, 147, 187. For defenses of speculation see also Hill, *The Gold Bricks of Speculation*, and C. Baker, *The Life and Character of William Taylor Baker;* for a restatement of the evolutionary defense of speculation see Brace, *Organized Speculation*, 8–10, 200–204; on the "sign of production" see Michael Denning, *Mechanic Accents* (London, 1987), 59, 82; on J. Laurence Laughlin and the academic attack on Populist economic proposals see Goodwyn, *Democratic Promise*, 517.

99. Brace, *Organized Speculation*, 180.

100. Brace, *Organized Speculation*, 149.

101. Quinn, *Gambling and Gambling Devices*, 289–290; or as Thorstein Veblen wrote: "Gradually, as industrial activity further displaces predatory activity in a

community's everyday life and in men's habits of thought, accumulated property more and more replaces trophies of predatory exploit as the conventional exponent of prepotence and success. With the growth of settled industry, therefore, the possession of wealth gains in relative importance and effectiveness as a customary basis of repute and esteem." *The Theory of the Leisure Class*, 37, 41–80. The passage from Lloyd is in *Wealth against Commonwealth*, 515.

102. *Board of Trade* v. *Christie Grain and Stock Co.*, 198 U.S. 250, 246 (1905); see also *The New York and Chicago Grain and Stock Exchange* v. *Board of Trade*, 127 Ill. 153 (1889); *Clews* v. *Jamieson*, 182 U.S. 461 (1901); *Central Stock and Grain Exchange* v. *Board of Trade*, 196 Ill., 396 (1902); and Boyle, *Speculation*, 89–96.

103. *Board of Trade* v. *Christie Grain and Stock Co.*, 252, 236, 237, 247; see also Brace, *Organized Speculation*, 223, and Ferris, *The Grain Traders*, 121–122.

104. Boyle, *Speculation*, 93–96.

105. Lloyd, "Making Bread Dear," 119. Walter Benn Michaels's discussion of the relations between capitalism and fiction and the particularly rich position of Realism is illuminating. See "Dreiser's *Financier*," 279–292, and "Sister Carrie's Popular Economy," in *The Gold Standard*, 38–39, 56–58. For a discussion of the morality of Realism see also Alan Trachtenberg, *The Incorporation of America* (New York, 1982), 182–201.

106. In a somewhat attenuated fashion I am following an argument advanced by J.G.A. Pocock in the last chapter of *The Machiavellian Moment: Florentine Political Thought and the Atlantic Republican Tradition* (Princeton, N.J., 1975): "The Americanization of Virtue: Corruption, Constitution, and Frontier," especially 540, 534–552; Henry Nash Smith, "The Yeoman and the Fee-Simple Empire," in *Virgin Land: The American West as Symbol and Myth* (Cambridge, Mass., 1950), 133–144.

107. J. A. Everitt, *The Third Power* (Indianapolis, Ind., 1905), 14, quoted in Lurie, *The Chicago Board of Trade*, 205.

Index

Index

Index

Index